What Men Want

WHAT MEN WANT

mothers, fathers, and manhood

John Munder Ross

Harvard University Press
Cambridge, Massachusetts
London, England 1994

Library of Congress Cataloging-in-Publication Data
Ross, John Munder.
    What men want : mothers, fathers, and manhood / John Munder Ross.
        p. cm.
    Includes bibliographical references and index.
    ISBN 0-674-95080-1
    1. Men—Psychology. 2. Fatherhood—Psychological aspects.
    3. Masculinity (Psychology) 4. Gender identity. I. Title.
HQ1090.R7 1994
155.3'32—dc20
93-46057
CIP

To the memory of my mother, Barbara Munder Ross, and my dear sister, Ellin

Contents

I dare do all that may become a man;
Who dares do more is none.

Macbeth

1

Studying Men

In this book I will attempt to integrate my evolving theoretical (developmental and clinical) notions about critical aspects of the male condition: fatherhood, aggression, and heterosexual love.

It was 1971 when I began to study what I would understand later to be the roots of paternal identity. I didn't know it at the time, but other researchers, most of them men, had also started turning their attention to similar matters—to the roles men play in the life of their families, to the vagaries in their development, to the complexities and paradoxes inherent in masculinity. Complementing what at first seemed to be my lonely and rather tentative study of would-be fatherhood were the efforts of investigators such as Ernst Abelin, Michael Lamb, Michael Yogman, James Herzog, Kyle Pruett, Stanley Cath, Alan Gurwitt, James Levine, and Joseph Pleck. Later we would meet to share our findings as our work began to appear in print. In the meantime, however, we found ourselves impelled by unseen historical forces to fill a remarkable void in the psychological and psychoanalytic literature.

The women's movement was very much in the air, demanding a reconsideration of gender stereotypes. Nothing seemed quite so inevitable in the differences to be found between the sexes, and women figured as powerful instruments for social change and revitalization. In this compelling ethos, it may have been unavoidable that I as a man of my times, both humbled and intellectually ambitious, should alight on male envy of a woman's capacity to make babies as the subject for my doctoral research.[1] Like the children I was about to study, at the outset I tended to equate having children and being a parent with being a mother.

The idea of "womb envy" seemed both new and nonsexist. It was not, of course. Other theorists had been there before me, only to have their discovery of men's feminine underbellies conveniently forgotten. Though they had failed to integrate their observations into their developmental theory, psychoanalysts beginning with Freud had written about a little boy's anxiety-laden identification with his mother. Following the lead of theorists such as Horney, Ferenczi, Jones, Boehm, and others, they had increasingly questioned the field's phallocentrism and defensive misogyny. The ego psychological approach to development allowed analytic observers, particularly Edith Jacobson and Margaret Mahler, to highlight the "mother in everyman" and the ways in which individuals of both sexes struggle to disidentify from her, making her mediating functions their own. Perhaps more than any other contributor, Judith Kestenberg underscored universal feminine currents in male development in her notion of an "inner genital phase." However, as late as the 1970s, the thrust of these scattered insights and their implications for a revised conceptualization of male development remained unappreciated. It was as if no analyst had ever said that men might want to be women—to have wombs, vaginas, and breasts and to bear and rear babies.[2]

And so at the time my speculation represented a self-conscious challenge to the status quo of sex stereotyping while also accenting the feminine side of manhood. Freud had said that women wanted to be men like their fathers or at least to have what they have—penises and all that was associated with them in the way of male power. Rather than dispute his clinical wisdom or presume to challenge women's insights into themselves, I would simply show how men envied women.

Moreover, I would go back to the basics, to a point in the growing individual's development when his consciousness is still relatively free from the influences of society—either the prevailing misogyny or the new feminism. Whatever developmental psychologist Lawrence Kohlberg might say about the conformism inherent in the child's consolidation of sexual identity—his or her need to be a good little boy or girl—nonetheless three- or even six-year-olds would still be less subject to the constraints of so-called political correctness. And so these children might be counted on to tell the truths of the human heart. A direct study of boys' birth wishes might serve to demonstrate how men wished for a womb of their own.

My subjects, over sixty boys between three and ten years old, turned out to be less fearful for their masculinity than many potential sponsors, who had felt that the subject matter was far too charged, and the research subjects too defended, to yield significant results. Not only did these children prove my initial hypothesis right, but their responses taught me more than I had anticipated about how a boy's wishes to be what he is not evolve over time into an ambition to achieve what is possible: fatherhood. Responding to the projective test designed for this research, one typical boy of three and a half spoke of the "special creases people come out of," gesturing toward his crotch. Another agemate tugged absently at his T shirt and said, "Boys want to feed babies from big pimples just like mommies." Still another boy, five and a half, became suddenly grave after his cavalier description of intercourse—"You flip her over and stick in your dick, stupid!"—when he contemplated the sperm's subsequent journey: "Up, up and up it goes . . . And then you know what happens—then, then the egg eats up the sperm!" Yet another child, at six years, mused: "You feel proud when you're a dad, like you got bigger!"

These swaggering and clearly masculine boys still had chinks in their defensive male armor. Not yet so rigid about their gender role, they could afford not to feel or act like superheroes all the time. And because of their ingenuousness, the research brought with it a new understanding of some of the paradoxes inherent in a boy's and later a man's unfolding sexual identity. It underscored the specific importance of fatherly ambitions in cementing a sense of masculinity.

Like primitive peoples who worship fertility goddesses before they understand a father's less obvious role in procreation, children at first believe that only women have a role in producing babies. For boys in particular, this means that the pride in their being a male with a penis precludes the satisfactions and powers that come with being a parent— a mother. Their virility seems to doom all males to barrenness. In making or "having" babies, boys think, they risk losing their penises.

My preschoolers intuited that when it comes to the mystery of life's origins, and what Freud believed to be the true riddle of the Sphinx, ontogeny recapitulates phylogeny. It is when boys begin to realize the father's part in what psychoanalysts have called the primal scene, the erotic meeting of man and woman as father and mother, that they begin to put womb and penis together and to attain a rudimentary understanding of procreation. Like their ancestors, they then go to the opposite extreme and deify the powers of the great phallus, as if it were the sole organ of fertility. In this phallocentric mythology, women come to assume a secondary role, becoming mere warehouses wherein men's magnificent creations are stored until their time comes—like little homunculi. Having wished to be big and powerful mothers, four- and five-year-olds now disavow their regressive and disorganizing identifications and become male chauvinists par excellence. In the life of the little boy, matriarchy once again gives way to an illusory patriarchy.

That is, until greater knowledge of the facts of life allows the sexes to become separate, equal—and complementary. Growing older and wiser in the ways that Jean Piaget has described, most boys can begin to draw from images of their fathers as caring and tender. If their fathers have been both present and nurturant, they come to see their parents as partners, mutually engaged in creating and sustaining a family. Having grasped the fact that adult men somehow help make and care for babies, boys can at last integrate their parental aspirations and their ambitions as men. By about six years, they want to be neither mothers nor "just men" but, quite specifically, fathers. That is how to have a baby, they understand at last; that is how to get close to mothers. In biological and psychological fatherhood, imagined in childhood and realized as an adult, one discovers the "sublimated motherhood" so essential, in Erik Erikson's terms, to the identity of a whole man.

Fathering

Having studied the evolution of paternal identity in childhood and publishing my work in the 1970s, I discovered the growing body of work by other researchers and practitioners. For the most part, they had looked at fathers from the outside, at what the male parents *did* for their children, rather than at what they felt or at how they came to be what they were. It was against a more intrapsychic backdrop that I joined in these efforts and began to look directly at parent-child behavior and the developmental dialogues taking place between actual fathers and their daughters and sons.

In the preceding decade, researchers such as Henry Biller had studied the effects on children of a father's absence. Now, following the leads of Loewald, Greenacre, Greenson, Abelin, and a few other analytically oriented developmentalists, many investigators began to look at his presence early on—at what he had to offer when he was there.[3] As the feminist movement also noted, a void had been left by the fathers who had fought in World War II and had then removed themselves from their families during the era of suburban commuting and momism. In this climate, fathers continued to be seen as material providers, bread-winners, and instrumental presences (as the sociologist Talcott Parsons had put it in the 1950s)—men who brought the work world with them into the home. But as researchers now sought to demonstrate, they were people and parents too. As the developmental psychologist Michael Lamb and the child psychiatrist Kyle Pruett were to demonstrate, fathers could take on caretaking roles once ascribed only to mothers, doing the "women's work" of childrearing without compromising their masculine modes of behavior.

Perhaps even more important were the distinctly male contributions men make to the child's earliest emotional and intellectual development. According to the pediatric behavioralists Michael Yogman and T. Berry Brazelton, infants seek out their fathers from the earliest months of life, almost as much as they respond to their mothers. Scrutinizing the interactions between fathers and their babies and toddlers from the perspective of Mahler, Piaget, and Lacan, Ernst Abelin drew inferences about the ways in which a father introduces what he called "the male principle" into the psychic world of the child, who in turn thirsts after such sustenance. Through a process of early triangulation, Abelin continued, a boy identifies with his father's difference from the mother and with his masculinity. "Father hunger" was the phrase James Herzog coined to describe the child's longings for his father. Without this presence, Herzog showed, young children, particularly boys, are hard put to express and to modulate their aggressivity.

Having published their findings in their different technical journals, these researchers joined with educators and policymakers, such as Joseph Pleck and James Levine, and began to talk about what had been learned of the phenomenon they came to label "fathering." Despite the different technical languages and diverging notions about the basic components of human nature and determinants of behavior, a common purpose energized these meetings. In fact, a whole movement began to grow up around the idea of the so-called New Fatherhood.[4]

Men wanted to change their family lives. By the late 1970s, like women before them, many men had grown uneasy with preordained sex roles. There was more, they sensed, to a man's life than work and competition. For one thing, men had not seen very much of their own fathers in the sexist days when they were growing up. They did not want to miss out a second time on the affectionate, sensuous, indeed libidinal satisfactions of homelife. If wives now demanded the right to work, husbands everywhere yearned to be parents too. They wanted more than the hours, minutes, even mere seconds that most fathers spent daily with their children.

Implicit in the plea for equality between parents, then, was a mounting generational challenge. Women had increasingly encroached on the older male generation's territory as coworkers, and the beleaguered men were reluctant to give up any more paternalistic prerogatives. Men in authority demand a filial devotion and held up the workplace or training program or university as a sort of family away from home, inviting transferences in kind. Like the collective fatherhood practiced in Papua New Guinea and elsewhere, the old guard commanded the next generation to submit to their more protracted rites of passage. Taken from their houses so much of the time, "living" with them in a western version of the men's huts, tyros were to be fashioned by their elders. Sadly enough, pediatricians, psychoanalysts, and child psychologists proved no exception to this rule. Now asserting their own paternal prerogatives, the "experts" of the younger generation took on the work ethic. They set about proving that fathers could be just as nurturing as mothers and almost as needful of their children's expressions of dependency and trust.

Divorce rates had not yet climbed to 50 percent. The media had yet to announce that 25 percent of American households were headed by single parents, mostly women. The average American family had still to shrink from over 5 members in the 1950s to 2.2 individuals in the 1990s. Work had not as yet taken precedence over love in a life of shrinking leisure time, and family values still mattered. It was the era of the "good-enough father." Psychologists borrowed this term from D. W. Winnicott's folksy descriptions of "ordinarily devoted" mothers as they held their babies close to body and soul. Up to this point, women alone had been entrusted by child psychologists with the physical survival, emotional vitality, and relative equanimity of their infants. At best, fathers performed the ancillary functions of protection and provision and so were cast in the role of outsider. Now the pendulum began to swing back to preindustrial days when, according to family historians, men lived and worked with their offspring and the *pater familias* functioned as the child's spiritual overseer. Once again fathers were to have a place in the parenting of their progeny.

Sometimes, in the newer views of fatherhood, the male parent entered the family drama as a White Knight, to borrow from the psychoanalytic pioneer Phyllis Greenacre, making up for inadequate or downright bad mothering. More universally, fathers also had their own "gender-specific" tasks to do in more or less normal homes. A child could suffer from too much mothering, and to this toxicity fathering would provide the antidote. Even the most well-meaning and competent mother's grasp tended to grow cloying with her son's or daughter's thrust toward autonomy. As the work on separation-individuation of Margaret Mahler and her coworkers demonstrated, mother love could impede a toddler's progress to independence and sexual definition. Fathers acted to disrupt this bond, introducing maleness into the toddler's life and inviting her or him to assume the roles set forth by virtue of an emergent gender identity. Adult men "jazzed things up," as James Herzog put it without ceremony, "kamikazeeing" their way into the serene homescape of women and children. A man's high-keyed style invited his child to participate in worlds other than the soft, warm maternal universe. At the same time, as a sexual man, a husband satisfied a wife's needs for adult intimacy and erotic pleasure. Thus he diverted a mother's attention from her child alone.

A father's dealings with sons and daughters came from the heart, I learned from my own observations, and provided prototypes for the dealings of the developing individual with members of the same and the opposite sexes. Furthermore, the man's manner of stimulating or containing his children's inborn impulses acted to release the Oedipus complex, giving it its particular stamp in each case. Infant researcher René Spitz had spoken of the emotional dialogue between mother and baby. Now I found analogous communications in the verbal and behavioral interactions of fathers with somewhat older children, albeit more complex in initial organization and more subject to the vagaries of defense. Fathers did indeed help direct a child's destiny while fulfilling their own.

The Laius Complex

Certainly there was more to a man's rough-and-tumble style than met the observer's eye—the observer of mere behavior. I sensed at times that this new man, constructed to compensate for the totemic tyrant of Freud's early theory, was missing something inherently and irreversibly male about men, something primal, repressed. My growing clinical experience repeatedly revealed those secret "wishes repugnant to morality" to which Freud had alluded in *The Interpretation of Dreams.* Exchanges with other practitioner-researchers, notably Herzog, persuaded me to look more directly into the darker side of fatherhood.

In the larger American society, an atmosphere of cynical self-interest gradually began to supplant the optimistic generosity of the early 1970s, itself an overcompensation for the collective evils of the Vietnam war and Watergate. The 1980s was an era of social disillusionment. Despite the so-called rediscovery of childhood, media attention made everyone aware of the horrors of wife battering and child abuse. And an even more systematic neglect of children crept into governmental policy with the Reagan administration's ruthless cuts in federal programs for the young and needy.

Men, research indicated, seemed particularly prone both to act on their aggression and to ignore the needs of their children. Whatever might be the legacies of their early histories in the laps of their mothers, male children were born to do battle, designed by nature to fight. Indeed, as Eleanor Maccoby and her collaborators found, this propensity for "intrusive hostility" proved to be the one consistent sex difference cutting across empirical study after study. The universal characteristic of males seemed to be aggressive behavior and their ability to do harm.

When Freud first published his analysis of Sophocles' tragedy in 1900, he related how Oedipus' relentless inquiry reveals that the evils that initially seem to lie outside really abide within himself. Searching for the killer of King Laius, like the patient in analysis who starts out blaming others and externalizing his inner fantasy life, the hero finds to his horror that it was he himself who killed his father and married his mother. And so Freud concluded that Oedipus the son, like all men, is guilty—of either actual misdeeds or sins of the heart. Psychologically, it does not much matter which. Tragedy is a matter of the mind, the mind in conflict.

Yet could it be that within this drama Oedipus is the only figure with such a mind and such a conflict? If he is not the only persona in the play—and myth—there must be more to the allegory than this one reading of it, and more players in real life than the son alone. Mothers and fathers also have roles in this universal drama, making it unclear just who is the victim and who the perpetrator.

Having heard the terrible prophecy that his son would kill him and replace him in his wife's bed, it is not Oedipus the son but Laius the father who has acted to set the tragic events in motion by demanding that his newborn son be left to die. It is Laius who later adds insult to injury by trying to run the adolescent boy off the road. Rising to the challenge and killing him, Oedipus acts out of preordained or, the post-Freudian psychologist would say, unconscious revenge toward the father who has turned his back. Orphaned by his real parents, Oedipus must rely on the kindness of strangers—the shepherds who rescue him from the mountainside and the king and queen of Corinth who adopt the foundling as their own. In the end, blinded and cast out again, Oedipus must depend on his daughter Antigone to care for him and King Theseus to exculpate him.

And not only does Laius try to have his baby boy killed and humiliate his teenaged son; in addition, as ancient Greek sources other than Sophocles reveal, Laius was condemned because, as a young prince on the run from the uncle who had usurped his throne, he had kidnapped and sodomized Chrysippus, the young son of his host and protector, King Pelops. Pelops joined the goddess Hera in condemning Laius for this violation and decreed that Chrysippus would be avenged by another young boy, none other than Laius' unborn son. Oedipus' later rebellion thus emerges as an inevitable response to his father's youthful perversity and to his adult depravity and tyranny—to Laius' exploitation of other children and to the attempted murder of his son and heir.

It is no wonder that Laius, narcissist that he is, fails to solve the Sphinx's riddle, fails to understand that man is mortal and must be moral.

Oedipus Rex could thus be interpreted as a story not only of parricide but of child abuse. As it had earlier in Freudian theory, the metaphors of the Oedipus myth again shed light on the dealings between real-life fathers and sons. To Freud's Oedipus complex there could be added the "Laius complex," a term I coined in 1982. The son's terrifying patricidal and incestuous wishes find a counterpart in his father's even more horrifying urges to commit pederasty and filicide. Repressed from consciousness, the existence of these aggressive impulses helps to explain religious sacrifice and submission, authoritarianism, child abuse, and war, in all of which the older generation threatens sons with exile and death and now and then actually sends them to their death. It illumines the psychological motives behind the neglect and exploitation of children throughout history and across cultures.

A father's aggression toward his progeny has many normal as well as pathological influences on a child's emotional development. Originally equipped to fight off predators and competitors, to guard their group's territories and maintain a stable dominance hierarchy within this unit, males of most species reveal higher testosterone levels, greater size and strength, destructiveness, and simple activity in their behavior (if not necessarily their thoughts) than females do. Their more aggressivized interactions with the young range from the exuberant games fathers play with toddlers (scaring, chasing, pretend fighting), which help them to escape the mother's gentler and more enveloping hold; to forthright paternal discipline; to more sensational acts of mental cruelty and physical violence. Even the Swedish and American "house-husbands" studied by Lamb and Pruett remained "male" and high-keyed in rearing the children. And where the individual man may not be so inclined, children themselves will actively seek out aggressivity from their fathers.

In reviewing the literature on the Oedipus myth, I discovered that my understanding of paternal aggression was not new to psychoanalysis—no more than my stress ten years earlier on "maternal instincts" in men had been. Like their colleagues who looked into men's hearts and found the mother within, psychoanalysts such as Ferenczi, Devereux, Kanzer, and Erikson had made similar excursions and assertions only to have their ideas and arguments forgotten. The murderous aggression of a little boy, an oedipal pretender, seemed easier to entertain than that of adult protectors with power over a child's life.

Later, during the 1980s, other psychoanalytic theorists did begin to ponder the more sinister communications between parents and children. Principles of adult development (or adaptation) found a way into their thinking—for instance, in the recognition of the fact that fathers and mothers react and accommodate to their growing children rather than remaining constant in their personalities after childhood. With this awareness, a stress on rivalry between the generations began to replace the one-sided idea of the son's unidirectional oedipal complex. The Theban king's story came to be seen not only as an individual drama but as a family tragedy.

Romantic Love

In studying the psychology of men, I focused on the impact of generational relationships. An appreciation of the son's conflict-laden internalization of his transactions with his mother and, subsequently, of his struggle to identify with his father served to orient my understanding of a boy's progression toward adult manhood. It was probably a natural extension of this initial preoccupation to consider next the gender relations in which the adult man found himself engaged, though at the time the shift in interest seemed more of a change of pace—an escape from the harsher theme of generational strife. Having looked long and hard at men's brutality toward one another, I returned to their dealings, internal and actual, with women and to their capacity for passionate love.

By the late eighties, in the era of sexually transmitted disease and sexual temperance, erotic and romantic passion, rather than sensual freedom, became a subject of philosophical, anthropological, and psychoanalytic discourse. And in this last sphere, a number of serious and original investigators—notably, Otto Kernberg, Ethel Person, and Martin Bergmann—began to ponder the preconditions for falling and remaining in love. No longer were such states of mind to be dismissed simply as rash adventures of a misspent youth, but were to be scrutinized as powerful developmental experiences.

In keeping with my basic perspective, it was the male versions of these inner upheavals on which I concentrated. Much of my own initial work on men's love of women was published in *Tales of Love, Sex and Danger,* a study of love stories coauthored with Sudhir Kakar, a psychoanalyst and student of Indian culture and religion. The poets, playwrights, novelists, and mythmakers had proved to be abler love theorists than clinical and social scientists, though their insights could be extracted, we found, and transposed to our field's conceptualization of development. Distilling these notions and juxtaposing them with psychoanalysis' appreciation of the dynamisms left over from early childhood, I then contributed a more or less official essay on romantic love for a "professional" volume on emotions.

Like fatherhood, with its roots in an ambisexual childhood, the mysteries of erotic passion also proved to be a rather neglected part of a man's life story. With women, I found, men might rediscover their own femininity while simultaneously exercising their virility. If their fathers had been present early on, I noted, leaving their male mark on them, their enduring presence allowed their young adult sons to identify with them. As mature lovers, fully capable of regression, such men could feel freer to cross over the boundaries of gender and self, daring to feel as women for a while because their basic masculinity was secured.

Further reflection on the uses of love provided the basis for my conclusions on the impact of falling in love in attenuating the late adolescent's ties to his past. Only when he has become basically his own man is the young man man enough for a woman, who, in her turn, teaches him to know his heart. Love, I have learned, helps men to rediscover the old femininity in themselves, gentling their consciences and making for a moral revolution.

What Men Want They Do Not Want

The tensions men experience—which derive from their basic instinctual drives, their sexuality and aggression, and from their relations with others—constantly impinge in paradoxical ways on men's sense of masculinity. As much as men *will* be men, as ingrained as their male destiny is, they must constantly contend with contradictory forces within themselves.

First of all, men also wish to be like women sometimes, or rather in the way they see women. Unconsciously at least, they long to have and to be charmed by children, to be passive, sexy, sensuous, feminine. Most men have been brought up by their mothers so that the first significant others in their lives, their models for being a person, were female. Their mothers' female aura, to borrow from Robert Stoller, has left a deep imprint on their son's psyches. So, later on in life, women's womanliness tends to seem both awesome and catching. Be with women, men fear, or do what they do, and they risk becoming female.

Men's psychological masculinization is analogous to the fetal androgynization that takes place in the womb. They begin their emotional lives in the orbit of women, whom they are like in many respects. Like hormones, psychological male principles have to be introduced into their experience and their psyches if they are to feel like men one day. In the case of the mind, it is largely the father who is the agent of a boy's masculine development. A consideration of fathers, like mothers before them, is essential to an understanding of the psychology of men. And one of the major characteristics associated with fathers, as with all adult males, is their propensity to display aggression and invite identifications in kind with their ability to do harm.

Thus, on the other side of the coin, men feel terrified of the haunting potential for violence that seems to go with being male. They recoil from the physical destructiveness they sense in themselves and other men. Aggression in men figures as a survival mechanism serving the community. Impelled by their testosterone, males were made to fight, and they are taught to do so by other men, notably their fathers. More than this, being aggressive for most men means being male, and they can exploit their hostility to reassure themselves that they are. The trouble is, their violence can also get out of hand.

Baffled by his female patients and colleagues, Freud is said to have once asked his disciple and benefactor, Princess Marie Bonaparte, "My God, what does woman want?" Men, we now know, are no less mysterious.

2

From Mother to Father

It is Erikson's view that a sense of identity, indeed the sum of what we are, is achieved by accretion, with each structure building on what preceded it. The paternal identity of little boys—their would-be parenthood—follows this general principle as well, revealing a succession of identifications with the nurturing and generative functions of both mother and father. In this chapter, I sketch the unfolding of paternal identity in early childhood, a progression that climaxes during the oedipal era, presaging the psychological paternity of the adult man.

As with any line of development, desires and convictions about procreation can represent an individual's attempt to resolve basic conflicts between active and passive positions, progressive thrusts and regressive longings. A boy's or girl's interest in childbearing will express simultaneously wishes to be a baby and to have one, to be nurtured and to nurture. Throughout life, the wish to possess a child will at some level emanate from strivings to be a big, strong, succoring parent (mother or father) as well as from longings to be an infant, cared for and freed from responsibility.

The ease with which very young boys shift roles in relation to their dolls and teddy bears illustrates the duality. As one patient in analysis recalled, his brother's birth initially seemed to promise the status of big brother. Yet it also reintroduced cribs and bottles into his home, the stuff with which he, as a near four-year-old, might settle back into the passivity that he always—then and thereafter—tended to find more comfortable. Similarly, one father-to-be, proudly furnishing the nursery, found himself seized by an image of himself at his wife's breast, pondering how her milk would taste.

Henry, a five-year-old, gives symbolic but poignant expression to this dichotomy. Full of boyish bravado, Henry was also, according to his parents, extremely concerned with babies. He loved them—his barber's, a family friend's, any baby at all. He was an only child, long awaited and much doted on by middle-aged parents, who joined with the child's teachers in wondering where, since his experience with babies was so indirect, his fascination came from.

I interviewed Henry in an early research project I conducted (1974, 1976), playing a game in which I pretended to be a genie who offered to fulfill any three wishes. Eventually Henry would ask for a baby and two dolls. But first he recast the play:

> *Henry:* No, No, No! I'm the genie and you're the Henry [the name, his own, that the child had given to a boy bear in a picture, who was portrayed holding a baby, dubbed by the subject "Henry Two"]. You have to tell me the three things you want and I'll give it to you! [Pause.] You tell me what you want! You're the baby!
>
> *JRM:* Oh, I don't know, all the M&Ms in the world, or is that silly?
>
> *Henry:* Silly . . . a baby?
>
> *JRM:* Well, what about a baby?
>
> *Henry:* Ok, a baby. Abracadabra, into a baby! [He points and grins.]
>
> *JMR:* I'm a baby? I meant having a baby.
>
> *Henry:* I mean a baby. [He points again.] Wham!
>
> *JMR:* Right . . . Tell me, what three things do you *think* Henry Two [the baby] would wish for?
>
> *Henry:* He would wish for a doll.
>
> *JMR:* And?
>
> *Henry:* Abracadabra, another doll!
>
> *JMR:* And what do I do with all these dolls?
>
> *Henry:* Give it to the little baby.
>
> *JMR:* And the baby plays with the dolls?
>
> *Henry:* Yeah, they just move them around in their mouth. [He

reaches for more candy, sucks on an M&M, and begins to crawl around pointedly, playing baby and grinning.]

Henry apparently wants both to be a baby himself and to have one. In having a baby, it seems he seeks power, not just an age-specific oedipal triumph but a more primary ascendance: the power to give, as a parent. In short, Henry aspires to improve on his generational status in some way, in one direction or the other.

Becoming Oneself

The infant has little choice in the matter, not to mention little equipment or inclination to make choices of any kind. The experience of being cared for by the mother, however, establishes the foundation for later acts of self-help and gestures of self-parenting. Indeed, indicators of the infant's purposeful efforts to elicit maternal attentions actively occur as early as two or three months of age.

The smiling response described by René Spitz (1965) signals a first organizer of the infantile ego in relation to the mother and, quite possibly, the dawning sense on the infant's part that he or she can act, in Mahler's felicitous words, to "extract" maternal care and support. No longer does a baby merely react to sensations of hunger or satiation; no longer is his or her world known by "coenaesthetic sensing," as Spitz dubbed the neonate's gut responsiveness. Rather, the child begins to perceive the gestalt of the mother's face in association with sensations of oral pleasure and bodily warmth. More important, an infant further reveals a rudimentary intentionality of sorts by returning the smile of a being who is, however, not yet clearly distinguished from the infant's own self.

I do not wish to ascribe too much in the way of intention to a behavior that is released by specific signs during a critical period and that is probably largely a function of instinctive patterning and maturational factors. Perhaps more telling are an infant's early experiments with transitional objects and phenomena, which begin after symbiosis proper, anywhere between four and ten months, according to Winnicott (1953), and which continue to serve a baby through differentiation and further separation-individuation from the mother.

Not only do transitional activities—cuddling, cradling, cooing—testify to some primal "object relationship" but, by betraying some of the major ingredients of their meaning and function, they also augur specific fantasies about having babies. Transitional behaviors define who the child is and where the child begins and ends. At the same time, they bespeak prototypic efforts on the part of children to *mother* themselves in the mother's absence—to comfort themselves with a soft blanket and gentle cooing, to cuddle and cradle it, to incorporate or recreate the mother's breast and to put it at their own disposal. Above all, these objects and activities serve to concretize personal relations in rudimentary or "proto-symbols," thus easing a baby's awareness of differentiation from the mother by perpetuating the illusion of continuing union with her. In a word, they enable the baby to create a "me" and, increasingly, to be its own baby.

No child at this stage is able to want a baby per se, of course. Inchoate wishes and imaginings are present only as ill-defined urges. But it is evident that the child has come to imitate motherly acts in the way that he or she understands them. In addition, although germinative impulses toward self-parenting share the fate of most preverbal and therefore diffuse and unbound experience—becoming inaccessible in their original form to verbal recollection or even direct reconstruction—still their derivatives and continuing impact may be inferred from the less primitive, more articulate utterances and activities of older children.

In my research, for instance, I found that many nursery-school children entertain the theory that babies are made from milk or some ingested substance or are born from breasts or carved out of the mother's body. Others reveal more open desires to nurse babies, to put them down and give them bottles, to have "big pimples." Such beliefs and wishes need not be seen as expressions solely of naked hunger and spite, of "breast envy" alone. Rather, this evidence indicates a young child's initial confusion and equation of nurturance with birth and productivity. It conveys, moreover, the vague sense that the child, or the child's ego, was somehow created from the love and gifts proferred by the mother—the *psychological* breast of the symbiotic era. When an older boy happens to see a baby fed and watches it grow, the notion that the two processes, nurturing and generating, are equivalent is confirmed.

An actual fantasy of bearing and suckling a baby requires the kind of symbolization in words, ideas, and images that is made possible by the birth of representational thought in the second half of the second year, and its growing ascendancy over coenesthetic sensing, participatory representation, and sensorimotor intelligence. To construct a fantasy of bearing or rearing a baby, furthermore, a child must have developed a more certain awareness of body boundaries and of self and others; for in this way, the child is led to represent both others and self as distinct objects, ultimately as full-fledged persons. His sense of gender has become more defined, as have his perception and definition of his own genitals, even though a child may continue to be more preoccupied with anal erotic stimulation and sensations emanating from the "inner body," as Kestenberg has dubbed it. For a boy, the perception of himself as a boy will enable him increasingly to distinguish himself from his mother and to gain some understanding of their specific relationship as mother and child, and perhaps as female and male.

In addition, a boy comes to appreciate the unique anatomy of his mother. He recognizes the existence of her breasts and genitals and aspects of their functions, although he may in turn adorn himself, in fantasy at least, with the mother's recesses and perhaps also her protuberances. In some instances, the birth of a sibling may provide inklings of the nature of nursing and, more dimly, of childhood. Defining bodies, his own and others', a boy can begin to intuit some of the connections between body parts and somatic sensations and the production and sustenance of babies.

Because so much of his thinking remains dominated by what psychoanalysts call primary process, the exact nature of the relationships cannot be understood. Nor, for that matter, can desires and discoveries be distinguished as either fantasy or reality. It is only in the wake of the rapprochement subphase of separation-individuation, the dawning of representational (if still preoperational) thinking, and (from the psychosexual point of view) the maturation of sphincter control and anal preoccupation, that a child may first articulate definite childbearing and childrearing fantasies. Even then, these fantasies may be most evident in a two-year-old's doll play, in a more active employment of transitional objects, or, perhaps, in pillows stuffed under shirts or mute cradling—and not in elaborate verbalizations for which the child is still conceptually and linguistically ill prepared.

Procreative desires at this stage will be related to anal urges in the broadest sense. The child would like to produce from within a part of the body that can never be known directly something that is alive and valuable and not summarily disposable. In the words of Van der Leeuw (1958), a child would identify with the "active, productive, purposeful mother."

Furthermore, possessing, bearing, or nursing a baby of one's own may symbolically allow the child to keep the mother near in the face of the painful but now irrevocable realization that the two of them are not one and the same being. It is a realization that elsewhere provokes the sudden, often desperate clinging behavior typical of so many once adventurous two-year-olds. Further regressive undertones are discovered in the notions of reproduction through oral incorporation, in instances of the cloacal birth fantasies that seized Freud's attention, and in the ease with which a boy of this age switches roles in scenarios with his teddy bear or security blanket—now enacting provider and parent, now baby.

To cite another example: Sam had never been a fearful boy, and his rapprochement crisis was not particularly troubled. Still, he did retreat more readily than before, running back and catching hold of his mother's or father's welcome hands on outings to the playground. More noteworthy was Sam's interest in his stools. Undiapered, he waved goodbye to them and, taken to the potty now and then at two years, he mumbled something to the effect of "Sam" and "Baba." In fact, babies became a preoccupation, and Sam would stare at younger children in the playground in rapt attention until exclaiming in delight, "Baby!" He loved his doll, William, and another doll made to resemble his father, both of whom began to attract him more than the blanket that previously had been his dearest love. By the age of two and a half, he would hold these to his breast or stuff them down the front of his pants while singing softly. And he would refer to the dolls, each of his parents, himself, and his penis, interchanging the names: William, Sammy, Daddy, Mommy, Baby.

Being Both Sexes

Playing parent soon becomes complicated by a boy's developing perception of sexual differences. His discovery of his genitals and his boyishness is beset by feelings of helplessness, ambivalence, the inability to understand simple relations, a reluctance to give up former objects, a terror of losing body parts. (Sometimes when Sam saw his feces disappear down the drain, he would frown in fear and grasp his penis with one fist while clutching his mother's fingers in the other.) His quest for omnipotence takes shape in what Lawrence Kubie called the "drive to become two sexes." His voraciousness further whetted by an unrelinquished identification with a seemingly all-powerful mother, a boy hesitates to confine himself to a single gender.

Kestenberg has suggested that the young boy passes through an "inner genital stage" characterized by heightened perineal and inguinal sensations, problematic testicular changes, and, gradually, the uncontrollable states of penile tumescence to which he becomes ever more attuned. The observer cannot know for sure whether he is responding to heightened inner sensations and a cathexis, or investment, in the internal parts of his reproductive apparatus. If he is, whether these are linked to more feminine feelings is also unclear. In all events, what I would emphasize are the little boy's *wishes* to be in possession of a mother's capacious recesses and resources, such as he imagines them. The child represents these internal and unseen body parts on the basis of his own sensorimotor repertory, anal, inner genital, or otherwise.

Cognizant now of anatomical differences, a boy between two and three years of age seeks at times to undo them through a variety of infantile fetishes—the sticks, marbles, toy horses, and other talismen that line boys' pockets and guard against the dreaded castration he believes to have been visited on females. Heirs to transitional phenomena, these serve to express the illusion, and dawning delusion, of the phallic woman.

A boy further seeks to endow himself with the gifts of both male and female and to fashion for himself an identity not simply, as Freud had it, of the polymorphous "little pervert" but somewhat more discriminately of a "little hermaphrodite." He would have breasts like his mother's and use them as he sees her use them, to feed with or simply to have. More intuitively, he would be full, possessed of her womb as he conceives of it, and bear babies just as she does.

Hermaphroditic and parthenogenetic motifs abound in mythology. There are carvings from the Creto-Minoan civilization in which vulva and penis are made to blend into each other as emblems of fertility. In certain societies in the South Pacific, the function of the man's penis in intercourse is misconstrued: his semen is believed to feed the fetus of the already pregnant woman. In the Hindu culture, the god of the hearth, Ganesh, is a male figure with the head and trunk of an elephant and a distinctly swollen abdomen. The impression is of a belly full of life, of self-contained providence and fertility. And there are the even more explicit ambisexual incarnations of Vishnu, alternating with his frankly phallic form in the great linga.

A boy's early wishes to procreate in the manner of a mother—to be filled up as if they had wombs and breasts and to give birth to a baby through one opening or another—may not emerge into consciousness at the time of their inception. Many boys, poised on the eve of the oedipal phase, lack a rudimentary knowledge of the facts of life and the cognitive wherewithal needed to articulate these relatively complex reproductive fantasies. In these instances, maternal strivings remain subject to a primal repression of sorts, so that they are betrayed in the faintest of derivatives. In what Piaget called the "vertical décalage," these urges find representational form only after the fact.

But enough in the way of motherly ambitions and identifications has been laid down to provide a template for their fuller elaboration later in development. Under the sway of regression, struggling to maintain a phallic stance in the face of feared retaliation and an uncertain masculine identity, many young boys will retreat from the more positive oedipal position into the safety of an identification with the mother and of more anal libidinal aims. It is in this circumstance that they will fall back on the wish to make a baby, adding to this more archaic aim their age-specific desire to submit to the father and to penetration by his penis as a means to achieve their ends. It is later, then, in the negative variant of the complete Oedipus complex and with the cognitive sophistication provided by more firmly established preoperational thinking, that boys tend to revive, refine, and more fully reveal their yearnings to mothers and, by extension, women—their father's women.

Among the boys I studied at these later stages of development, many tugged absently and dreamily at their T shirts while speaking of women's "big pimples" and of nursing babies. One of these children, Chad (age five), virtually deserted by his mother and cared for by his father alone, declared that he indeed was going to have a baby, which was growing in his belly and would emerge from what a classmate of his called "the special crease that people come out of."

Henry, the boy described earlier who wanted to be the genie and not the baby, in an act of imagination and imitation also expressed his envy of "woman's painful prerogative." Perhaps this was exaggerated by dim notions of a cesarean section. Moreover, in his reference to "two babies," he may have been alluding to the testicles and to a wishful equation between these occupants of the scrotal sac and infants *in utero*.

Asked how a baby is born, Henry puffed himself up and blurted:

Henry: And then it grows and grows and grows and grows, and then it comes to be like that! Whush! [Looks behind him.] I can see what's in back there.

JMR: How do you think she [the mother bear in the pictures shown to these children] feels having that thing growing inside like that?

Henry: She's going to get fat . . . [He puffs up his cheeks, laughs.]

JMR: But where does it come out of her, do you know? [Points to his mouth.] Out of her mouth?

Henry: No! They have to open her tummy . . . They make it open and then they put some more blood in, and then it's out. [He "operates" on himself by crisscrossing his belly with his hands.] He's getting fatter, see! [In a later picture, Henry points to the father bear.] He's going to have the baby . . . The door's open there. [Points to the door to the room, which is ajar.]

JMR: Do you want it closed?

Henry: Yes, so nobody sees me. [He looks nervous, his attention appears to lapse, and then he whispers.] He's going to have a baby, too . . .

JMR: So he's going to have a baby, and how does he feel about that?

Henry: He's going to put him right in there. [Points quickly to the father's belly, then to the baby carriage in the picture.]

JMR: He's going to put him right in there? So he can have a baby, huh?

Henry: [With great passion.] Yeah, two babies!

JMR: What about the little boy, how does he feel?

Henry: He's going to get a baby too . . . and he-she too. [Indicates the girl bear in the picture.]

JMR: How are they going to get their babies, do you know?

Henry: I just told you. [In a hoarse whisper.] They just open it up and they get a baby out and then they sew it back in again!

JMR: And how are they going to feel about having those babies? Are they going to like having them or not?

Henry: Yes . . . [Absently.] I got my new big wheel . . . [He turns away.]

Matt provides further evidence of how one boy, deprived of the normal family triad, struggled to relinquish his wish to be a mommy in favor of becoming a daddy. At three years of age, the parents having separated, Matt was living with his mother and seven-year-old sister. Matt did not know what "a woman's" was and in fact first equated her with the person who had one day stolen his mother's handbag. "Woman" was not synonymous with thief, his mother informed her son. Rather she was a person with no penis but breasts. He, a male with a penis, would grow up to become a man instead. "No," the boy countered, "a doctor." Such were the confoundings of category, of classes and relations, in his unformed epistemology.

Once he had assimilated these distinctions of gender as categories, Matt believed that he had a choice in the matter. First he decided that he would someday rather be a woman like his mother. His mother noted in her diary, "Matt has got the sexes straight at last [when he] reeled off a list of all the humans he knows who have penises . . . including himself." With this discovery, however, the child was seized by a new anxiety. Naked from the waist down one blistering day, he grasped his penis and exclaimed, "It might come off!" That was what had happened to his sister, he declared, for all she had left was a hole. It was at this point that his mother explained to him "where babies come from and why girls are different." More specifically, Matt's mother wrote:

When I was telling him about the place inside the mother where the baby grows, he said he wanted a place like that and a baby to grow inside him too. So I explained the father's part in making a baby and that you couldn't have a baby without a father. Sybil [her daughter] wandered into the room and so I asked Matt if he could explain it to her; I wanted to see if he understood it. He hadn't.

The daddy has semen in his tummy, he told her, and the mommy has an egg and—"Mommy what about chickens? They sit on their eggs."

This morning Matt was getting dressed when he passed gas. "Oops," he said, "that must be the baby I have inside of me." I asked if he still thought he'd like to have a baby inside him, and he said yes. Then he added that, as a matter of fact, he did have a baby inside him, "Right now."

The birth fantasies of older boys like Chad, Henry, or even Matt appear to have been somewhat protracted by special life circumstances and their impact on the child's oedipal phase. As noted earlier, a later accent on submission to, longing for, and love of the father, rather than competition and identification with him, may heighten a boy's emulation of his mother in her sexual role as a woman. This will call upon earlier and more specifically maternal identifications with her, reviving regressively a little boy's ambisexual wishes. The point is, these have been with him from the near start of his emotional life, influencing the evolution of his sexual identity in a variety of ways.

In their original form (in boys of two and a half or three), such fantasies already serve several psychic masters. They can express the wish to have the mother's special power and yet presage a father's procreativity. They may represent an attempted mastery of toilet training: of the stools passed, the anxieties attached to their loss, and a restiveness at parental power over the moving of one's own bowels. In addition, because of the connections in the boy's mind between his feces and his penis, and the mother's strength and her imagined penis, the wish to have a baby defends, anticipates, and helps to master a boy's dread of another potential loss through castration. Thus it facilitates the difficult transition into the next libidinal stage in psychosexual development—the phallic phase.

Becoming a Boy

Between approximately 22 and 36 months, then, depending on both psychosexual and overall ego development, a little boy may reveal wishes to give birth to babies. At the very least, he will interest himself in rearing and even specifically nursing them. Just how sustained, acceptable, and conscious such fantasies of pregnancy, birth, and ambisexuality may be for any given child remains to be determined. In most instances, though, childbearing fantasies and, to a lesser degree, the desires to succor babies quickly become problematic for boys. Whatever their residual and subliminal effects, maternal strivings are short-lived as conscious ambitions. In this respect, a "typical" boy differs from a "typical" girl, embarking on a diverging path of sexual and generative development.

Witness Matt's fear for his penis and Henry's secrecy is not wanting his wishes for a baby to be made known. Even motherless Chad asserted that not only did he wish for a baby but also for "wings so I can fly . . . like a pilot." Stereotypically manly ambitions and constraints have begun to impinge on wishes now perceived to be feminine.

The phallic phase proper emerges as a result of a preordained maturational thrust, an identification with the father, further progress in gender identity—but also, I believe, in a certain sense of resignation and loss. Unable to compete with his mother's parental ascendancy over him, a boy must find an alternative route to parental authority. So he makes use of what he has. Wanting babies no longer means having power, power that is within reach. A boy gradually learns not only that his mother lacks a penis, but also that he will never have a womb or breasts. In this regard he feels destined to be shortchanged all of his life, to be physically barren or empty.

For a while he may (like Freud's Little Hans or like Matt) believe that he can determine his sexual destiny. But in time a boy will move from the "hermaphroditic" position and anticipate that to have babies is to be a woman and requires the sacrifice of his masculine attributes, specifically his penis, leaving him not with a womb but a wound. Rather than relinquish the symbol and prime organizer of his masculinity, palpable and present as it is, he cedes the fantasied and elusive baby.

Subsequently a boy may come to invest his tender yet ambitious maternalism in his genitals or inner spaces. At times he even may imagine that they are his womb. He may cherish them as if they were the child he cannot have (Henry's two babies may be his testicles, his scrotal sack a uterus). Some of these urges become diffused and are displaced onto infantile fetishes that have roots in transitional objects but now also embody a boy's pride in his penis as well as his anxiety about preserving it. Many boys try to hide their femininity and their sensuality and tenderness behind hypermasculine caricatures.

For example, one five-year-old I tested in my research, Charles, had a mother who remained at home most of the time and was pretty much available to him; the father was a businessman without a great deal of time for his child. Confronted with the theme of reproduction, he seemed to fear for his fragile maleness. Indeed, this boy revealed the kind of aggressiveness and defensiveness which had been anticipated as the typical response of children to the projective procedure—though, mostly deprived of a father with whom to establish his masculinity, he proved to be the exception rather than the rule. "How does he feel right now, do you think?" I asked while showing the picture of the little male bear holding a baby bear.

> *Charles:* He feels stupid.
> *JMR:* Why does he feel stupid?
> *Charles:* I don't know.
> *JMR:* Is it because he's holding the baby? Does that make him feel stupid?
> *Charles:* Yeah. That makes him feel stupid. That would make *me* feel stupid.
> *JMR:* To hold the baby, why?
> *Charles:* I don't know, maybe it's for *girls.*
> *JMR:* A baby is for a girl? What is he going to do with that baby?
> *Charles:* Give it back to the mother. This baby is terrible. Ha, ha, ha! [Laughs.] I'm going to make a *big hole* in his pants. Yeah. Baby bottom has a big hole!
> *JMR:* What's he going to do after he gives the baby back?
> *Charles:* He's going to go up to his room and shut the door and go back to sleep, because it's the middle of the night.

Charles cannot answer any questions about the boy bear, but instead simply refers to him as stupid and asks the examiner to get lost. At the end of this, I ask whether there's anything else he wants to say. He responds, "No, Ma'am."

JMR: All right, there's one more picture which I'm going to show you. There's Petunia. [This is the disparaging name Charles has given the sister in the picture, who is now seen holding the baby.] How does she feel?

Charles: [Letting down his guard and changing his tune.] Nice. Yeah, she feels nice.

JMR: [As if not hearing.] What does it feel like for her to hold the baby, do you think?

Charles: I don't know, like it's her baby.

JMR: What's she going to do with the baby?

Charles: She's going to hold it until the mother says, "Give it to me."

JMR: And then what's she going to do, give it back?

Charles: No, nothing, she's going to put it in its bed . . . in the beddy bed, in the crib.

JMR: And if the genie came to her and gave her three wishes, what would she wish for?

Charles: A grown baby! That's all!

JMR: What would she do with her own baby?

Charles: And she would wish for a crib, and a knife . . . and a husband.

JMR: A husband?

Charles: I'm not going to get a husband! Uuuh! I'm going to be a husband!

JMR: You're not going to get a husband, you're going to be a husband?

Charles: [Laughs, again defensively.] When you're going to be a husband, I'll be a husband. I don't know what I'll do then, 'cause I'll have two of them then. [Points to the two children.]

JMR: You'll have two children?

Charles: Yeah, and I'd be scared. [Laughs.]

At the close of the session, Charles looks in toybox. He pulls out a red wagon and leaves it out; then he removes the tractor and the horse, exclaiming "I did it. I found it." He connects the wagon and the tractor and causes an accident in which the tractor collides with the box of crayons he had just used for coloring.

Again, some inferences: In this instance, perhaps as a function of the father's relative absence as a nurturing figure in this boy's life, the themes of childrearing and tenderness pose terrible threats to the boy's gender identity. They stir his castration fears and hark back to whatever glimpses he may have had of the primal scene, conceived by him to be a destructive, dangerous collision. More than this, child care and procreation, associated as they are with a woman, tap underlying homosexual urges, intensified by the identificatory void and erotic longings that are a result of the father's absence. To be interested in babies for this boy means to be a girl, or, more specifically, a wife for the father. He attempts to master his castration anxiety, furthermore, by projecting its imagined consequences and by portraying both women and babies as derogated and emasculated figures, hiding his wishes to be in their position by assuming a phallic-sadistic posture.

Many aspects of a boy's increasingly outmoded childbearing wishes are repressed by a rapidly developing defensive repertory. In a more adaptive alternative to Charles's misogyny, they are defended against and gratified by way of certain projective identifications that allow a future heterosexual to externalize his femininity by finding and empathizing with it in his love object—his mother, a woman. This strategy ideally lends to the primal scene, conceptualized by a boy like Charles in more sadomasochistic terms, a sensuous and inviting quality. It is the father's inner presence that enables a boy, and later a man, to immerse himself in a woman and her sexuality.

Another five-year-old, Jake, revealed an altogether different attitude from Charles's toward the process of procreation, birth, and childrearing. This boy's father, an artist, is very much a presence in the child's life and shapes his interest in the reproductive process. For Jake, having babies comes to mean being big, strong, grown-up, and male.

> JMR: How does this brother bear feel about being a boy?
>   Would he have any feelings about that?
> Jake: I think he feels that he wants to have a baby. Like his
>   mother and father did.

Here he indicates not a violent and exploitative conception of sexual relations, but rather an intuition into the mutuality of the persons engaged in them and their creative consequences. Later the child looks at the card in which the baby bear is portrayed being held by the boy and exclaims, "Baby bear's getting big."

JMR: Who's that holding baby bear?
Jake: Papa. [Long pause. He looks puzzledly at the picture.]
JMR: Looks like Papa, but look closely. Look who's getting big.
Jake: Him. [Very excited and lively voice.] That's who it is, that's brother bear. He's getting pretty big, he's getting to be a Papa Bear!
JMR: How does he feel about holding his baby sister?
Jake: I think that is his baby, maybe.
JMR: What is he going to do with the baby?
Jake: I don't know, if it's his, he'd probably take care of it.
JMR: How does it feel to hold her like that?
Jake: I think it feels grown-up. [Plays with his pen, pushing the point in and out.]
JMR: What is he going to do after he puts the baby down?
Jake: Maybe he'll go to the kitchen to get her a bottle.
JMR: Does he like to do that?
Jake: I think he sometimes likes to, and sometimes he doesn't like to, when she cries.

At a later point in the interview, I asked Jake, like the rest of my subjects, to say what he would choose should a genie come to him and offer three wishes. The child answered, "To be rich. And to go to Jamaica, and also that's where I went once."

JMR: Was it nice?
Jake: Yeah.
JMR: And what did you do there?
Jake: Swam. You know what? I have an exciting story. [Proceeds to speak in a very fast and excited voice.] When we went out on the coral, we saw two squid hanging from a rope . . . my father was with me . . . and they were shooting a jet of ink!

In all events, should a boy remain bent on being a mother, dissonant as this identification becomes with current psychosexual aims and cognitive capacities and with the fact that he is a boy, then the presence of such aspirations augurs a denial of sexual differences and of his own actual gender. Ultimately, such maladaptations may paradoxically come to inhibit the very procreativity for which a boy strives. That is, such inhibition may occur if his residual underlying maternal urges are not in some way largely satisfied. Based on my research, this resolution seems to be most prevalent among sons of single mothers, boys whose fathers are altogether absent.

To Be a Father

A boy's perceptions of his father have made sex differences evident in the first place. Having long ago singled out his father as a figure in his own right, indeed as a person of unique importance, a boy witnesses in him his own psychosexual fate and the impossibility of changing his gender. But if the masculinity promised by the father's presence entails certain losses, it also offers undeniably sweet rewards. That same admixture of love and incorporative yearning a boy once felt within his early symbiosis with the mother draws him away from her toward a father who becomes in his eyes less and less of a strange and peripheral figure. Identification with and attachment to his father facilitate separation.

A son at this stage seeks more and more to drink in and enact for himself what he experiences as his father's manly strength. He too wants to be intrusive, erect, angular, mobile—phallic.

First, I believe, during rapprochement and somewhat later during that particular phase described by some analysts as a period of girlish dependency on the father, a son would merely be with his daddy and share adventures with him. Homoerotic longings or, better, a more nonspecific object love for the father intermingle with strivings to be like him. Second, I conjecture that when the ambivalence of rapprochement has been superseded, then the aggressive urges initially directed toward the mother are displaced and projected onto the father, who is cast as a rival to be pushed aside in a boy's newfound quest for his mother's exclusive admiration. It is now that the positive oedipal complex is set in motion.

Thus, I would differ with Ernst Abelin's notions about early triangulation, emphasizing as he does the toddler's gender-specific rivalry with father. What I would stress instead is the presence from the start of the son's father in two guises, analogous to those of the mother. The "good father" is there to be loved, imitated, and introjected, and makes himself available as a model for the boy's developing gender identity. There also exists in the boy's experience a "bad father" who is absent, frustrating, punishing, tough, and eventually rivalrous, a stereotypical he-man. Contending with this father allows the boy to exercise his muscles, expressing and modulating his aggression, and is useful for many aspects of development. But these felt confrontations also make for conflicts that further complicate the evolution of a son's masculinity.

Whatever the illusions of strength and promise of greatness an identification with this aggressive, sadistic, or even bad image of the father may appear to offer, it remains an "identification with the aggressor," a primarily defensive maneuver designed to ward off a boy's fears for his nascent and fragile virility and to counter his sense of inadequacy and incompleteness as a male. Such an identification is fruitless as well. Even some measure of success in his effort to be strong in a bold but unproductive way will not enable a boy to feel fertile and creative, to fulfill his sensuality, to assuage the hurts suffered as a consequence of his body's barrenness. Another sense of the father and of his own future is needed if a boy is to atone for these (potential) lacks within himself.

A father's physical and emotional availability to his son, to the family in general and to the child's mother in particular will influence his son's understanding of the parental relationship, the so-called primal scene and the attitudes the child projects onto both participants. If the father seems remote, hostile, or authoritarian, his son may very well seize on sex as an altogether self-serving act of aggression, one that is more or less isolated from familial love, and he may contrive for himself a variety of violent fantasies about it. As with the mother of infancy, parental absences tend not to make the heart grow fonder. Instead they excite rage and projections of aggression, coloring the child's representation of the missing father. But if the father presents himself as a relatively caring, tender, and benign figure, able to absorb his son's hostilities without openly or implicitly threatening retaliation, then a boy will experience his as a nurturing presence. Such a relationship will, in turn, offset a child's more destructive conceptions of intercourse, which spring partly from the sadistic, intrusive components of his own phallic impulse. A boy may then intuit the more sensuous, pleasurable, indeed creative and generous aspect of the father in his sexual role. Having further acquired primitive logical capacities and thus more sexual knowledge, he may identify with the father as a procreator possessed concretely and metaphorically of a "giving penis."

Norton, a four-year-old with a reportedly nurturing father and a rather sad and less available mother, gave eloquent if still symbolic expression to the oedipal boy's search for masculinity and indeed for a penis that are distinctly providential and nurturant. At the close of an interview session during a free-play period, Norton wanted to stay in the room and play with the toys. He started pulling a tiny tractor onto which was attached a cart and said it "was pulling things to eat at home." He also held a toy cow that was going to "go into the rain and stand." He continued speaking about the "rain being nice" and the "rain stopping." Then he picked up a toy horse with a man on it and declared that the man wanted to "plant a seed" and would "dig a hole and drop the seed in." It was raining all over, he added, and seemed mournful for a moment.

> *JMR:* What can the rain do?
> *Norton:* [The boy was holding a toy cannon and matter-of-factly said:] The cannon ball is broken . . . [After a pause, he responded to the question] . . . The rain gives plants something to drink.
> *JMR:* The rain gives plants something to drink . . . And what happens to them?
> *Norton:* [With delight.] They get bigger! [Playing with the cannon, exclaims] POW!

Still pulling things out of the toybox, Norton found a balloon and asked me to blow it up. He left, clutching the balloon to his breast, grinning, eyes sparkling. Later he was observed cradling the balloon and, his teacher reported, "cooing to it."

A whole generative history seemed to be condensed in a few moments. Above all, it appears that Norton's wish to be succored, together with his desire actively to nurture, found expression in what he envisioned as the power of men to sow seeds and water them, to make things grow. Thus, maternal and infantile aims, now outmoded, might be fulfilled by way of an age-appropriate masculine modality. This identity remains precarious and uncertain: Norton's cannon ball remains at least momentarily broken. Yet Norton himself remains secure, his integrity assured by a continuing recourse to transitional supports, which now also preserve his boyishness.

Once again, Matt is a case in point. His mother relates how her son came to accept his sexual fate:

> I pointed out to him that he could be a daddy when he grew up and do all the same things to take care of a baby that a mommy does. The only thing he missed was carrying the baby inside him before it was born. He still looked a little forlorn, so I remarked that he'd never had a baby doll and would he like one? So he could play daddy and change its diapers and feed it? And he said eagerly that, yes, he wanted one, and seemed suddenly indignant that he's never had one before. [Three days later she made the following entry.] Matt finally has the facts of life straight, and with a vengeance. Last night he paraded around with his socks stuffed down the front of his shorts, saying proudly: "Look how my penis has grown." He started asking me about his father's new wife. "Does she have eggs inside her to make a baby?" I told him she does have but reminded him that she can't have a baby by herself. There has to be a daddy too. "Yes," he explained patiently, "but she has my daddy! And he can put his seed in her, and it gets squashed together with her egg and makes a baby." He's beginning to feel good about his part—the man's part—in the whole repro-ductive process. This morning he spent 20 minutes with his new baby doll, walking around with it, rocking it and singing to it, and he finally tucked it into bed using his own precious security blanket. "Are you pretending to be a baby's daddy?" I asked him. "Oh, no, I'm the baby-sitter," he said. "And baby-sitter is good too." I've just started using a 15-year-old boy as a sitter and Matt is very taken with him.

Beneficent though a father may be, he cannot altogether quell the castration anxiety inevitable during the phallic and oedipal phases of psychosexual development. Nor will even the gentlest of fathers pre-vent his son from becoming for the time being an aggressive little male chauvinist, for such is the spirit of a boy's initial discovery of what it means to be a man. Thus even Norton, more ready with images of nurturance than many of his peers, is very much preoccupied with cannon *balls* that are broken. And Matt too is alternately proud of

displaying his penis and anxious about losing it. Still unable to integrate bits of information into a complete understanding of stages in
the reproductive process and unsteady in his burgeoning masculinity,
a son even with a "better than average expectable" family, with a father
who is a genuine libidinal provider, must struggle to organize sexual
and nurturing images of himself that are still fragmentary and potentially contradictory.

This is a transitional period, then, a state of "dynamic disequilibrium," in Piagetian terms, a phase before styles of defense have
crystallized into a distinct character structure. During this transition,
a boy will entertain a variety of wishes and identifications that will
probably remain with him in more or less unconscious form throughout his life; they may become pathogenic as far as his eventual genitality
is concerned. Reaction formations, inherent sadism, and denials of
maternalism or tenderness may predominate, leading to the phallic
fixations so often associated with the stereotypical unfeeling, ungiving,
often unproductive male.

On the other hand, a boy may retreat from assuming the man's role
because it is unavailable to be internalized, because he fears retribution,
or because he feels somehow that his mother does not accept him as
a man. Homosexual longings and defenses may then serve to stifle the
possibility of actual parenthood, and a boy may revert to the wish to
make the baby in his own bowels.

For instance, Matt's case poses problems about the fate of maternal
aspirations in a boy whose oedipal triangle is left incomplete. Certainly
it leaves many unanswered questions: Did the mother's intervention
catalyze latent pregnancy wishes that had perhaps contributed to Matt's
castration fear and had found some fulfillment in Matt's pride in his
penis, that is, *his* baby? Or was it, as Freud might have suggested, Matt's
fear of losing his penis and longing for his father that forced him to
retreat into a feminine identification in which having babies served as
compensation for emasculation? We cannot say. Neither possibility
excludes the other, in fact, and evidence for both is suggested. Actually
Matt's childbearing fantasies are probably bolder and balder than
many, and may result from the sporadic presence of his father, who
had left his son at a crucial stage in sexual development, causing the
mother to serve as a primary object of identification. She, in turn, by
her well-meaning efforts to discourage male chauvinism and her evi-

dent rejection of Matt's father, may have appeared to devalue men and masculinity. Still, as his mother herself points out, father and son continued to spend weekends together, and other men, uncles and friends, were available to the boy. Nor did she actually frown on her boy's delight in his maleness.

Above all, Matt's mother provided her son with an understanding of a man's fatherly relation to his children. And it was, as she declared, "just what Matt needed." What the boy required was some awareness of the man's part in reproduction, of a man's sexual relationship with a woman, and of his active caretaking role whereby he might imagine himself to be a creative, nurturant "daddy" who shared in making and tending babies. With this sense of purpose, Matt might now overcome life's typical hardships as well as those peculiar to his unique circumstances, reconciling aspirations to generativity with the constraints and pleasures afforded by his being a boy.

Along with the good father, then, a boy's mother must be present during the oedipal phase as an essentially admiring and worthy, if not altogether available, object of her son's aspiring love. Her receptivity plays a vital role in determining the nature and quality of his libidinal object choices and of his sexual identity, and hence the possibility for future procreativity. Such a mother remains a constant figure who is both warm and appropriately detached: that is to say, maternal, womanly, sensual, and authoritative, all at once.

Also she must, so far as her son can see, love and admire her husband, his father. If she does, the mother can be seen to be essentially the same person within her sexual relationship with the father as she is in her mothering. Neither she nor her son becomes split in their sexuality, with pleasure divorced from caring or conception. She does not, however, become so accessible to her son (at least not directly) that she lets him take his father's place, thus depriving the son of ideals of what she would like him to be and of the sort of woman he would choose to love.

Even a motherly mother and a fatherly father cannot altogether spare their son from residual and persistent exaggerations of feminine or homosexual wishes that divert him from his heteroerotic and fatherly ambitions. Nor will even the least sexist parents be able to forestall his anxious, defensive, and often overcompensating hypermasculine protests against these threats to a new sense of masculinity. With luck, however, these and other potentially regressive, self-absorbing, and isolating responses will be transformed by the successful sublimations that accompany the oedipal resolution. Whatever their form, preoedipal urges toward productivity, along with selective maternal identifications, may now be subordinated to the overarching paternal identification that climaxes the oedipal crisis and constitutes the first avatar of a boy's male sexuality. It is this assumption of would-be paternity, I am convinced, which promises to atone best for lacks inherent in being any one sex, and which thereby resolves inescapable conflicts in a boy's general sexual as well as his more delimited gender identity.

The Riddle of the Sphinx

Of crucial importance in this evolution of these interwoven progressions is the so-called latency period. Middle childhood, the interlude between the oedipal years and adolescence, is a time when cognitive advances and the father's actual mentorship permit a boy to comprehend the facts of life and to foresee his heterosexual and procreative destiny.

Just how and when does a boy come to comprehend what it means to father a child? As a boy's general ego development proceeds, his increasing intellectual abilities enable him, in Piaget's terms, to discover laws of causality for occurrences evident in the world. It is a child's emerging capacity for concrete operations that allows him to grasp some rudimentary facts about the reproductive process and to glimpse at least momentarily the chain of events connecting these elements.

The timetable is variable and debated by psychologists. In my own empirical studies, I found that boys between six and seven years of age, now freed from many of the preemptive impulses and anxieties that still dominate their younger brothers, begin solving the riddle of the Sphinx. A middle-class, relatively savvy six-year-old in our culture intuits that father and mother, male and female, conjoin in some way to produce offspring. A male, he himself will one day participate in a sexual relationship with a woman whereby children are reproduced and tended, though, of course, the personal knowledge conveyed by ejaculation eludes him.

The trouble is, such knowledge remains vulnerable to the kind of lapses and splits in awareness which, as Freud (1927) pointed out, may characterize even an adult man's perception of the facts of life, particularly when it comes to anatomical differences. The degree to which contemporary children merely parrot the knowledge fed to them by sophisticated, liberal elders, parents, and teachers, without integrating it to pertain to themselves and those close to them, also remains uncertain in many cases. How much children want to know what they are told, and how much unwanted, burdensome facts are liable to distortion or repression, are still more elusive questions. And, of course, even a schematic understanding of what adults construe as "lovemaking" may serve other ends, becoming more associated with the machismo and bravado typical of boys this age than with erotic union and surrender.

Tough-talking Simon, six and a half years old, was the son of an aggressive businessman to whom he felt very much attached. Teachers and parents remarked on his "smart, hep" style, his braggadocio, and his unabashed striving for power. He was not, they said, among the more gentle boys in his class. And yet:

JMR: [Showing a picture of a mother bear with her baby.]
  How'd she get that baby, do you think?
Simon: The doctor pulled her out of the uterus. How else,
  Dummy? The vagina, it came out of!
JMR: And how did it get in the vagina, do you know? How
  was it made?
Simon: They first . . . the father that has sperms . . . and the
  girl that has eggs . . . [Rapidly.] I have a book all about be-
  ing born, do *you?* Do *you* know that?
JMR: You do? so it tells . . .
Simon: [Interrupting.] So when the sperm's alive and it turns
  into an egg, it moves over to the uterus when it's black [sic].
  The baby moves over, rolls overboard! Man overboard! You
  see there's a cord attached to your body button that will
  grow and live. And then she is starting moving in the
  mother's body. So, she felt it. Right?
JMR: Right!
Simon: And then she knew that a baby would come out soon.
  [Thumps his abdomen.]

JMR: Because she felt the baby move?

Simon: Yep. And then!! You know what happened? [All this is said with an air of great authority and drama.]

JMR: What happened then?

Simon: The doctor pulled the baby out of her vagina!

JMR: How do you think it feels to have the baby inside, do you think?

Simon: I don't know, but *she* does! Dummy! She's a girl!

JMR: Right. How does it feel to have a baby come out?

Simon: Well, she wouldn't even see it. 'Cause she would be asleep—*Kook!* That's what you have to do, to be *asleep*, to pull a baby out from a *vagina!*

JMR: How does it feel to hold that baby then? How do you think she feels?

Simon: She feels happy, good inside.

JMR: Why does she feel happy?

Simon: Ha, ha, ha!!! That's a *simple* question. [Very loudly.] 'Cause she has a new baby! Yeah!

JMR: And that makes her feel happy, and what else?

Simon: What else? And what else?! Except *love!*

JMR: Love . . . Okay, let me ask you: So who can have babies then?

Simon: Only girls can but [quickly, definitely] the father has to help, and the girl has to be turned over sideways, and then, you see, the father sticks the penis into the vagina, and the sperm starts coming out into the mother' vagina! And then you know what?

JMR: No, what?

Simon: Then the egg eats up that sperm! Yep, it does. [Later.]

JMR: How would *he* feel if he didn't have any role in making the baby?

Simon: Sad. She [sic] would feel sad.

JMR: Sad? Why?

Simon: 'Cause no baby would come out of her!

JMR: Shall we see the next picture?

Simon: Hold on a second! I know how dogs were born too. The same way! They need sperm seeds.

JMR: Right. So that the man has . . .

Simon: And also chickens! And also things like that.

[Later he looks at a picture showing a mother, father, older brother, and sister on an outing with a new baby. When asked to describe the brother's and sister's states of mind, he says they feel "fine." He continues.]

Simon: But, except they're mad too, 'cause they get a better, 'cause they [points to the parents] own the baby and they don't. [Points to the children and frowns, adds triumphantly.] 'Cause if she gets a baby, then they [children] will also own one and they [parents] won't.

JMR: Huh? And the parents won't?

Simon: And I know what happens. When they're 18, they can't have any kids. You're too old to have kids, dummy!

JMR: At 18 you're too old?

Simon: Yeah, when you're 80. Tee-hee. I think when they're grown-ups, these kids will be their father.

JMR: Uh huh . . .

Simon: And so their kids will be their father to the kids! When he [the brother] is a grown-up, the baby would be a kid . . . And he would own the kid. [Starts to turn pages again. Minutes later he looks at a picture of the brother bear holding the baby.] He's fat. [Muses for a moment.] He's going to grow up when he's a father—and take a nap in the park!

In closing Simon endows the baby with "special spider powers," speaks of his wish to own a baby leopard cub, and then describes the feline pet already in his possession, a cat he has named "Black Power." As Simon implies, being a father means to grow up, although he remains unclear as to whether, so to speak, the "poppa chicken" or his "egg" comes first. Nor is he so certain, it seems, that such responsibility will be altogether welcome.

No oedipal or postoedipal boy actually achieves the paternal identity expressed in his masculine ideal. A little boy is still, after all, a child. He is excluded from the bedroom, from adulthood, and from acts of creation for which his body is not yet prepared. Compared with his parents, no matter how attentively they applaud his gestures at manhood, biologically a son *is* inadequate and infertile, and he must discover other modes of feeling strong and productive. Otherwise his only recourse would be that regressive, passive, and at the same time mysterious and powerful "nap in the park." When one is asleep, anything can happen.

One such mode of productivity may be found in the creative play that typically occupies postoedipal boys and that, in most societies, ushers in their status as schoolboys. Much boyish play bespeaks phallic, intrusive contours and strivings, as Erikson has demonstrated. At the same time, however, certain activities at this stage hearken back to the boy's imitation of his mother's domestic, feminine activities. Still other creations, both plastic and dramatic, betray what appear to be transparent bisexual or ambisexual motives. In fact, they express exactly that union of identifications with both father and mother which Freud hypothesized in 1923.

By seven or eight years of age at the latest, most boys have focused on gunplay, tower building, and other activities associated with phallic ambitions. But they also have begun to construct castles presided over by kings who sire royal families. They pirate and pilot rather womblike boats. Perhaps they manage hotels in which food and drink are served. They play doctor. Moreover, in some of these games, chauvinism aside, girls may be invited to join as active coworkers and playmates. In many of their productions, intrusive, inclusive, and inceptive forms and modalities are intermingled.

Sometimes, preoccupied with the world he has helped to create, a boy will drift away and give up the helm. When he does so, enacting the role of patient rather than doctor or simply snoozing away in his buccaneer's galleon, he may be revealing the kind of passivity that is a response to childish failure, inevitable and temporary though it may be. He may be acknowledging, wordlessly, the sense of littleness and insignificance that strikes children of this age.

To Become a Parent

Confronted by the futility of his generative ambitions, the postoedipal boy embarks on a regression in the service of the ego, as Ernst Kris (1952) once put it in describing the creative process. In part, this is a defensive measure. But it is also age-appropriate and adaptive, both springing from and, in turn, fostering progress in other realms, specifically in a boy's ability to explore and to act in the ever-widening world in which he finds himself.

Thwarted in his wish to produce offspring as his mother has, a son further finds himself unable to possess her and, in having her, to be productive in the manner of his father. Denied erotic passion as well as the privileges of parenthood, a little boy may then decide unconsciously to be his own inseminator, his own parents, and, more regressively, his own child. Thus a fantasy of parthenogenesis may be born, expressing a boy's inability to accept his generational status and, with it, his delayed generativity.

Less tolerable at this stage, nonetheless, a procreative fantasy has become repressible. Ideally, wishes to produce babies and to be as nurturing as the idealized mother can now be sublimated in the form of a general productivity, in impulses to learn, act, and create as if independent of adult interference or advice. The aims of such residual oedipal ambitions—to be both mother and father, to be big, strong, and triumphant over both sexes of the older generation, not to need them or anybody else but rather to do it all oneself—are naturally unattainable. Once more, child that he is, the would-be parthogenitor is doomed to fall short of his mark. Yet there is a telos as well as a dynamism in these concerted efforts at mastery and self-sufficiency, and a boy's labors mean much more than they did at the start.

To describe the postoedipal period merely as a time of latency, in the sense of dormancy, is misleading, especially in light of what Erikson has described as a boy's thrust toward industry (Erikson, 1963, 1964). The sensual appetites and aggressions of middle childhood and the fears these engender seem tamer and less transparent than those of earlier stages. Even where the child is subject to the overstimulation provided by the contemporary media, his parents, objects of his oedipal impulses, have typically become less important in his consciousness and instinctual life.

But the superseded desires and anxieties of the prelatency years never go away completely. Most significantly, a boy's general interest in creativity remains with him, rendering the years of middle childhood a time of great excitement and accomplishment. The schoolboy is now impelled to discover skills that will enable him increasingly to move freely within and occasionally act on his surroundings, to build a sense of competence, which Robert White (1959) believes to be a prime mover and psychological mainstay throughout one's working life. Unable to "make people," a boy becomes instead a student, a worker, a producer. At least this is one adaptive solution to his abiding feelings of insignificance and infertility.

Middle childhood further encompasses a cognitive revolution during which a host of new realizations—many of which seem at once forbidden and disheartening as well as uplifting or fascinating—must be integrated into the child's developing worldview. New modes of thought are called on; with new problems come different means of reasoning. The intense efforts of so many boys of this age to arrive at "right" answers, and their chagrin at minor failures, indicate not only thinly veiled fears of oedipal catastrophe and preoedipal demands for perfection, but also a more autonomous, adaptive struggle to acquire knowledge and mastery. The arena of interest and conflict has shifted, but life tasks have not become any less pressing.

Specifically, the issues a boy now confronts are matters of life and death. On the unconscious level, his growing concern with knowing and manipulating the extrafamilial environment may originate, at least in part, in his striving to feel more potent and productive than he did within the family and its oedipal triangle. Outside this context, however, a boy also discovers his limits—that is, the finitude and relativity he must share with all creatures. Of vital importance, as both Piaget and Freud suggested, is the child's crucial preoccupation with the origins and ends of life itself. However inchoate his emerging personal philosophy may be, an eight-year-old encounters the basic facts of life. Like everything else in the world, he was conceived; he was born; he lives; he will die.

In a boy's struggle to solve the problems of life, issues of content resonate with modes of understanding. Challenged now is his egocentrism of feeling and thought, a self-centeredness that becomes increasingly untenable and unserviceable in the real world. By eight or nine years of age, a child requires an unprecedented objectivity, a decentering, if he is to become detached enough to classify himself with other beings and define his own limits in both time and space. Without such an appreciation of limits, as opposed to infantile or even later phallic omnipotence, effective action would be impossible.

Indeed, far from being all powerful, a child's sense of self may even become momentarily lost in the dryness of style typical of latency boys.

At times a businesslike, cool demeanor suggests affective isolation or even a false self. But this apparent emotional vacuum is adaptive, granting a young boy potentially painful, conflict-laden realizations about his human powers and inner limits without his either succumbing to despair or reawakening those self-seeking motives that continue to impel his curiosity.

A child of this age may err in the other direction from the self-reference of his earlier years, now removing himself from the problems with which he grapples, as if they had nothing to do with him. The primal scene, his parents' relationship, his own sexual feelings, his bodily sensations in general and, for that matter, his wishes to be nurturant or generative—these no longer interest him. Or, if they do, than he is loth to admit it. He is concerned instead with mates, that is, the male and the female, chickens and anatomical tubes, as well as responsibility, work, and life's continuity. Finally, the boy's practiced use of concrete operations, which he has applied to the physical universe, finally enables him to resolve more fully the riddle of the Sphinx. His capacity to form classes and relations allows him to begin to cope with life's complexity and to interrelate its various elements: anatomical differences, the origin of babies, the complementarity of man and woman, and the finality of death.

During adolescence these ideas will be personalized once more to include the boy himself, thereby regaining their emotional impact and instinctual meaning. In the meantime, he forgets what he once knew so well and felt so much. The fact that his parents "did that" (to quote at least one nine-year-old boy), and by doing "that" made him, provides the greatest shock. The origins of at least a portion of his conceptual endeavors in his repressed procreative strivings remain sublimated. Nor does he seem to recognize that, intellectually, he is discovering how one day he will in fact fulfill his biological destiny.

To Be Fathered

Throughout middle childhood, the possibility of tending babies is redemptive. Although a boy cannot yet father a baby, nor feed it from breasts he will never have, he can care for a child or other creatures in a variety of ways. In fact, many boys in this age group enact and express an avid interest in caretaking, more readily than younger children still in the throes of oedipal conflict, and more so than early adolescents beset by renewed conflicts in gender identity and the need to compensate for their confusion. Many eight-, nine-, and ten-year-olds manifest this nurturance by growing plants, succoring pets, and otherwise shepherding animals or children.

Some boys find the prospect of these activities effeminizing; others find such inclinations more tolerable and desirable. Once again, the presence or absence of an involved father seems to be a major mediating factor, helping to determine both a son's readiness to tender love and his freedom to learn to produce work.

Throughout development, as noted earlier, good and bad fathers present discrepant models of masculinity. During middle childhood especially, a father as mentor comes to serve specific functions. A father may now help his son discover the skills with which to satisfy pregenital aims in a more acceptable fashion, to explore and experiment in the service of competence rather than to be driven or inhibited by excessive competitiveness. He may actually help his son become stronger and more adult, more of a man and potential rival. Or, for reasons of his own, he may not.

Indeed, this stage of the relationship between fathers and sons appears analogous in some respects to a boy's early rapprochement with his ambivalently held mother, though the structural implications are, of course, less far-reaching. Having been alienated from the father by his own rivalry and projections of his hostility, a son then returns to him for renewed guidance and instruction. It is closeness with the father and trust in him that ideally allow a boy to temper the aggressivity of both his curiosity and his assertiveness. And if his father is there, there for him, he will feel less inclined to destroy for himself the man he loves and needs in his own mind's eye. He will be less likely to risk the loss, in an imagined retaliation for his initiative, of his own boyishness.

More secure in these ways because he experiences his father's care and because his father does indeed help him become masterly and manly, a boy may be further freed to fulfill creative wishes. In addition, he may deepen his concept of manhood to encompass a variety of affects and activities which might otherwise become associated with the mother's exclusive province, with being womanly.

When a boy has as a model only a rivalrous "bad" father, it is often much harder for him, unless an alternative mentor is found, to modulate his phallic aggressions in the service of discovery or industry. Nor can he integrate needs to produce or nurture with a sex-linked aggressivity. Heightened bravado, displays of aggression, and denials of tenderness or a recession into an outworn feminine identification and a homosexual orientation may be the consequences of this sort of failure.

In cultures other than our own, this mentorship is more often institutionalized. Boys are handed over to the tutelage of fathers or their collective male representatives after having been wrested from the virtually exclusive care of women (See Kakar 1982; Lidz and Lidz, 1973). In our society, patterns of paternal involvement with sons (and daughters) during the ontogenetic "age of reason" are more variable.

One boy, Willy, living alone with his mother and visiting his father perhaps once a month, passed through a particularly irksome phase during which he attacked, assaulted, and shouted down all comers while accomplishing very little on his own. As his father made himself more accessible, Willy, by the age of nine, had become calmer and also less inhibited in his work.

Jimmy, a sixteen-year-old boy whose father lived with the family but seemed to take little interest in it, found himself indifferent to school, work, sports, sex, or any active pursuit. His inertia compounded his sense of inferiority, and a vicious cycle set in of inactivity and sterility. Only drugs could capture his attention until, through treatment with a male therapist and an idealizing paternal transference, he found himself increasingly drawn to interests, schoolwork, and sex, which previously had been, in his words, "irrelevant."

Active fathering helps to reconcile another division, again originating earlier in development. In part, a boy's generativity may be seen to follow two courses. One is object-oriented, involving desires for the opposite sex and eventuating in genitality and fatherhood. The other more or less follows the "narcissistic" line, to borrow from Heinz Kohut (1971) and his followers; at least in part, creative work stems from a sublimated love of self and the self's productions. It is not that these two directions constitute diverging, distinct lines of development, but that a *potential* tension exists between work and love.

This conflict is evident in the proverbial complaint of many adult men that involvement with family will erode their effectiveness as workers and material providers, or that being a father will rob them of their freedom to create. In our society there is a measure of truth to this: shop and house are no longer blended, and jobs do take men from the home. Still, this reality can serve as a resistance. Absorption in work may be tantamount to self-absorption; conversely, an exclusive interest in family may represent a retreat from a legitimate narcissistic pleasure in work achievement. Both are based in disappointments with respect to the preoedipal or "just-oedipal" mother: arrests, fixations, and regressions. But a father's comfort in being a father, his familiarity with the child, and his own self-fulfillment as a man may do much to heal old wounds and fill in the gaps, to repair the splits within his son's sexuality, and to offer future ways of adapting to the compartmentalizations inevitable in modern life. His presence may not synthesize a boy's procreative and creative identities as one—that is simply not realistic—but fathering may certainly make them seem more compatible.

It is not quite that simple, however. When one envisions the "ideal mother" during her toddler's rapprochement crisis, one sees her arms opening in welcome but then unfolding to let her child go, leaving the child free to feel independent once more. The danger is twofold. For whatever reason, she may reject or rebuff her child; or she may seduce and engulf him again, thwarting his move toward autonomy.

Fathering presents analogous problems during middle childhood, for not only may a father ignore or avoid his son but he may overcontrol him. His guidance, which is a form of nurturance, may become a force-feeding, an intrusion that disallows privacy and freedom of choice. Because of their own narcissistic needs, many men drive their sons, push them to succeed, steer them into uncomfortable activities. The effects may not be so profound at this stage as they were earlier, during rapprochement with the mother or even during the oedipal era, because so much has intervened. With capacities such as object constancy secured, too much structuralization has occurred to permit so great a transformation as the one whereby the good mother is internalized. Still a boy's final assimilation of the good father and his triumph over the bad father are vital in divesting his images of, and identifications with, a masculinity of excessive hostility, filial defense, or isolation. In so doing, he engenders a male identity, not merely phallic and intrusive but caring, competent, fatherly in itself.

Back to the Future

As Bettelheim, Blos, and others have remarked, puberty is presaged by a resurgence of regressive and ambisexual yearnings, and by an increasing sense of uncertainty and defensiveness. The tightening of defenses in preadolescence represents an overcompensation and a protest against the crumbling of a boy's brittle, posturing detachment, the false maturity of so many late-latency children. Less consciously and less completely than before, children recapitulate many of the transformations in sexual and parental identity that are so visible and intense in three- and four-year-olds.

The differences, of course, are pronounced. For example, with the coming of puberty, boys anticipate realizable sexual impulses and social independence. In the interim, they suffer fragmentation and seek solace in allies, including fathers and their various incarnations outside the family. Peers also provide points of anchorage in the midst of these upheavals. At least these boys have behind them a decade of mothering and fathering, and of identifications, from which to forge an identity that is their own and eventually to assume their status as a caretaker for the next generation.

The major achievements of a boy's adolescence are the consolidation of his work identity and his capacity to fall in love, both of which reorganize personality in many ways. I will reserve for the concluding chapters of this book a discussion of the transition from what Erikson called the "morality of childhood" to the "ethics of the adult." It is a passage in which romantic passion and the whisperings of a woman's more temperate voice of judgment play vital roles. In the meantime, let us turn to the relationship of men to their inner male presence, specifically to the identifications and psychic integrations that secure a man's sense of himself as a father.

3

Becoming a Father

In his *Three Essays on the Theory of Sexuality* of 1905, Freud detailed the progression and penultimate objectives of infantile sexuality, with its changing libidinal zones and aims. Initially linked to the survival of the self and less tangible narcissistic necessities, slowly becoming invested in others for their own sake, an individual's quest for pleasure eventually became focused on the genitals and on intercourse with a person of the opposite sex. Ultimately, sex serves and ensures the reproduction of the species. Freud had introduced his theory of genital primacy.

Implicit in Freud's concept of genitality and its childhood *Anlagen* is a view of a simultaneously evolving generativity. The adult individual's potential biological and social parenthood is foretold in the erotic and sensual activities and sexual identifications of the growing child, destined to become not only an adult individual but the vehicle of his or her species' "germ plasm" (Freud, 1914b). For the grown man—as much as for the woman—parenthood is both the outcome of his psychosexual history and a testimony to his manhood. Paternity and masculinity are inextricably interwoven.

As I have suggested, a man does not come to fatherhood in a vacuum. His paternal identity, expressed in fathering his children, is embedded in a life-historical, intrapsychic, and interpersonal context. Fathers have been sons. They have a stock of experiences with their fathers and mothers from which to draw in synthesizing their own representation of parenthood. In childhood are discovered the pre-stages of paternity, the successive parental identifications that accrue to the self-representation, preparing the way for the active nurturance and generativity of the adult man.

Biological fatherhood and the ongoing responsibilities of childrearing often precipitate an age-specific crisis, one in which repressed conflicts and outmoded identifications are reactivated and reworked. Confronted by a new significant object and a new role, a father endeavors to integrate the images of the child and of himself as parent by way of both assimilation and accommodation.

A man identifies in part with his baby's infantile needs and modes of expression, experiencing and enacting these for himself. And he translates and interprets these events according to the existing configurations, either current or outmoded, of his representational world, fitting them to fantasies and memories of his own parents and of himself as a child. But in the end, the novelty and immediacy of fatherhood engender a state of dynamic disequilibrium, which cannot be mastered by assimilation alone, referred to the extant past. An accommodation to the actual experience is demanded, an active adjustment, which resonates through and reshapes the man's representational world, altering images of the self and parents and the relations among them.

Thus, the adult crisis provoked by the birth and presence of children needs to be elucidated from the vantage of the integrated dynamic and object-relations perspectives of current psychoanalytic theory. The adaptational demands placed on a man when he actually becomes a father further require reference to the guiding principles set forth by Hartmann in his explication of the individual's relation to his internal and external environments (1939) as well as in the genetic structuralism elaborated by Piaget and others. In addition to the interplay between accommodation and assimilation, coming to terms with fatherhood and fitting in to the new generational role that this brings set in motion the processes of differentiation and integration emphasized by the early ego psychologists. Ideally, even as he enacts his paternal fantasies in the real world, under the sway of his new responsibilities, the new father ultimately achieves that higher level of internalization and autonomy that is the sine qua non of successful adaptation. I invoke the concept of adaptation rather than development to describe these psychic reorganizations because with fathers, unlike mothers, the biological contributions to the changes taking place are minimal. The sequences and outcomes are less predictable, and the individual father is freer to approach the challenges of parenthood in any number of ways.[1]

A new father will influence and in turn be affected by the development, which *is* maturationally impelled, of his child. A unique individual with particular capacities, needs, modes of apprehension and expression—a growing child will nonetheless pass through a typical and predictable sequence of psychosexual and psychosocial phases. A father will attune to these by seeking an emphatic foundation in his own history. As he finds many of his childhood struggles revivified and vicariously resolved again, he will in turn help to determine the course of his child's psychological growth. That fathers do many of the same things with the child is a function more of the child's than of his own prewiring. Thus, within the dyad of father and child, there transpire mostly implicit communications many of which spring from the deepest and most basic motives of each participant. These require mutual adjustments that ideally answer at once the needs of both child and man. Under less than optimal conditions, father and child can make the best of what they have and what is offered—a testimony to human resiliency.

The context in which this dyad is embedded cannot be overlooked: the elaborate network of familial relations among father, mother, and other siblings as individuals, pairs, triads, and so forth. All are further anchored in a culture replete with the myths, proscriptions, and workaday routines that order a man's life. Let us now turn to what fathers themselves have to say.

Fathers Speak

Just what does it mean to a man to be a father? I have put this question directly and fairly systematically to fathers of young children on several occasions, on visits to their homes and in discussion groups consisting of three to eight men. These inquiries were conducted as part of larger research projects having to do with child development in general: first, Louis Kaplan's observational center at New York University, modeled on Mahler's Masters study; second, Judith Kestenberg's Port Washington Child Development Research Center, geared as well to prevention and parent training. By and large, the population was middle-class and white, most of the parents ranging in age from twenty-five to thirty-five. A further bias had to do with the avowed interest of the group in child development, an interest that moved them to volunteer to participate in the first place. In addition to clinical interviews and general group discussions, these men were observed by myself and by graduate-student assistants in interaction with their children. The children were preschoolers, boys and girls ranging in age from a few weeks to three years.

As my subjects, individually or together, began to reflect on what being a father meant to them, certain themes and problems emerged. For one thing, most of these men were new in their role and found it hard to articulate their sense of it. For another, rarely had they had the chance to collect together, as mothers often do, and share their parental experiences and questions. So the idea of having a sounding board of their own was a novelty. In general, they said, their wives had "done the reading" and seemed the more competent and instinctive parent. For many of the men, the baby was a strange, foreign, or inanimate body on its arrival, random in its movements and unrelated to them, "a thing," as one put it, "that ate and defecated a lot."

One might be tempted to say that these were men out of touch or unconcerned with parenthood, were it not for the fact that all had chosen to have themselves and their children participate in the projects, carving time out of busy schedules to ponder exactly that aspect of their lives. Instead their uneasiness seemed to stem from a general void in the social consciousness of the times, the seventies, about fathers and their familial functions. More important, the inability to embody in words one's paternity bespoke darker conflicts and uncertainties, many inherited from childhood.

Once again the Theban Sphinx rears her head, the oedipal motif in its broadest sense. Becoming a father, the son at last rivals his father, albeit with a certain fear and trembling: "I can't explain it, but the first time I went to see my parents after Seth was born, my wife and I were driving up to their house and I was seized by this terrible anxiety, shaky and confused and I couldn't pin down why, just that something had changed—at least between my father and me . . . I got over it in an hour or so, and the second visit didn't upset me." Another young father put it more benignly and yet more explicitly: "When Billy was born, and I became a father, well then my father became just a man, a guy

I could understand. Before that, I sort of worshipped him, you know, or else I blamed him for all the things he hadn't done or understood about me. But now I was just like him." The father's father loses some of his luster, his omnipotence, his culpability and responsibility, as his son becomes no longer merely a son.

Along with an enhanced generational status come rumblings that portend a destruction of the old family order—not simply by virtue of the man's unsettled aggressions from childhood, although their veracity cannot be denied, but also because the father's and one's own mortality now presents itself as well. A new life, like the act of procreation itself, invokes its opposite, death, dispelling the illusion of an omnipotent and mystical parental force ensuring personal eternity. Having a baby renders inescapable the place of a single life cycle in the cycle of generations, no matter how inchoate or inarticulate a young father's understanding is of this fact. In any event, the prospective birth and, later, the presence of children called to mind, for several of the men interviewed, their own finitude. As one man put it, "When Rachel was pregnant, I stopped being the carefree old soul I'd been. I began to think about security, my dying, providing for her and Jennifer . . . I don't know why, but I hadn't thought about my dying before, at least not in that way—just the way all teenagers worry. Now, I guess, it doesn't seem to matter so much, that is, not for myself."

Another, the father of three young boys, lamented: "From what I've seen, in other families, the parents aren't all that indispensable. I mean, kids can go on without you . . . at least without the father . . . I guess I find that a real blow, that they could just forget me like that." His remarks stirred the other members of the group, one of whom retorted: "Gee, that doesn't bother me at all. I mean my dispensability is precisely what I would want for my family. I feel secure knowing they could manage without me. And I've done much to accomplish exactly that." Still another father intervened: "You're simply all wrong about that. Men matter to their families and aren't forgotten just like that." The talk became an argument, a power struggle in the guise of assertion and proof.

Underlying the rationalizations being bantered about were the projective identifications made by all these men with their children, who revivified in them memories of their own oedipal strivings, further stimulated, and perhaps even fulfilled, by their paternity. If they could triumph over their own fathers, why couldn't their child in turn displace and destroy them? Perhaps, as much as they might yearn for and then cherish their children, they might also seek to discard and orphan them, like Laius, before it's "too late." Fathers are also sons—hence they fear the inescapable fate and guilt of Oedipus, while at the same time recoiling from the possibility of a father's more intentional and, by virtue of the power of age, more dangerous malevolence. Repudiating death wishes of this kind, they introject the son's would-be fate as their own, visiting on themselves images of a terrible abandonment.

At times, it seemed that the fathers interviewed bent over backward to negate their own narcissistic needs in the face of their children's demands. And yet, in certain important areas, their own urges to ascendancy won out. For example, in the name of sexual honesty, most of the men insisted on the right to appear naked before their girls and boys, and occasionally on the value of explicitly using themselves as exemplars of anatomy and its functions. No doubt it is an uncomfortable business suddenly to cover oneself in the privacy of the home, especially in a culture increasingly tolerant of public nakedness. Nor could these men be expected to emphasize with the child's-eye view, since they are not privy to those recollections of awesome genitalia, male or female, that come the way of the clinician (see Greenacre, 1953, and below). Yet one could not help sensing the demonstration of supremacy in the act of exhibition, the picture worth thousands of words to the contrary: "You see, I give in to you, but after all that, look how much bigger I really am."

Not only did the fathers aspire to supremacy in displaying their penis, but they also seemed to be asserting a wish to return to the innocence and freedom of their own childhood. At the very least, these men seemed to be asking if they were not just as deserving of maternal care and its pleasures as their children. "Counteroedipal" or more broadly sexual promptings were evident as well in such acts, in the dead earnestness with which one somber father reportedly demonstrated the moving of bowels to his two-year-old son. In this case, one might pinpoint his reciprocal counter-negative oedipal wishes toward his son. A more explicit acknowledgment of these wishes would likely shake the sexual identity of most men, bent as they are on parading and thus finding a mirror for their masculinity.

This raises another issue. Together with aggressive strivings, regressive longings, and both negative and positive oedipal or more generally sexual impulses, pregnancy, birth, and the presence of children also seem to awaken the maternal promptings and archaic feminine identifications that most fathers had long ago repressed. As one man put it in describing his participation in his wife's natural childbirth: "I felt it all as if it were happening to me . . . You know, with the fetal monitor you can get on top of the contraction before the woman does, you know what's going on in her body better than she . . . *You* feel the strain." Another man described outright his envy of the wife's ability to give birth and then nurse her child. And many husbands were moved to compete with their wives for parental authority. One, a man deeply immersed in all of his two-year-old's doings, looked condescendingly at a dripping, crumbling sandwich. In an only half-humorous conspiratorial tone, he told the boy: "We're going to fire mommy! We can do it better, can't we!"

The deep love a child stirs in his parents may revivify the man's yearnings for a renewed intimacy with his own mother, along with its attendant confusion of identities. He may find both his sense of separateness and his masculinity threatened, depending on the degree to which he can allow himself to cross over sexual boundaries without violating them and to encompass a sensuous and to some degree feminine tenderness within an essentially male identity. Among the father-child pairs studied, I noticed some men who seemed both to become infected with their child's rhythms, baby talk, and movements and simultaneously to adopt a distinctly, almost caricatured maternal manner that often was not evident when I spoke to them separately. Furthermore, these were the fathers who, like overprotective mothers, appeared most caught up in their children's wanderings and wonderings, unwilling during the hours together to grant the child much space or time of his own. Other men hung back warily, retreating from group activities like dances and songs, stiff in their postures and unable to flow with the inclinations and impulses of the children. One sensed in these fathers an effort to fortify a masculine identity in the face of the maternal and symbiotic pressures being exerted upon it.

Obviously, different men contend with such tensions in different ways. Some may run away from their families into a more stereotypically manly work identity. Thus, several of the fathers described working harder and harder after the children were born, complaining about their busy schedules, which, since some were self-employed, were to a certain extent of their own making. Others retreated from work, absorbing themselves in the family instead. For most, in fact, finding a balance between loving their children and working for personal success was problematic.

This was, I believe, a partial recapitulation of an earlier crisis in sexual identity. I have said that, during the oedipal period, boys must struggle to resolve the conflict between urges to maternal power and the need to feel fertile and productive, on the one hand, and phallic strivings and the need to preserve a nascent virility on the other. An identification with the father's fatherhood—intuitions and inchoate imaginings about his creativity within the primal scene, the child's would-be participation in it, the knowledge that males can be strong and tender at once, a sense of the paternal future—all these are major steppingstones toward a vital male identity. Biological fatherhood brings to light the six-year-old's hazy fantasy of parenthood, sharpens it, and makes it real even as it reinvokes the dynamics that entered into its composition.

Interestingly, most of the men interviewed assiduously disavowed any projections for the future with regard to their children. They claimed that they demanded no great achievements for them but merely hoped that the child might become happy and good. And yet these men were so specific in naming what they did not want for the child, and what they did *not* want for them was so closely tied to what they *did* want for themselves, that the disavowal seemed transparent. Further constrained by a liberal ethos, many young fathers seemed to strive against reflexive tendencies to impose their values and ideals on their children, betraying them instead nonverbally or by communicating their opposite (see Burlingham, 1973).

To say, then, that fathers expect the fruition of their own ego ideal in children may be an oversimplification. For one thing, paternity and the hard commitments it necessitates begin to demonstrate the fantastic nature of idealized and grandiose self-images that in the past may very well have been retained as secret goals. Their unreality becomes inescapable with the appearance of a dependent being who asks above all that its caretakers be real, be what they are. For another, notwithstanding his grand expectations, a father may also be moved to compete with and even belittle his child, devaluing him in order to preserve his own self-esteem and security. He may feel morally bound to deny his desires that his child be special. And his projective identification with the child will be affected by both his sexual impulses toward him as well as by vacillations and fluctuations in his sense of sexual identity. The possibilities are many. Thus, for a man, a child presents itself as a narcissistic problem, rather than simply an extension of self, invoking a host of contradictory self and object representations, affects, and wishes.

Among these conflicts is a man's struggle to extract the best from his relationship with his own father. If a man experiences fatherhood as a conquest of his own father, vanquished and then lost to him, he will also seek to resurrect the father's image as a source of identification, a foundation on which to construct his own paternal identity. In this regard, a large portion of the men lamented their own father's absence or failure to participate in their growing up. Furthermore, often they remarked that only by fulfilling the standards he set for them, by meeting his expectations, and even doing his work could they find any kind of relationship with him. They had experienced their father only on his terms. In contrast, they said, their children would suffer neither the paternal intrusions nor the paternal vacuum they had experienced as sons.

But the insubstantiality of their paternal object representation, hence the deficiencies of their "paternal ego ideal" (Blos, 1985), seemed to baffle many of these men (though not all). To discover the wellspring of both the nurturance and the fatherly authority asked of and excited in them by their children, many might turn only to selective identifications with the mother. The trouble was that these revivifications, mostly at the preoedipal level, appeared to be even more threatening to their sexual identity. Impoverished experiences of their fathers, who had not lent themselves completely to internalization, made transient identifications with the females in a young father's life all the more troubling. As one subject put it:

> I guess I was just like the other boys in my suburb. We never saw our dads much, just our mothers. And yet our dads wanted to make so much of us, wanted me to win, to get the prizes, to go into his business. It's a funny thing, but I resented him not being there and yet being there all the time—know what I mean? Both

things at the same time . . . I just want to be there for Andy. But I don't quite know how—it seems easier for Beth [his wife]— maybe because she's a woman—and maybe because mothers don't ask their children to be anything. That's what I'd like to do, but it's hard.

Ultimately these young men, like all fathers, must make their own parents all over again and make them their own. As Benedek, Kestenberg, and Erikson have all underlined, parenthood constitutes a life stage, or better an ongoing progression, unto itself—a series of relentless challenges during which an individual's personality is beset and revolutionized by new exigencies from without and needs from within. Becoming a father and taking care of a child can transform an individual's multifaceted identity as an adult man in a variety of ways, depending on his instinctual proclivities, his inherent gifts, his history, life circumstances, the roles and opportunities opening up or closing before him, and the disposition of the child to whom he must attune. Generativity in procreation counteracts a potential sense of stasis, vanity, and futility. But it requires care, curtailing infantile license and diminishing certain real and otherwise legitimate adult freedoms. In a word: "I looked at that baby, and my whole life changed. I was a different person."

To summarize, becoming a father provokes an adaptational crisis in an adult man that may have to do with one or more of the following interwoven psychic threads: uncertainty about the identity of a father and his actual role; a changed relationship to his wife and his family of origin; revivification of oedipal rivalries and desires and the fear of their realization or reciprocation; regressive, often preoedipal, symbiotic longings; a crisis in sexual identity calling up maternal and feminine identifications and the defenses against them; a sense of narcissistic limits and injury versus the possibility of self-extension and immortalization through one's legacy; the search for a man's own father; and the demand for a new ego identity, integrating object representations of the child and self-representation in the role of father.

Defining Paternal Identity

Throughout, I have made reference to the boy's sense of paternal identity without saying what I mean by this construct. *Identity*, of any kind, is one of those psychological "star words," as Pruyser (1975) notes in his discussion of splitting, which capture a great deal but elude definition and thus invite controversy. So precision-minded analysts argue for a more restricted use of such delimited concepts as self or self-representation. I do not share this view. Rather, I believe that the sense of identity remains a most valuable and encompassing psycho-analytic concept, one at the intersection of phenomenological experi-ence and theoretical reflection. Still I agree that such terms must be more explicitly defined.

Phenomenologically speaking, identity (in the sense of ego identity, in Erikson's more articulate rendering) may be viewed as an individ-ual's sense of wholeness, sameness, and continuity. In psychosocial language, this is an internal consistency over time, which in turn is mirrored, affirmed, and facilitated by the demands and opportunities afforded by other people, as well as by the roles, cultural traditions, and institutions that constitute the social environment. In more devel-opmental and genetic terms, Erikson says that identity unfolds as an "evolving configuration . . . established by syntheses and re-syntheses throughout childhood . . . gradually integrating constitutional givens, idiosyncratic libidinal needs, favored capacities, significant identifica-tions, effective defenses, successful sublimations and consistent roles" (1959:116).

Compared with character—personal style observed from without (Moore and Fine, 1990)—identity may be articulated as an individual's own sense of the themes and modalities that shape personal integrity. Thus identity is a construct that is at once experienced and explanatory, self-referential and recognizable.

Finally, an object-relations perspective might have it that a sense of identity is the reciprocal of object relations proper. Evolving in inter-dependence, both object relations and identity describe the various configurations of and relations between self and object representations, with the accent falling in the one instance on the object and in the other on the self. Hence an individual's identity, in contrast to a role, is fundamentally a private psychic experience, an experience of self in relation to others, one with conscious and unconscious dimensions. But as with object relations, it is realized and observable in its deriva-tives in the societal realm, where others recognize you for who you are.

By *relations* are meant the affects, cognitions, instinctual wishes, attitudes, guiding principles, and felt obligations that link self and others (Kernberg, 1976). It is the relations between representations of objects and of the self, rather than the representations themselves, which the growing individual internalizes.

The various aspects of identity organize one another. *Core gender identity,* Stoller's concept (1986), which is consolidated prior to the phallic phase, refers to an individual's cognitive and emotional conviction of being male or female in relation to members of the same and opposite sexes. Gender is an inclusive and dichotomous category (perhaps the basic category, as linguistic convention suggests). As such, it becomes an organizer of the confusing pluralisms in the surrounding world and provides a means of situating the self within the world. With the exception of transsexualism, an individual's gender identity is less subject to workings of desire, conflict, and paradox than is her or his sexual identity.

Sexual identity is at once a broader and a more delimited concept, evolving through the course of the life cycle and pertaining to an individual's sense of the particular kind of man or woman he or she is, especially in the sexual arena. On the one hand, it represents an integration of the internalization of the culture's prescribed gender role. On the other hand, this sense of one's sexual self derives not only from the certainty of one's given gender but also from transformations of preemptive, if most often unconscious, ambisexual and indeed cross-sexual identifications and desires.

Generational identity is another pertinent dimension of identity as a whole. It refers to an individual's appreciation of the place of his or her life cycle within the generational flow or, more concretely, of one's felt status and attributes as a child, a parent, a grandchild, and so forth. One begins life as a son or daughter, a definition of self in relation to others that remains throughout its duration, but later becomes a father or mother and subsequently a grandparent. There are attributes, mostly having to do with power and responsibility, associated with these various conditions. Furthermore, a person's gender has a far-reaching if often opaque impact on the sense of generational authority and position, especially when the social implications of maleness and femaleness are also considered. In any given society at one or another junctures in its history, becoming a father carries with it different implications from those of being a mother. To the extent that biological parenthood is generalized and analogized to include professional or social ascendancy, the roles available to the sexes further color the meanings of identity. The patriarch is not simply a *pater familias.* Similarly, the matriarch of the family may hold little sway in the world of work even as she rules the roost. So both mother and father tend to provide complicated and contradictory models for sons and daughters to emulate, even as their children's own social contexts change.

In any event, generational identity is not quite equivalent to parental or paternal identity, the subject at hand. Parental identity pertains to one's fantasies, ambitions, and actual achievements in the role of a generator and nurturer of products, human and otherwise. Paternal identity, in particular, represents the dovetailing and synthesis of paternal, sexual, and male gender identity. For a man, his parental sense of himself, his feeling of fatherhood, represents his conviction that he has been man enough, actively heterosexual and sufficiently mature, to sire and father a child. His paternal identity describes his sense of self as a masculine procreator, producer, caretaker—a personal equation of parenthood and manhood with fatherhood.

Fruition of a Developmental Line

Earlier I outlined a ideal progression for an "ideal type" of boy, a construct serving heuristic purposes without any direct manifestation in reality. Of course, no such child exists. Other, real-life boys may pass through the stages posited, each with a different timetable, occasionally altering or even reversing the sequence of these stages. Perhaps most important, in isolating a series of individual steps, one inevitably ignores the impact on a child of his actual caretakers, to whom he must adapt, and does a disservice to the reciprocity between parents and child. Overgeneralized, the "average expectable environment" (Hartmann, 1939) may ultimately amount to no environment at all.

With these caveats in mind, I left this hypothetical boy, and father-to-be, on the verge of fulfilling his genital destiny as he begins adolescence. Before turning to actual fatherhood, however I must pause and briefly consider some critical turning points in the adolescent passage.

As puberty approaches, the pseudo-detachment of latency falters, revealing conflicts and ambisexual currents hitherto submerged. The teenager relives the central crises of his early years—the rapprochement struggles that climax the separation-individuation process, the feminine identifications and homosexual object choices that precede the oedipal period, the Oedipus complex itself. Beleaguered from within and overwhelmed at times by his surprising bodily feelings, an adolescent may seek refuge in group stereotype and conformism, shunning all that does not jibe with a gender identity once more in doubt.

At the same time, however, he discovers altogether new developments in himself: the ejaculatory capacity first manifest perhaps in wet dreams and later in masturbatory activity and, with this, a variety of fantasies about the import of the ejaculate; the maturation of his genitals and secondary sex characteristics; the perfection of deductive thinking; increasing autonomy and intimacy outside the home. All lend new substance to his gender identity and deepen sexual identity with the foretastes, as it were, of genital love. And these advances are accompanied by the imminence of psychosocial independence.

Fatherhood is now within the realm of biological possibility. Yet as far as parental identity is concerned, adolescence indeed constitutes a moratorium when paternity, possible at last but now unwanted and potentially irresponsible, is to be avoided. The power of the maturing body finds its counterpart in that of the mind and in the exercise of the will. With exceptions here and there, biological parenthood is typically delayed until the boy can cement his sexuality and his selfhood, ready himself for choices in work and love, and become a man. Before he can take care of others, he must prepare to take care of himself. Ideally at least, before a young man can reproduce and tend his young, he must learn to love and work and, in so doing, consolidate his own inner authority. (This is not to dismiss the epidemiological problem of teenage parenthood, one pertaining to boys as well as girls. Indeed, fears of sterility may emerge as heirs to an earlier castration anxiety, compounded now by concerns about the vitality of the ejaculate and a more general preoccupation with the adolescent's mortality.)

According to Erikson, there is at least one further waystation en route to the generativity and care—in procreation and work productivity—that are the hallmarks of generational ascendancy. Again recapitulating his early development, a young man must strive to sustain a capacity for intimacy with a woman, as he "trains" to be an effective father. Such intimacy presents a number of paradoxes. Sexual union entails a temporary traversing of boundaries, requiring both flexibility in identification and firmness in essential selfhood. Empathy in sex implies that one integrate cross-sexual identifications with one's actual gender identity, for it is only then that a male lover will flow with the needs and rhythms of a woman, and vice versa. In sex as in childrearing, a modicum of feminization helps to steady and enhance a man's sexual performance. An ongoing mutuality and working union with a woman, a workaday intimacy along with the erotic one, serve to intensify a man's needs along with the demands made of him, burdening, threatening, but once again challenging not only his sense of masculinity but also his independence. The interchanges between a man and a woman are such, moreover, that an assumption of both active and passive positions, of both initiative and receptivity, must be embraced by each partner. More specifically, in intimacy a man will reexperience his own childish dependency as he is mothered by the woman he loves, as well as the parental urges held in abeyance until now when he mothers and fathers her. Important in their own right, to be sure, intimacy and love nonetheless serve to prepare the way for a man's forthcoming parenthood. They build strength and create emotional elasticity, facilitating adult responsibility even as they encourage regression in the service of empathy and insight.

At a certain point, even so seemingly complete an experience as genital love needs fruition if it is not to end in stasis. The decision to have children is, ideally, a choice to participate in the generational process, a choice that is an embodiment of the union itself. This is not to dismiss the narcissistic satisfactions and problems imposed by procreation—the unconscious parthenogenetic fantasies, the anticipation of self-extension, the sacrifices of freedom and privacy, the confrontation with the limits of one's own life cycle. My point is to emphasize the mutual act of love in insemination. No one sex has the unilateral physical ability to make babies. Nor do children conceived in order to fulfill this fantasy on a father's part enter life with receptive, complementary, and differentiated parents. Mothers and fathers need each other, and babies need them both.

The Paternal-Identity Crisis Proper

Were I to distill an essence from the successive strivings for paternity during childhood, I would cite a truth derived by Erikson from his study of Gandhi, namely, that a sublimated maternalism is crucial to the positive identity of a man. A fatherly identity in adulthood provides for just such a self-completion, even as actual fatherhood reactivates the various sexual ambitions, ambiguities, and anxieties that have accompanied the quest for it. Fatherhood attests to one's manhood while it allows for a transcendence of the limits inherent in a single gender identity, thereby making for what one gratified and successful father spoke of as a sense of an expansive, irreducible "security." Nonetheless, for these same reasons, because fatherhood recapitulates its prestages, becoming a father shakes most men's foundations.

Fatherhood cannot be taken as a particular state tied to one moment in psychological time. Up to a point, this adult adaptational stage may divide into substages, with external reference points—for instance, the phases of a woman's pregnancy, the child's birth, and the major stages in the child's development—at least for some fathers. But the lack of a maturational blueprint for fatherhood makes such generalizing suspect. The construct of a psychological developmental phase in the absence of physiological correlates also poses difficulties. Once more, the generalizations tendered here have more heuristic value than empirical validity. Like the free-floating expectations that inform the psychoanalyst's hearing of a patient's associations, such patterns of meaning serve to orient us, alerting us to possible meanings that might otherwise elude our attention.

A man's identification with his pregnant wife has received much attention (Gurwitt, 1976, 1982; Trehowan, 1965; Boehm, 1930; Horney, 1932). Authors have underscored the womb envy precipitated by the new-found power of a woman's body as well as a man's longing to enter as a child into the symbiosis taking shape before his eyes, a mystery from which he is excluded. Few men consciously entertain the meanings of the spectacle. Rather, these are revealed in concrete if symbolic form—in abdominal and other somatic complaints and in rituals like couvade—all of which express wordlessly a man's wish to be privy to a union that is fundamentally organic and therefore not quite subject to representation. A father-to-be may only identify with his wife's motherhood, an age-specific adaptation harking back to his beginnings in the dual unity of mother and infant. Thus, apart from gestures at provision, and some nesting, most first-time expectant fathers find it difficult to envision themselves in the paternal role.

Boehm long ago suggested that the expulsion of the child from the vagina is a far more potent act than a male's ejaculation. Prepared-childbirth methods have enabled men to witness parturition in recent years, to be awed by birth, and to achieve a semblance of equal power as they assist their wives in overcoming the pains of labor. Some describe or at least betray their envy of a woman's productive and nurturing powers. And some suffer castration horror. Many feel the strain and agony in their own viscera, affectively initiating themselves into parenthood. Still others report a sublime, joyous, nearly orgiastic response to the birth and the later sight of the newborn at the breast. (The British researchers, Greenberg and Morris, 1982), have also noted the new father's feeling of "engrossment.")

The new status, authority, and attendant obligations implied by pregnancy and birth further signal the end of childhood. With this, paternity portends the inner loss of one's own parents as parents, with so many of their functions being adopted, willingly or not, as one's own. Certain men, sound and therefore flexible enough to entertain competing, seemingly incompatible, images of themselves and others, embrace the profundity offered by their paternal role. Others, less mature, cannot withstand the contradictions and flee by retreating into childish states, by avoiding contact or by denying the affective impact of it all.

Becoming a father, especially if the child is a son, renews a man's confrontation with his own father in all his intrapsychic manifestations. Gurwitt (1976, 1982) has demonstrated the revivification during pregnancy of a multifaceted intergenerational rivalry and other aspects of the charged relations between fathers and their parents. These strains can become acute with the baby's actual appearance and especially with his increasing demands for handling and emotional responsiveness. A man holds in his hands a tiny being on whom converge conflictual affects and intentions, some of which are not in the infant's best interests.

With the appearance of the baby, the "Laius complex" is born, a transfiguration of the childhood oedipal constellation. A man will recall through his child his erstwhile ambivalence toward his own father. Anticipating that a son, or a daughter for that matter, will be similarly moved, a man may be secretly tempted to abandon or to hurt the baby. If he is capable of loving him, he will of course recoil from his darker and more terrible promptings. Perhaps he will perform a reversal and foresee Oedipus' tragic fate as a baby and old man—abandonment—visited upon himself. His horror of such exile may then be betrayed in feelings of being somehow left out, of being but a vehicle for child support, in images of himself as unneeded and unloved, useless and ineffectual.

And a man fears his child *as a child*. Remembering his secret and unwanted ambitions and seeing them realized in his biological fatherhood, a father not only suffers oedipal guilt but, further, glimpses the ironies implicit in the generational cycle. His child is at once his crowning achievement, his legacy, and the harbinger of his mortality.

The struggle to resolve the conflicts rife within him moves a new father to discover another unsettling truth about his origins. Making his way through a maze of competing and incompatible paternal representations, looking into himself, he happens upon the reality of his father as a man, a man who until now he may have idealized, dismissed, or devalued, but in all events has pretty much relegated to his paternal function and little else. With fatherhood, primal fathers—good and bad, oedipal and otherwise—fall away to expose simply men with all their various frailties and virtues.

Exacerbated by this inner loss, a nagging sense of his father's relative absence from his childhood and youth may then supplant the childish complaints and veneration to which the man has been subjected. Pondering how much he himself will do for this child at the same time that he has been deprived of his own inner father, negatively or positively aggrandized, a man may find himself as if suddenly orphaned. He may cast about urgently for memories and fantasies about fathering from which to synthesize a paternal ideal for himself, a partial self-image with which to replace his representation of an all-powerful good father. He needs such a figure with whom to identify as a guiding force if he is to offset the maternal identifications revived in him, the regressive pulls exerted by the child, and the hostilities excited by the child, which may be associated with images of the bad father. Negative oedipal strivings, now potentially reciprocated, also require modulation. Above all, the child himself appeals to the sustenance and direction provided by a good father who has been internalized and transmuted as an aspect of a man's own identity.

The success of a man in these respects is, to some degree, dependent on his success in traversing the developmental passage that typically precedes his negotiation of first-time fatherhood. He must have relinquished his dependency on his father's protection and moral guidance in late adolescence and consolidated his own ego ideal. In other words, paternal identity is best created in the solid crucible of an adequate ego identity, which permits the individual to maintain his self-esteem according to his own lights.

Indeed, bound up with these struggles, which recapitulate the preoedipal relationship of mother and son and the later competition with the father, are many narcissistic problems. As Freud and later analysts suggested, children can serve as would-be embodiments of idealized selves or simply as extensions of the self. Moreover, defenses may be mobilized to subdue strivings in this vein. Projectively identified with sons and daughters, many men remember parental intrusions into their life choices, those moments at which their wishes were overridden because they were not distinguished from those of the parents' inner world. In the face of these recollections, many fathers may conscientiously retreat from articulating any values or expectations for the child (failing to recognize that their wishes and goals will be embraced or not by a child who becomes ever more his or her own person). Many parents seek to disavow the narcissistic pleasures proffered by children, so much so that at times they may deprive their families of ethical guidelines and of spontaneity in enjoying the children's beauty and accomplishments. Ironically, it is the child's self-esteem that is apt to suffer most.

This is not to say that children do not require attention, interest, and a certain disinvestment in the self. And they present the specter of one's own mortal limits. In such inevitable circumstances, can a man shift his focus from himself to a concern for the future of another person? Can he give love knowing that this will never be completely repaid by the child, who by nature is egocentric and consumes generosity (and who later forgets what he once took in)? Only the man who is more or less secure in his individuality, integrity, and worth, and who has not withdrawn either into an illusory grandiosity or, conversely, into self-abnegation and pathological abstinences—only he will be able to love parentally without either martyring himself to the child or reconstituting in his offspring a reflection of the man's own grandiose self.

These, then, figure as some of the leitmotifs from the past revivified by fatherhood. During the course of the child's growth, other issues will come to the fore: oral hunger and the incorporative prototypes of both love and destruction—the Kronos motif; the ability to say no; reactions to the child's anality, active from the start in the father's need to adjust to the infant's incontinence and disruption of routine schedules; what Nathaniel Ross discovered to be "rivalry with the product" (1960); masturbatory conflicts in which the child becomes a phallic substitute and potential incestuous object; tolerance for the derivative incestuous and homosexual inclinations and a more general capacity for sensuality without sexual seduction, for what Stoller called "minimal seduction"; modulation of aggression—most specifically, the ability to refrain from retaliation (so often moralized) and yet to discipline the child; acceptance of responsibility without omnipotent guilt. In all instances, the assimilation of the good father as an aspect of the self-representation provides the crucial counterpoint, facilitating an optimal detachment (a decentering) without emotional disengagement.

This recourse to the good father of childhood actuality and fantasy makes for a viable paternal identity, which allows a father to contend with the age-specific demands besetting his parenthood. He must accept and, ideally, take pleasure in a radically changed relationship with his wife. He must meet her needs and his own in addition to the child's. At the same time, work and financial security, so often serving the purposes of resistance, are pressing realities; he must provide. As a mentor and model, he must know his limits without interjecting the kind of unwanted confession of impotence that robs children of fodder for self-invigorating and sustaining idealizations. He must modulate his affects and impulses, without rigidifying restraint.

A father's tasks are many and hard. Only with a solid foundation will he be free to appreciate the real object that is his son or daughter and, as a good-enough father himself, to care adequately for the child. Only then can he enjoy fully the deep parental love that is now his, the absolute pleasures afforded by children—pleasures that cannot in the end be reduced to anything but themselves.

Further Notes on Context

Intrapsychic occurrences are an important and, to the psychoanalyst, the most interesting part of the narrative. But when it comes to fathers and their families, they do not tell the whole story. Attention must also be paid to the environment—the other people, the societal norms and mores, the cultural values, the constraints of work, and more—all of which impinge on the realities of fatherhood and are internalized to influence the psychological experience itself. The father does not exist in a vacuum. A word or two on the impact of the family as a whole and of the surrounding cultural context may therefore be in order.

Earlier I indicated that a boy's image of his father in his sexual and procreative role is very much a function of what he witnesses in the partnership of father and mother. Of course, the mother is an active participant in these triadic interactions. In addition, she is a personal mythmaker who further conveyed in word and deed distinct impressions of who the father is and what he should be. A man's wife is a potent family force who is often more influential than he is within the home and who does much to determine the amount, quality, and circumstances of a man's interaction with the children. Just as internal objects and external people cannot be fully defined without reference to the self, so too they cannot be apprehended independently of one another; mother and father reflect each other for their children.

Expanding on Abelin's concept of the parental couple as a "double mirror" in the eyes of the toddler, the child psychiatrist Richard Atkins developed the notion of "transitive vitalization" to encompass the ways in which, from infancy on, mothers act to set out images of the father in the eyes of the child. Alluding to fathers in their absence and orchestrating their encounters with children when they are present, wives act to tell their children in word and deed who their husband, and child's father, is. And they do so for better or worse, as the French psychoanalyst Chasseguet-Smirgel has noted, either valorizing the male parent or derogating him as a worthy subject for interaction and identification.

A mother's womanly relation to men in general, the notions, stereotypes, and fears she gives utterance to, and the use she makes of her husband as a parent will confirm, negate, or prejudice a child's unfolding representation of the father. Some women actively devalue spouses; others passively defer to their husbands; still others find mutuality in marriage; and even more mothers constantly contradict themselves. Mothers may discourage a child's involvement with a father or welcome the relief he provides. Fathers may be cast by mothers in the specific roles of playmate, authority, or disciplinarian. Children may be made to feel that they should approach admirable and loving fathers or be punished for any overtures on either their own or the father's part.

Add to these contributions by the mother a father's different transactions with siblings, no two of whom have phenomenologically equivalent parents, and the various paternal impressions falling within the child's purview become exceedingly intricate. His needs to repress or deny aspects of his own self or perhaps to split off elements of certain objects, notably the mother, and to reconstitute these in other persons (the father, for instance) along with a whole gamut of other intrapsychic motives and distortions—these complicate matters still further. Once more, a child's basic vision of his father comes primarily from a preconscious communication—to some elemental and emotional declaration of paternity that underlies more elaborate and occasionally obfuscating superstructures.

Finally, the cultural ethos and the mechanics of social organization inform the hours a father spends with the family. Collective archetypes of masculinity and prescriptions about a father's importance obviously affect a man's attitude toward his children and his freedom to be affectionate with them. In our own society, for example, radical notions about androgyny at one pole and traditional views about a father's virilized responsibilities at the other have been synthesized in the form of a new consciousness about a man's invaluable role with children.

In other societies, paternal and filial relations may be regulated by various rituals, such as rites of passage. Many of these may be seen to symbolize simultaneously affirmations of a boy's new adult male status, of the castration threat posed and indelibly retained as scars of circumcision suffered in its achievement, and of the collective fatherhood's claims to birth-giving power. (See Nunberg, 1947; Freud, 1912; Bettelheim, 1954.) In cultures like these, ritual, prescription, and proscription take the place of the Western man's conscious reflection and discretion—or at least modern man's illusions about his ability to know himself and the freedom of his choices—in fulfilling his functions in the generational cycle.

Not only variable norms and complex values but simpler social realities may influence fatherhood in more straightforward ways. There is the contrast, for example, between the exigencies of urban work, which typically remove a man from his home for many hours, and

those rural or village livelihoods—crafts, husbandry, farming—undertaken in collaboration with the whole family, with fathers serving early
on as concrete mentors and sons as essential helpmates. Occupational
choices and restrictive roles, with the time demands they entail and the
priorities they hold up as "male," do much to influence the quantity
and quality of fathering. The artist painting at home, the lawyer working into the wee hours, the blue-collar laborer who proverbially quits
working at five but then goes drinking with the boys, will spend
different kinds of time with sons and daughters. Thus the sociology of
fatherhood cannot be dismissed by even the most avid advocate of
psychic determinism.

Even some of these patterns may be changing—modified as more
and more urban middle-class men and women begin to lobby for the
kind of part-time employment that permits a more equitable distribu-
tion of domestic responsibilities and satisfactions. And this occurs even
as all over the world the men of rural areas continue their migration
to the cities.

This last point raises many important class and economic issues of
the kind all too readily dismissed or simply ignored by the analytic
movement and psychologist of the individual. The facts of sociohisto-
rical life do indeed conspire to shape men's destinies. They do so in
coloring and impinging on their sense of fulfillment and self-esteem,
the opportunities they may offer to their families, their expressions of
accomplishment and failure, and the ambitions held out for their
offspring. Although all individuals are, within the dictates of biological
and social fortune, at least partial masters of their lives, their lives still
cannot be accounted for on a purely individualistic or intrapsychic
basis. At some level, the analytic theorist must acknowledge the purview of disciplines and kens other than his own.

4

Fathers in Action

Having probed the father's internal state, I will turn to the matter of what a man does with his paternal feelings, how he acts as a father, and what his actions add to his child's emotional life. The attunement of the man to his growing child will receive special emphasis, along with the child's part in eliciting the fathering they need from him. Against this backdrop, I will also touch on trends discovered during my observational research in the interplay between fathers and children during the third year of life. In this context, I will scrutinize some of the ways in which men invite their sons and daughters to assume their sexual identity and act to "release" the Oedipus complex.

Father Absent, Father Present

The oedipal father of classic and patriarchic psychoanalysis had been destined to be dethroned during the 1950s and 1960s by the preoedipal mother of ego psychology. Infant observers such as Bowlby, Escalona, Spitz, and, most of all, Mahler studied the first two to three years of development, stressing interchanges within the dyad of infant and mother. In part, their emphasis was an inevitable outcome of the facts themselves. During these years, the typical mother is indeed ascendant in her baby's experience. Working with the forces of maturation, she serves as chief midwife to the birth of the self and its sustaining executive functions.

But other factors also seem to have led to this preemptive focus on mothering. For one thing, men were hard to get into observational settings with any regularity. They could be observed with their children in the lab only incidentally or described second hand—through a mother's eyes. Then too, with increasing numbers of women rising to prominence within the field, observers and developmental theorists were moved to counter what Ernest Jones dubbed the phallocentric bias of psychoanalysis. If women were to be cast as passive, receptive, somewhat masochistic pawns within the oedipal drama, as the mothers of infancy they had become supremely active and potent. Indeed, with babies, no mere man could hope to rival them. Those innocuous queens, Jocasta of the Oedipus myth or Hamlet's mother Gertrude, so easily led, receded to reveal the guardians, earth goddesses, huntresses, and she-demons noted, but not dwelled upon, by Freud. A silent feminist revolution had overtaken psychoanalysis, further influencing its theory and practice along a variety of different lines.

But what became of fathers in all of this? Had analysts and observers gone too far in letting the pendulum swing back toward the laps of mothers as they held babies who could not yet speak and for whom the workings of drive and conflict were but a fleeting shadow in the gleam of her eye? It was not that they dismissed the father's role during the preoedipal years, but rather that the students of early childhood development took him for granted.

When the crystal breaks, its structure is revealed. For example, it was from an examination of his neurotic patients, together with the analysis of his own dreams at the height of a personal crisis, that Freud first glimpsed the workings of the so-called normal mind and the universality of unconscious psychic processes. In much the same way, psychologists' dawning appreciation of a father's importance to his children came from studies of the deleterious effects of "father absence."

Indeed, before 1970 (a watershed year, it seems), the research on fatherhood consisted of just this—an examination of paternal deprivation. Along with psychoanalysis, the annals of developmental and social psychology and behavioral pediatrics revealed a dearth of literature on the subject of fatherhood. When they did study fathers, empirical researchers tended to focus mostly on the unfortunate corollaries of their failure to fulfill fatherly functions, or simply to be there for their children during the formative years.[1] Where fathers were missing, researchers joined with clinicians in remarking on the associated pathological consequences in their sons' and daughters' behavior and personalities: disturbances in sex-role identity (especially for boys); deep-seated cognitive deficits and a general depression in intellectual functioning; poor school performance; and compromised impulse control and resulting behavior problems.

In correlational studies such as these, causation is more suggested than proven, of course. Thus, no responsible researcher could say for sure whether the lack of a father made for these results or whether these difficulties as well as his absence itself were the results of other confounding variables, among them family dysfunctions and more encompassing social ills. In fact, most of the research failed to explore the interpersonal much less the intrapsychic precipitants of absence itself (Sprey, 1967). And some of the samples were so specific, indeed idiosyncratic—in studies of the absence of Scandinavian sailors, for instance—that generalizing to other populations became suspect. Yet these investigators had begun to remark on a significant lack—in theory as in life. It was a void, both real and representational, of which the professionals trying to help people, as well as the social scientists who studied them, were becoming increasingly aware.

Noteworthy were the pervasive and abiding omissions by most private practitioners and clinics to include fathers systematically in their clinical formulations and treatment plans. Implicitly relegating responsibility for children to "women's work," clinicians succumbed to the cultural limitations of their era. At times they seemed to fall unconscious prey to those covert archaic myths, explicit in both young children and simple societies, whereby women remain sole agents of procreation. Their nurturance and fertility treated as incidental matters, or equated with some austere, remote authority, fathers were tacitly and *de facto* excluded from the treatment of their children, as they had been from the obligations of biological parenthood. Their children continued to suffer in turn, denied a vital birthright. Profound, long-standing inner resistance diverted attention from the actuality and significance of father-child relations.

In this era of general father absence—of matricentric theory, the feminized clinic, and the momist home—the pioneering investigations of Henry Biller and others began to have a seminal effect. Their provocative studies planted seeds in the minds of both developmental explorers and clinical practitioners. Empirical psychologists as well as psychotherapists began to review the matrifocal bias of their work to date and to wonder about the obverse of what researchers had found in their unfathered subjects. Investigators began to ponder the effects of a father's presence on the sexual, intellectual, moral, and overall ego development of his offspring. And, observing behavior and analyzing the derivatives of intrapsychic events, they began to describe and conceptualize the modalities in which his influence took effect. Putting theory into practice, individual and family therapists actually began to target failures in fathering both in their patients' reminiscences and in their strategic interventions.

A Meeting of Minds and Methods

Following Freud, most formulations of the father's developmental import were based on the recollections of adult patients' childhoods during the course of their analyses. Increasingly over the years, many clinically minded psychoanalysts have restricted the data on which their conceptualizing is to be based to the evidence of the consulting room and to what their patients have to say about their free associations. Distrusting both the application of analytic notions in other arenas and the inferences drawn from other sorts of data, they have cast a particularly skeptical eye on the fruits of infant observation. How can we determine what babies feel, imagine, or want from how they behave? They themselves cannot speak, tell us in words what they are conscious of in themselves. Looking at babies, we can attribute any number of meanings to what we observe about them without regard to the lawfulness or mere fancy guiding our inferences.

In all events, these more classic critics continue, most adult patients cannot recall their preoedipal years and those sensorimotor and chaotic representational experiences, which they encoded in a lexicon very different from the visual imagery and verbal communications of the adult and, indeed, the older child. It is oedipal fantasy and feeling that come back to grown-up patients during the course of an analysis. And so it is the Oedipus complex that shapes the transference neurosis and determines how the clinician renders his disciplined constructions of the unconscious and reconstructions of the extant past. Hasty attempts to ferret out preverbal enactments in a patient's state or actions, and to take at face value myths about their unremembered infancy and toddlerhood, may lead the practitioner to overlook the unconscious

Oedipal and regressive fantasies betrayed in these phenomena. In so doing, in making imaginative leaps or higher-order inferences about preverbal experience, the analyst will collude with the patient's abiding self-deceptions. Or, worse still, the clinician will create new and comforting illusions, mostly of victimization and deprivation, which serve to obscure the psychic truth and thereby to discharge individuals of responsibility for their mental productions. So much, then, for the preoedipal father.

Notwithstanding these critiques, other psychoanalysts, most of whom continued to conduct their adult analyses in the classic fashion, found merit in looking at children. Spitz, Mahler and her collaborators, Galenson, Roiphe, and others spent fruitful years looking at mothers and babies. And they refrained from schematic transliterations of their findings into the clinical setting. They did their looking with the naked eye, however. Instead of systematic measurement, they relied on the observing team's consensus to provide checks and balances in substantiating, refining, and qualifying their inferences. Arriving at some crucial emotional truths about the dawn of mental life (psychic symbiosis, for instance), these observational pioneers inevitably ignored others that could not so readily be seen. Thus, when psychoanalytically minded Daniel Stern entered the scene of child development with his frame-by-frame analyses of mother-child interactions during the first six months of life (1974), he was able to show that infants do indeed distinguish and respond to caregivers as distinct objects in their purview—at least some of the time, in one or another state, and under certain conditions.

Presaged in the Piagetian anecdotal observations of Abelin, who examined not only the subjects at the Masters Center but also his own son and daughter, a number of nonpsychoanalytic researchers introduced observational media that, more and more, illuminated a figure on the periphery of the dyad—the father. Their instruments revealed how a father introduced difference and what seemed to be a kind of proto-maleness into the mother's encompassing orbit. As gender-defined selves, sons and daughters might then be moved to find ways out of a world equated with her alone.

From the outset, even Margaret Mahler had highlighted the importance of the father in facilitating individuation. Other analysts, including Hans Loewald, Phyllis Greenacre, and Ralph Greenson, also remarked on the place of a father in providing an alternative to the mother. They emphasized his early incarnation as an emerging figure for identification and as an object of awe, excitement, and attraction. No longer were fathers to be seen initially or primarily as despots threatening castration. Outside the mainstream of American psychoanalytic thought, too, Fairbairn, Lacan, and Chasseguet-Smirgel highlighted the part of fathers in the unfolding of early object relations, the crystallization of the symbolic function, language development, identificatory processes, and self-replenishing idealizations.

But it was the use of videotape, film analysis, and more systematic quantification in the study of infant development that most persuasively revealed the father's parenting style. The utilization of these techniques by researchers like Brazelton, Yogman, and Stern on the extraordinary social responsiveness and interpersonal repertory of the infant—even the neonate—called into question the discrete developmental sequences and timetables postulated by Spitz and others on the basis of their inevitably cruder methodologies. Among other things, these newer devices enabled observers to isolate the behavioral interactions of infants with significant adults other than the mother.

Drawing on these instruments, a number of subsequent researchers began to focus specifically on the behavior of babies with mothers, fathers, and strangers.[2] Michael Lamb, in particular, examined the attachment and affiliation behaviors of infants and toddlers with fathers in contrast to mothers at different ages and in different circumstances (home/laboratory). According to him, fathers figure as prominent and stimulating beings in a baby's world, easily as much as mothers do. Infants and toddlers relate to them differently, "affiliating" more with their fathers from afar and showing greater "attachment" behaviors with more proximal mothers.

Even where fathers opt to be the primary caretaker, as with the Swedish father who exercises his right to paternity leave, these characteristic interactions still obtain, Lamb continued. Their toddlers still treat them as fathers, not as mothers manqué. Indeed, this may be one reason why the children of such househusbands, studied in the United States by Kyle Pruett, far from succumbing to any maternal neglect or inherent deficiency in a father's parenting, actually revealed developmental IQs that were higher than the norm. Whereas mothers more readily accept their infant on its own terms, permitting and sustaining its assimilation of environmental shifts to tried and true modalities, fathers, distant and on the go, demand change, performance, and a reaching out to new experiential frontiers. With fathers, both by virtue of their masculine style and because of the initiative the babies increasingly take when they engage with them, children are forced to adapt by way of accommodation, stimulated to grow more quickly.

In collaboration with T. Berry Brazelton at Harvard's Childrens Hospital, Michael Yogman demonstrated how these transactional modes are present from the very outset of life. With two cameras trained on six babies, secured in their infant seats, and simultaneously on adults who were asked to play with them, Yogman produced a series of split-frame videotapes contrasting the impact of mothers, fathers, and strangers on the behavior of a baby during the first months of life—from two weeks to six months. The effects were eye-opening. Yogman showed how infants attune to both parents more than to strangers, revealing almost as much "conjoint" or synchronous behavior with fathers as mothers. Differences are to be discerned essentially in the greater excitement provided by fathers. Whereas mothers tend rhythmically to envelop and enfold their infants, reestablishing homeostasis, fathers arouse them, providing what Yogman terms "a base for play."

In time, as these sequences of comparative images demonstrate, the babies seek out father and mother—more so than the strangers who come into view—and each for different things. With fathers, who are more motoric and intrusive than mothers, more "male," they become more animated than comfortable, wide-eyed, bushy-tailed, and altogether alert. With men, the viewer begins to infer, babies can satisfy what presents itself as an unmistakable stimulus hunger. The comings and goings of parent and child, which are gradual when it comes to maternal engagements, tend to be more abrupt in confrontations with fathers, disruptive at times. The visual impressions, set before both the researchers and their audiences, including interested psychoanalysts, are further borne out in the graphs accompanying the moving pictures, charting the kinetics and the behavioral helloes and goodbyes of the adult and infant subjects.

As I have said, there is no sure way of determining the correspondence between what is shown in action by an infant in these rather artificial scenarios and what the representational or intrapsychic underpinnings of this behavior may be. So it is difficult to determine just how important the father we glimpse in these brief slices of laboratory life is to his young child. When a baby is brought "into alert" by a father, for instance, does it mean that it attunes to an entity which is recognized and remembered? What, if any, are the memory traces being activated? Or is it rather the father's recognition of and active response to the child, his high-key style, which momentarily motivates the vivacity of their encounter in a playful but time-limited contagion? And if the father rather than the baby's nascent impression of him is the central determinant, what about the performance artifacts of the laboratory situation where parent and offspring are on display? Do fathers interact with children as much, or as intensely, at home?

The statistics indicate that they do not. For example, conservative estimates have it that fathers spend only about 9.7 hours weekly tending home and family. Pedersen and Robson (1969), who had some stake in emphasizing the importance of fathers to babies, believe that fathers play with nine-month-olds a mere 8 hours a week. More dramatic are the findings of Ban and Lewis (1976), who concluded that the average play time of their interviewed fathers of one-year-olds was only 15 minutes a day. Finally, there are the distressing results of Rebelsky and Hanks (1971), whose subjects spent an average of 37.5 *seconds daily* interacting with infants three months and younger—the age range focused on by Yogman (see also Atkins, 1981, 1982). And what about socioeconomic variables and further sampling errors? The fathers studied are mostly middle-class, white, professionals, academics, and the like. Such men are more at home in the home.

Despite these questions, research has found a correspondence in the more "ethological," longitudinal efforts of analytic observers, especially when it comes to their understanding of the child's capacity to represent his or her senses of self and gender. Most notable are the contributions of Ernst Abelin on the laying down in behavior and the subsequent elaboration in mental representation of some fundamental male principal. By the second year of life, the father brings to his child, particularly to a boy, vistas of an other-than-mother space, which, in identifying with both his person and his maleness, his son can then explore. Boys' thirst for their father intensifies as they visibly strive to define their self and their gender identity. At the height of the rapprochement crisis, toward the end of the second year, they are better able to single out and name the male figures they would emulate than the mothers from whom sons now endeavor to disidentify.

A father's importance at this crucial developmental stage is vividly demonstrated in a study of labeling by Brooks-Gunn and Lewis (1975). At fifteen months, only 20 percent of the infants studied labeled the pictures of their fathers correctly. But by eighteen months, 100 percent of the toddlers identified the pictures of their fathers and, further, began to generalize his designation to include other male adults. Representations of the mother lagged behind, and it was not until two years that all infants labeled her without errors. Lamb's, Yogman's, and other empirical studies discriminate more between fathers and mothers than between sons and daughters. Children of both sexes seek out their male parent early on, they found, in much the same ways and for some of the same reasons. Both sexes thirst for his maleness.

Drawing from this work and from their own observations, investigators have tried to conceptualize the father's role in the psychosexual development of girls as well as boys. The father serves a vital mirroring function for female as well as male toddlers, according to Galenson and Roiphe. His appreciative presence is quickly enough internalized to affect a little girl's esteem for her body and the sexual anatomy of which she is becoming more aware. Thus the work of Parens and his associates has suggested that by two and a half years what Stoller terms "primary femininity" may become linked to a heterosexual love for the father and to procreative or maternal ambitions with regard to him.

Core gender identity is determined during this period for both sons and daughters, and not later for girls, as Freud once asserted. And it must be properly consolidated before a child reaches his/her third birthday if subsequent psychosexual development is to stay on course. A father's physical being and active, empathic involvement with children of both sexes seem to be the critical elements in this process, as the research and clinical data of such diverging theorists as Stoller and Socarides demonstrate. As noted earlier, father absence, actual or emotional, is inescapably associated with severe disturbances in gender identity or, at the very least, in sexual orientation.

The kinesthetic quality of a father's dealings with his infants and toddlers, set in relief in empirical investigations of his behavior with them, is also suggestive when it comes to the part he plays in organizing drive development and organization. Along with his impact on gender identity, a father also acts as an elicitor as well as a container of instinctual impulses in general. He is a disciplinarian, an external source of control, and a wedge between child and mother. Inviting and then limiting aggressive displays, he aids in the modulation of aggression. Corroborating earlier investigations, Herzog's poignant studies of two-year-olds bereft of fathers through divorce captures the child's longing for protection from his/her projected destructiveness, from the undeflected urges of the remaining parent, and from the real dangers of the unknown environment (1982a). In some agreement with Abelin, Herzog concludes that boys seem most vulnerable during this period to father absence, though he has also underscored the importance of men to their daughters early on. Herzog's parallel studies of the rough tactics of fathers playing with children demonstrate how he, specifically as a male, functions to make aggressivity manageable for sons and daughters alike.

The father figures as an alternative object to the mother, according to Abelin. The toddler can turn to him with split-off or otherwise inadmissible and inchoate feelings and desires. And children can identify with him as an *object related to mother but not fused with her*—an identification that helps to buttress, demarcate, and stabilize the self-representation, consolidating the foundations of primary self-identity. Research has suggested that a father's comings and goings also help to solidify object constancy. Talking with the mother, he facilitates the language development so vital in the representational process itself (see Gunsberg, 1982; Brooks-Gunn and Lewis, 1975; Clarke-Stewart, 1977).

Finally, as family theorists have noted (Lidz, Fleck, and Cornelison, 1965; Forrest, 1969; Anderson, 1968), fathers serve as alternatives to the child for the mother, helping her anchor her adult womanhood and parental identity in the midst of the regressive currents stirred by the child's infantile object world, pregenital demands, and primitive modes of communication.

I have considered only a few of a father's unique contributions during infancy and toddlerhood, as these have been adumbrated by researchers from different disciplines. Thereafter, the relations of father and child deepen and expand, in both fantasy and reality as the oedipal phase approaches. Before describing my own work on this transitional era, I must return to the psychology of the fathers themselves and the nature of their gender-specific attunement to the child.

Paternal Attunement

In the early days of developmental theorizing, the personalities of parents were treated as constants in what Heinz Hartmann called an "average expectable environment." Over the years, however, clinicians and researchers became aware that parents react to their children's expressions of need and that their reactions are influenced by the children themselves as well as by their own conflicts and defenses (Anthony and Benedek, 1970). The mother who responds with sensitivity and joy to a cuddly baby in the first months of life may have a harder time empathizing with a toddler's thrust toward autonomy and fail to meet his or her needs in this regard. Indeed, according to Stern's early studies of mother-child interactions, she may fail to recognize her baby's subtle shifts in stimulus hunger and reactivity from month to month or week to week. Both Escalona (1963) and Brazelton (1975) have underscored the various fits to be seen between babies of different activity levels and the niceties of a mother's capacity to attune to her growing and volatile child.

Although their involvement with each other is less continuous, and the failures less ominous, fathers must also intuit what their sons and daughters want of them. If he is in command of himself, a father can tune in to his child's evolving needs and modes of communication. These are both predictable, in the sense of the maturationally unfolding perceptual and object-related capabilities, and variable, dependent on the child's constitutional activity level, temperament, and inherent proclivities, which lend different meanings to apparently similar encounters. As I have noted, from the early months babies seem to respond and behave differently with fathers than with mothers, whatever the representations of these interactions may be. An affective interchange between father and child is established fairly early on, both paralleling and counterpointing the child's communication with the mother. Typically, of course, the interchanges within the maternal orbit are more intense. But the paternal dialogue exists as well and can also become "derailed," in Spitz's word, all the more easily, since a father and child usually have less time to know each other.

That a father and child know each other differently is self-evident. Before six months, in Spitz's view, or even twenty-five months, according to Mahler, babies and toddlers lack object constancy (the definitions differ). Thereafter, even with relative object constancy in Mahler's sense, perceptions of and attitudes toward parents change with the winds of fantasy, desire, and fear. A more or less well-adapted father, in contrast, pretty much knows his child for who he or she is.

Yet, up to a point, a father will mirror the wants of his children as well as their peculiar modes of expression and representation. During the first months, for instance, he too must bond to some extent with the child by sharing the baby's tactile and only gradually visual object experiences. That is, he must be close to his infant if he is to remain "imprinted" to the child, impressed with the child's concrete presence, and thereby keep his feel for the baby. Thus it makes sense that even men who later cement profound and tender relationships with an older child should recall the formless physical functions of that child as an infant—forever, it seemed to them, merely crying, eating, and defecating.

Later, when the child begins to differentiate, to single the father out and then to imitate his sounds, to reach, crawl, walk, and finally run toward him, the image and connection become more durable. Indeed, for some of the men I interviewed there may even have been an encapsulated moment affirming paternal competence, akin to that experienced by mothers, perhaps released, as it were, by the word "Daddy." In any event, the object relationship deepens with a child's greater mobility, increasingly complex and intelligible communications, the recourse made to the father during rapprochement, and those delicious identifications, adventures, and romances that serve to consolidate gender identity between the ages of two and three.

As the child develops, the father becomes more of a character in his fantasy life as well as a caregiver in reality. In a sense, a man must play out both roles at once, allowing ambitious desires without requiting them, facilitating psychosocial progress without abetting a precocity that is so frightening that it disrupts internalization and forestalls future growth. In Erikson's words, the father, like the mother, helps a child dream the imaginable and expect the possible.

The very fact of the father's receptivity to the child's expressive modalities is thus essential. At the same time, a child is alerted to a host of cues, many of them nonverbal, which express a father's understanding and expectations: postures, shapes, and rhythmic patterns; unique ways of holding, comforting, or containing the child; characteristic roughhousing and other play; a mirroring of the child's movements and bodily gestures that are in opposition. Words, of course, are significant, as are the implicit paternal fantasies betrayed in tell-tale games and make-believe.

In this regard, fathers, demanding accommodation as I have noted, may differ from mothers in a more general sense. Men who are parents, consciously and unconsciously remembering their own childhoods and responding to later developmental phases than the one through which the child is currently passing, tend to foresee that child's future—though they often take pains to deny that this is what they are doing. Most of the time, fathers are ahead of the game, a whole lot ahead or perhaps just a little, yet enough. They convey to their sons and daughters their expectation or at least their hope that they perform in ways beyond their current capacities. If such demands are not excessive, overwhelming children so that they shut down, retreat, or even regress in the face of inevitable failure, these projections on a man's part, complementing a mother's, push the process along and encourage emotional growth.

That many of a father's messages are emitted emotionally and preconsciously suggests that his "doing the right thing" in this and other regards must emanate from the wellsprings of a deeply paternal sense of himself. Lip service and role playing only confront a child with real-life contradictions of the kind that abet splits in self and object representations. Again, let me stress here the contribution of a man's internal state to his functioning as a parent. A father must be in possession of his own wishes and uncertainties if he is to resonate with, as well as contain, a son's or daughter's intense yet delicate instinctual stirrings. His relationship with the child's mother and her view of him are also vital—not only in shaping the child's view of gender relations, and of relationships in general, but in providing a base from which the male parent can function comfortably and effectively.

Even as a father, of course, a man is not only a male or a father but also an individual. He is another person in a growing person's contacts with people—a person to be perceived and understood, loved, admired, emulated, learned from, hated at times, disparaged, and simply recollected, a person whose closeness to the developing child in the most formative years makes him of unique importance.

When psychologists or social scientists write about a topic—men, fathers, paternal attunement—heuristic constraints compel them to generalize, to organize variables into categories they can manipulate and to speak the language of "ideal types" (Weber, 1947). For reasons of conceptual clarity, my emphasis has not been on the infinite variety of father-child pairs but only on the significance of the father's paternal identity as felt by him and responded to by the child, an inner consistency that sustains the father's part in his child's development.

On the Eve of Oedipus

In following observational paradigms, I have singled out only one dimension in the ongoing, encompassing relationships between these parents and their children: the sexually specific exchanges between a father as a man and his boy or girl. But this is not to dismiss the broader context of parenthood—the desires and identifications of the child in relation to the father as an individual who is, of course, more than his given sex denotes. In highlighting sex differences, it is not my intention to disavow an even greater individual variation. We cannot reduce a man's fatherhood to the fact of manhood or proclaim that sons and daughters make use of him only insofar as they are boys or girls.

Jake and his son Richard, aged two and a half, sit by the table where they and the other fathers and children in the observation center are in the midst of hammering pieces of wood, plastic, and metal into objects. Like the other fathers, Jake tends not to face his son directly but rather sits to the side and slightly in back of him. Nor is this position a function of the seating arrangement alone, since it will be maintained throughout the morning, even while the pair are standing in the wide-open middle of the room. Many fathers do not confront their sons face to face, instead moving beside or behind them. For that matter, they do not seem to say all that much to each other—with a few exceptions—choosing to interrelate through various more inanimate media.

Richard wants his nail to protrude in perpendicular to the side of his construction. When his father affixes it in a less patently phallic manner, the boy, somewhat histrionically, yowls in a show of disgusted rage, which culminates in half an obscenity hissed through his lips. With mock sternness and transparent glee, Jake scolds the boy, who frowns coyly in retort. Momentarily, his father hoists him, end over end, heaving the compact little boy up toward the ceiling, where it arcs barely short of it. Richard squeals and squeals, as the onlookers witness the ritual, silently aghast at all the near misses, until finally he is somersaulted and rolled across his father's chest and landed safely in his seat once again.

Nancy, several months Richard's senior, is only fleetingly distracted by these goings on. Her mouth drops for a moment as she stares up at the boy, but then she quickly settles back into her own father's easy lap and arms, which encircle her and then release her to allow her to fetch a piece of wood from a nearby bin. She runs to it and returns, gazing adoringly at her father, Douglas, who acknowledges her accomplishments with a few soft words and a low-keyed smile. She snuggles back into his lap once again, turning to her father, murmuring to him, engaging him in her make-believe.

During these moments at least, both men, Jack and Douglas, fall into the category of good-enough fathers. They are present, engaged, loving. Yet their behavior appears overdetermined, reactive to inner conflicts as well as to the child's communicated requirements of them. They tend to relate to the child in different ways—and here the reader must take on faith patterns that impressed themselves on me—depending on the child's sex. As I will argue, their mode of interaction is specific also to the developmental phase through which their child is passing.

First, Jake and his son Richard. According to Judith Kestenberg (1956a, 1968), between two and three years a little boy may be seen to pass through his inner genital and urethral subphases of psychosexual development. At the very least, he is in transition from the rapprochement subphase of separation-individuation to the phallic era. His relationship to his father will intimate the salient features of this transitional stage between his earlier love affair with him, and the world in general, and the growing sense that they are both males who will become engaged in a rivalry for the mother's love. A father such as

Jake, sensitized at some level to the urges and fears abating and awakening in the boy, will respond in kind to his son's silent "ambitendencies" toward him. In addition, he will impose on his son certain of his own conflicts, ambivalences left over from oedipal and postoedipal developmental phases, thus pointing a way toward the future.

In this instance, we might speculate that Jake's tendency not to position himself face to face with Richard springs from his sense of the boy's impetus toward increasingly autonomous functioning, which the father encourages as indicative of a budding masculinity. At the same time, as he adjusts to his son's needs, Jake defends against his own more problematic temptations, avoiding face-to-face and thus genital-to-genital contact, with all its aggressive as well as homosexual implications. It is safer for the two males to communicate through impersonal if also rather phallic activities, which further assure both participants that they are acting as two males together.

Paternal love, expressed more easily during bygone eras, is not entirely submerged. Rather it is left unstated, physicalized. Indeed, other fathers, who found it harder than Jake to talk with their boys or to participate in their activities, nevertheless would absently fondle them. In this instance too, Jake continued to love and stimulate Richard in characteristically fatherly fashion, tossing the boy up into the air.

But this act now conveyed an opposing meaning. It was also a statement of limits, a demonstration of phallic power, exciting identification and affording pleasure to the son, if at the cost of a certain submission on his part, betrayed by the boy's squeals of delight tinged with anxious and helpless defiance. Invited to be manly, a boy is enjoined by his father to go only so far lest he crash into the ceiling and fall to the floor. Remember, the father seems to say, ever so playfully, it was Icarus the son, not Daedalus the father, whose wings melted in the heat of their mutual overreaching, who plummeted to earth. One day you may fly like this, but on your own—one day, but not now. My love for and authority over you are one, a benevolent despotism. (See Weissman, 1963, on the meaning and impact of father-son play.)

Granted certain commonalities, the variations were also striking among these fathers in what was to be exaggerated and what suppressed. One father simply ignores his son, four months older than

Richard, letting the boy bump and thrust wildly about until his efforts end in a lonely crash, accompanied by screams of enraged pain. Another hovers about his son, watchful of his every move, both proud and cautious. A quiet, rather sad man, disappointed in his work life, retreats from the group with his son into corners where the two mumble together, intimate with each other and apart from others. Yet another man appears and disappears without notice, hardly greeting his two-and-one half month-old boy verbally but simply settling in behind him, caressing the child while his gaze wanders off to spaces beyond the room.

The interaction between Nancy and her father seems to express the best features of the dance between fathers and daughters on the eve of a little girl's oedipal romance. At other times she, like Richard, will be tossed high and about, though perhaps with greater anxiety than is evident in the boy. She too will build things with her father's aid, though enclosures rather than protuberances predominate in her constructions (see Erikson, 1963). But for the most part Nancy will seek to engage her father more directly, sensuously, and somewhat flirtatiously. She will face him either to present herself or to show something she has created, often undulating in response, Kestenberg would say, to the ebb and flow of tensions within her "inner body." Or she will fit her body to his, languishing there, close against him, for longer times and in greater proximity than the boys with their fathers. And she will talk more with her father, her language development having progressed more rapidly than that of most boys.

With her mother, in contrast, Nancy appears more ambivalent and independent. She is, in her presence, able to concentrate on activities without much recourse to those momentary refuelings that are legacies of the practicing subphase of separation-individuation. She tends to be more impatient with her mother, quicker to anger, perhaps prone to sullen despondency, which seems unprovoked but expresses a sense of some disappointment. It is her father now rather than her mother whom she seeks out most of the time, reveling in their moments alone together, specifically refueling with him by letting him in on her productivity, in the process playing out in action her burgeoning sexual identity and arousing her eroticism, which still does not have the full intensity of the oedipal phase ahead.

The child's input already demands a delicate balance in the father's expressed attitude, one that is further affected by his struggle to master his own attraction to his daughter, without lapsing into overstimulating and potentially frightening seductiveness and without abdicating his masculinity. He provides fuel for an idealization that is necessary to lure the girl from a potentially consuming involvement with her mother. In addition, a father will perhaps have to contend with the narcissistic injury and castration threat posed by having a girl. Loving as she is, she is not a boy and is thus an incomplete embodiment of himself.

For all these reasons, many men avoid or disparage a daughter at this critical point in the inception of her sexual identity and basically male object choice (just as earlier, observers noticed, during diapering, a man may perceive a baby's vulva with a mixture of attraction, fear, defensiveness, disgust, and disappointment). Once more, a feeling of paternity is what enables a man to integrate his images of his girl child into his representational matrix and to approach her as a tender, available father.

Again, different fathers behave differently with their daughters. One ignores his girl's endeavors, indifferent while she tries to engage him in play, listless as he halfheartedly pushes her swing, habitually communicating only resignation or limp gestures of approbation. Another tries to take over the parental role altogether; he fusses over his daughter, concerned with minute details of her appearance, prim in his parenting. A certain father may tease his little daughter repeatedly, scaring her, tickling her, almost unable to meet her on any but seductive, covertly sadistic grounds. Still another man seems to encourage masculine modes of play almost to the exclusion of more stereotypically girlish activities.

In the examples just described, the fathers have acted to consolidate the gender identity and to stimulate the broader yet more individualized sexual identity of their sons and daughters during the last stages of the preoedipal period. Earlier in development as well, a father treats his child in unique ways according to his or her sex. Inadvertently he has encouraged his son to build frustration tolerance (a commodity boys may tend to be inherently shorter on than girls) in the name of independence, whether uttered or not. For example, one observer noted how a loving enough father let his eight-month-old son lie on the floor, get knocked about, and cry for a moment while another—no more or less anxious or nurturant—would tend to retrieve his daughter far more quickly (see Rothbart and Maccoby, 1966).

It is generally only by about eight months that a father will seem more careless of his child than the mother, more ready to jounce the baby about than she. Before this, the reverse holds. Perhaps it is a function of his (culturally determined) inexperience with babies, possibly because of a sensed incompetence or underlying ambivalence—but, whatever the reasons, most fathers are at first more wary in their handling of infants than mothers, more tentative and uncomfortably angular in their movements. At the earliest age of life, it is most often mother who conveys an aura of strength and confidence.

It is difficult to understand how babies or even toddlers construe their father's handling of them as compared with the mother's. Obviously, the children themselves do not respond to sex differences as we understand them. But these passive experiences must enter into precursors of active fantasies. For example, excitement and the flirtatiousness of girls in the father's presence occur as early as eight months, become remarkable with the bipedal locomotions of the practicing period, and become quite intense with rapprochement. Is this evidence of Melanie Klein's notions about a prestage of oedipal triangulation or of a girl's sense of sexual deficit and search for a penis? Or does it also have to do with her father's more intentional messages that she be as girlish as possible? At any rate, a father probably quickens a little girl's thrust toward womanhood, long before the goal is in any way comprehensible to the child herself. In similar ways, fathers tend, as I have suggested, to behave in ways that masculinize their sons before the formation of his core gender identity and before a boy himself is able to recognize distinctions of sex.

The father's role is also bound up with functions not directly related to sexual identity. From the age of a year or so, I observed that in the centers children of both sexes tended to become elated and to display a more high-keyed mood when fathers and male adults were present. Some toddlers seemed more focused in the father's presence than they were with the mother. But this appeared to be very much a function of the degree to which the caretaking parent, male or female, allowed the child the greatest separate space. Where the father intruded on his son's or daughter's autonomy, the reverse held. Individual differences proved as important as divergences along sexual lines.

Invitations to a Sexual Identity

To sum up: The father first figures prominently in the child's experience during differentiation from the mother, beginning at roughly six months. He then becomes a special and exciting figure with the practicing subphase and the rapid spurt in muscular activity that accompanies this, when he comes to stand for "nonmother" space, enhancing a child's love affair with the world.

During a child's problematic rapprochement with the mother, which marks the death throes of the illusion of omnipotent union with her and solidifies object constancy, a father serves many essential functions. He provides an alternative to the mother, a target both for ideal love and, later, for rageful defiance as a toddler struggles by splitting his increasingly internal objects to come to terms with his inevitable ambivalence toward single objects in reality. Most important, a father now offers to a child an image of another integral object in relation to but not fused with the mother. A toddler can gradually liken himself to this distinct object, whose presence thereby lends its support and constancy to a child's nascent, tenuous, and labile representation of self.

With individuation come the beginnings of triangulation. A child becomes cognizant of two parents in addition to himself and of his own increasingly differentiated affects and desires with regard to each of them. The stage is set for the consolidation of gender identity and the assumption of an even more dynamic sexual identity between two and three years.

During this period, a father's presence complements the mother's, crystallizing a child's notions about the male gender and sex differences. Furthermore, a father must appreciate his son's and daughter's burgeoning efforts to express their sexual identity in relation to him by being genuinely receptive and admiring in ways that permit them to enjoy and esteem their own sex, their bodies, and the very selfhood with which these are associated. At this point and during the oedipal phase proper, a father may seem indifferent to a daughter's wooing of him or may make apparent promises of exclusivity, only to disappoint her later. Many little girls attribute such indifference to their own deficiencies, suffering a mortification that becomes associated with their femininity and genitals. Alternatively, a father may overstimulate a daughter, cast her as a coquette, or move her to renounce assertiveness for a caricatured girlishness. Similarly, fathers may either thwart or abet their sons' increasingly phallic aggressions. They may also invite or else disparage an object love and identificatory longing that take on quasi-homosexual overtones.

In all events, a father must be in possession of his own wishes and uncertainties if he is to resonate with, as well as contain, a son's or daughter's intense yet delicate instinctual stirrings. His relationship with the mother and her view of him, especially during the oedipal phase, are also vital in counteracting, for instance, the sadistic imagery surrounding a man's sexual role—fantasies of the kind to which both boys and girls fall prey and from which they may retreat, substituting various condensations of pregenital and phallic aims.

Failures in Fathering

Advancing technology, occupational specialization, the vastness and complexity of the modern economy, and, most recently, the decline in real wages have dealt successive death blows to the viability of the family as an essential socioeconomic unit. With this, a man's loyalties shifted to his corporation or institution as the owner of his life, well-being, and energies, indeed as his family away from home. Their vital childrearing functions minimized or ignored, many wives responded to the aggression implicit in their husband's abandonment by getting away themselves. In what was probably a distortion of feminism, an acquiescence to a tacit bribery on the part of the extrafamilial power structures governing our lives, and a rationalization in ideological terms of economic necessity in a bankrupt capitalist society—women also came to value work achievement as more fulfilling and creative than the production and nurturing of human life itself. Like men, they immersed themselves more and more in their jobs, relegating the sustenance of sons and daughters to hired housekeepers and custodial centers, which have no deep commitment to and certainly no special love for them. Beneath it all, a variety of disavowed financial factors have continued to impel these centrifugal forces and the dissolution of family bonds.

Where in the past they recoiled in protection of their masculine prerogative, men gradually came to support their wives in their newfound Protestant ethic and endorsed their spending long hours at work and away from home. And they did so without themselves filling in the gaps left by working mothers. Significantly, with exceptions here and there, husbands of working wives have not opted for "co-equal homemaking" or childrearing. Like Oedipus on the mountain, their children have been left to the capricious kindness of others. Indeed, the result seems less an equality of the sexes and a real valuing of women's identities than a neglect of and loss of love for children whose development is shortchanged at the very beginning of their lives.

When they are left at home and choose to stay there, many women, embittered at the maltreatment they have suffered, may avenge themselves on sons who recoil from their grip even as they are deprived of any model of masculine nurturance. An underlying fear of women and postures of bravado propel such children out of the home, further compromising the future of the family. An atmosphere of selfishness, indifference, and sadistic pretension to power envelopes the lives of all within the unfathered family, compounded by a lack of clear moral teaching and consequent values. Such myths as the story of the House of Atreus and the Agamemnon trilogy, Medea's filicide, and the Oedipus legend might all be read as family tragedies deriving from failures in fatherliness.

When fathers manage to be present and active within the family, they bring with them a number of virtues which serve all of its members and endow them with a sense of unity and direction. Girls, whose sexual and self-identity is very much dependent on a father's appreciation, feel worthy as women and aspire to be wives and mothers. A boy's almost inherent terror of, and rage at, male authority is modulated by way of familiarity and a mutuality of love as he further learns that an essential dimension of masculinity is parenthood. Men themselves may not be cognizant of the blow to their manhood in missing out as parents, but their children will be aware of what they did not get.

In fact, from Agamemnon on, fathers have been both blamed and exculpated by the sons and daughters who suffer their sins of commission and omission and who continue to long for authority and love. So it was, for instance, that in 1919 Franz Kafka penned his studiedly disembittered "Letter to His Father." To read it is to find, all at once, the trials and terrors, the nameless and unwarranted guilt afflicting his fictional protagonists, falling into place, in the image of the arbitrary tyrannies of the writer's father.

In much the same way, neurotic and more disturbed individuals continue obliquely, almost deviously to suffer their fathers' failures, omissions, and impositions. The guilt Kafka expresses is a veritable presence in the lives of many people, bespeaking the secret hatred and fantasies of murder leveled unconsciously at a father who is an over-lord, real or imaginary. This guilt is also his representative, as it were, in the child's personality, an introjection of his punitive power into the self-representation. Furthermore, self-condemnation of this kind on the part of a conscience rampant in its excesses (what analysts call an archaic, sadistic superego) serves to substitute for a self-love never achieved because the foundations were wanting in love from without. Something, even a bad part-object linked to an equally fragmented self by hatred and remorse, is better than nothing; the enraged and fear-some father may be, therefore, more tolerable than the insufficient and absent one, another of his protean manifestations.

Slowly, it seems, Kafka came to a realization of his terrible father's basic weakness. He recalled the man's ultimate abdication: "all one gets from you is: 'Do whatever you like . . . I've no advice to give you,' and all this with that frightful, hoarse undertone of anger and utter con-demnation that only makes me tremble less today than in my child-hood because the child's exclusive sense of guilt has been partly re-placed by insight into your helplessness, yours and mine." It occurs to Kafka, as it will to the analytic patient or to the insightful man en route to his own paternity, that his father is limited, fallible, and human. Such knowledge does not discharge the parent of responsibility or absolve him of culpability. Instead it tempers the effects of his wrongs and failures by removing the wrongdoer from his elevated position, a sinecure in which a father is ensconced partly by virtue of the child's sense of his immediate world's enormous proportions, but also be-cause, wanting in self-assuredness, feeling tiny, he finds it safer to have him up there. Laments to a less than perfect father and unjust excru-ciations before his dark and secret eyes, now within the self, will give way before what Erikson called a "paternity of self."

These matters take us to the paradigm of the Oedipus myth, to questions of conflict and the more sinister side of fatherhood.

5

Oedipus Revisited

In previous chapters I have emphasized a man's wish to be a parent and his role in releasing rather than inhibiting his child's developmental potential. As a result of my own work and that of other theorists, the "new father" came to be seen as a potential nurturer during the preoedipal era, the oedipal period itself, latency, adolescence, and beyond. Most recently, for example, Michael Diamond has schematized the father's facilitative functions throughout the life cycle, from the first months of life through grandfatherhood.[1]

But these good fathers, like other conceits of theory, tended to be more responsive to their conceptual antecedents than to real-life people. In compensating for the early psychoanalytic images of the father as oedipal tyrant, investigators tended to overcompensate. Few writers on fatherhood attended systematically to pathological features in fathering. They failed to tell the whole truth. Even the threat of castration at the father's hands—part of the daily fare of the working clinician, whatever the research and ethos outside the consulting room—continued to be seen as a product of the child's own imagination and inherent psychology, almost independent of actual paternal influences. Scrutinizing specific fathers, analytic authors and practitioners alike most often failed to explore the personalities and specific *parental conflicts* of the parents involved, and this even when they did underscore their more manifest pathogenic actions.

There is, unmistakably, a regressive potential in becoming a father, and a heart of darkness in any man to whom the lives of growing children are entrusted. In some who do not also have the good father within themselves, destructive forces will erupt in a variety of pathological actions. The ways in which such disturbing impulses are enacted (whether, for example, directly in a father's own behavior or through his influence on the mother's ability to take care of her children) will vary according to a host of factors. Some of these include the father's physical presence and emotional closeness with the child; the child's developmental level and its implications for the nature and intensity of the father's importance to him or her; the mother's impact on the father-child dyad and on the family climate as a whole; and other, more characterological features of the specific man. Their effects will also differ for similar reasons: that is, according to the degree and manner in which a child is primed, both individually and epigenetically, to experience the father's presence and to have recourse to other caretakers to fill in for a father who is failing that child. Paternal failures may be active sins, as it were, of commission or more passive omissions in parenting, as in the epidemiological problem of father absence.

Yet, in one way or at one time or another, in fact or fantasy, fathers may be guilty of some variant of psychic infanticide, some kind of abuse. They may be moved to commit "soul murder," to borrow from Leonard Shengold and from the memoirs of Schreber, brutalized by his father.[2] The statistics certainly, even in this age of enlightened attention to childhood, attest to the reality of parental aggression. In Brandt Steele's estimation in 1982, one million children are abused each year, while 2,000 to 3,000 die of neglect and injuries sustained at adult hands. According to the National Committee for the Prevention of Child Abuse, reports of abuse and neglect have risen from one million instances in 1980 to 2.1 million in 1986 to 2.4 million in 1989, with 42 percent of these reports substantiated. Though they spend less time with their children, men are more likely than women to lash out at them. For example, in 1983, 88 percent of the persons arrested for offenses against family and children were male and, of the offenders, 62.7 percent were between twenty-five and forty-four years old—typically the age of fatherhood in a man's life.

King Laius, Oedipus' father, was one of the prototypic perpetrators of child abuse. He may be seen as an embodiment of a veritable web of paternal disease and its terrible consequences, the paradigm of the bad father. It is to Laius' forgotten story, itself embedded in a whole generational history of children betrayed, to which I now turn. At times I shall treat this personage as if he were a real person with an unconscious rather than a figure concocted by the collective imagination. For this violation of the metaphor, I hope I may be excused. I am not a classicist; my aim is to exploit the myth and make of it a psychological parable of the darker dealings between fathers and sons.

The myth of Oedipus, the son, is also the story of Laius, the father. Laius is destiny's cruel and capricious human agent. Oedipus, the unwitting patricide, has also narrowly escaped infanticide. If Oedipus forces himself to play out the role of prime actor in his tragedy (and he does so initially for noble reasons, for the general good), he has remained the passive victim not only of some abstract fate but also of his father. Finally, the son Oedipus is himself a father and, generally, a good one—at least until he discovers the unwanted truth about his own parentage. Indeed, the whole legend can be viewed as a portrayal of parenthood both in its aspiring, nurturing, almost selfless aspects and as a breach of deep personal trust, a blind and sinister corruption. It is a corruption, moreover, born of generations past and continuing on, breeding guilt and fouling the lives of future children.

Freud drew on Sophocles' *Oedipus Rex,* of course, in illuminating the secrets of neurotic symptoms and dreams. Written within a week of the anniversary of his father's death in 1896, a letter to Fliess conveys Freud's excitement at the discovery of what he later would dub the Oedipus complex (1910:170):

> I have found love of the mother and jealousy of the father in my own case too, and now believe it to be a general phenomenon of early childhood . . . the gripping power of *Oedipus Rex* in spite of all the rational objections to the inexorable fate that the story presupposes, becomes intelligible . . . Every member of the audience was once a budding Oedipus in phantasy. (1954:223–224)

Two years later, in *The Interpretation of Dreams* (1900), Freud formalized the anecdotal allusion, discerning in the tragedy a metaphorical rendering of the conflictual fantasies of the child and the adult's unconscious mental life. He was to make of Oedipus a new myth, the "shibboleth," he would say, on which future psychoanalysis would stand or fall. He wrote:

Oedipus, son of Laius, King of Thebes, and of Jocasta, was exposed as an infant because an oracle had warned Laius that the still unborn child would be his father's murderer. The child was rescued, and grew up as a prince in an alien country, until, in doubts as to his origin, he too questioned the oracle and was warned to avoid his home since he was destined to murder his father and take his mother in marriage. On the road leading away from what he believed was his home, he met King Laius and slew him in a sudden quarrel. He came next to Thebes and solved the riddle set him by the Sphinx who barred his way. Out of gratitude the Thebans made him their king and gave him Jocasta's hand in marriage. He reigned long in peace and honor, and she who, unknown to him, was his mother bore him two sons and two daughters. Then at last a plague broke out and the Thebans made enquire once more of the oracle. It is at this point that Sophocles' tragedy opens. The messengers bring back the reply that the plague will cease when the murderer of Laius has been driven from the land . . .

The action of the play consists in nothing other than the process of revealing, with cunning delays and ever-mounting excitement—a process that can be likened to the work of a psychoanalysis—that Oedipus himself is the murderer of Laius, but further that he is the son of the murdered man and of Jocasta. Appalled at the abomination which he has unwittingly perpetrated, Oedipus blinds himself and forsakes his home . . .

His destiny moves us only because it might have been ours—because the oracle laid the same curse upon us before our birth as upon him. It is the fate of all of us, perhaps, to direct our first sexual impulse towards our mother and our first hatred and our first murderous wish against our father. Our dreams convince us that that is so. King Oedipus, who slew his father Laius and married his mother Jocasta, merely shows us the fulfillment of our own childhood wishes . . . The contrast with which the closing Chorus leaves us confronted—

Fix on Oedipus your eyes,
Who resolved the dark enigma, noblest champion and most wise.
Like a star his envied fortune mounted beaming far and wide:
Now he sinks in seas of anguish, whelmed beneath a raging tide.

—strikes as a warning at ourselves and our pride, at us who since our childhood have grown so wise and so mighty in our own eyes. Like Oedipus, we live in ignorance of these wishes, repugnant to morality, which have been forced upon us by Nature, and after their revelation may all of us well seek to close our eyes to the scenes of our childhood. (1900:261–263)

And to the sins of our fathers, I would add.

The veracity of Freud's formulations has been attested to repeatedly in clinical practice over the more than eighty years that have followed. Children, sons especially, harbor murder in their hearts, however benign their fathers in actual fact. As adults, they suffer anxiety, guilt, and conflict as a consequence of their hidden sensuality and malevolence. Much of the drama's power to move its audience to pity and terror resides in its resonance with the onlooker's own unwanted and repressed childhood wishes and his identification with the hero.

Yet it is remarkable that Freud should have ignored Laius' active part in the narrative, and that all but a handful of analytic authors after him should have omitted to fill in the gaps. The blind spots are reminiscent of Oedipus' own assumption of the entire burden of guilt for the drama's tragic events, as if exculpating the dead father altogether.[3]

In a note appended to the dream book when he was fifty-five, older and an established father himself, Freud may have touched on these forgotten themes when he remarked on the "constantly gnawing wishes of a man who is growing older . . . for youth" (476). A dream, eight years later, that his son had been wounded at the front he subjected to deeper analysis and discovered the "concealed impulse . . . which might have found satisfaction in the dreaded accident to my son: it was the *envy which is felt for the young by those who have grown old, but which they believe they have completely stifled*" (560; my italics).

Freud had, first of all, to find the unconscious in himself before he would trust its veracity. The trouble is that insights of this kind were not integrated into general psychoanalytic developmental theory, which remained essentially a psychology of sons and their filial conflicts.

Prehistory of the Myth

It is clear that even Sophocles' play itself portrays a terrible resonance between Oedipus' deeds and Laius' acts. By extension of the metaphor, the character of Laius and his role in his son's fate imply that a father's motives and actions constitute at least one precondition for, or "releasor" of, the Oedipus complex, certainly in its most aggressive and pathogenic forms.

Furthermore, the Greek audience to whom Freud refers would have heard the drama within the context of an oral history of the myth and a series of now-fragmentary written documents, including works by Homer, Hesiod, Pindar, Praxina, and Aeschylus, and such epics as the *Oedipodeia* and the lost *Thebaid*.[4] Indeed, the play served as a ritual catharsis for the Greeks, who knew perhaps as much about Laius as about Oedipus. They knew of his genealogy and legacy, his own history of expansion and suffering, the misdeeds he committed long before Oedipus' appearance on the scene, the hubris or trespass for which the oracle was his punishment.

Without its prehistory, Oedipus' story might remain mysterious and apparently unmotivated. Ultimately, behind *Oedipus Rex* lies a generational saga that depicts an ominous convergence of impulses and misapprehensions, an articulation of object worlds between father and son ending in mutual disaster. From the ethical point of view, the fundamental responsibility for this, the tragedy, must fall on the former, the adult father, as the more sentient and powerful of the two. Taken as analytic allegory, the chronicle portrays the Oedipus complex not merely as a four-year-old's psychic fiction but as an outcome of generations of bad parenting.

Laius and Oedipus were direct descendants of Cadmus, founder of the city later named Thebes. As in the famed curse on the House of Atreus, Cadmus' line also had been blighted by crimes against nature. With these as background, the terrible tragedy that was to consume the father and his legendary son is played out. These original sins involved not fathers at first, but mothers and sons. Insofar as they set in relief the relations between them, they may help to explain Laius' filicidal disposition.

Mount Cithaeron, near Thebes, on whose slopes Oedipus, fresh from the womb, was left to die, had witnessed a breach of parenthood, a crime against nature, long before this infant's birth. King Cadmus had several daughters, among them Semele and Agave. Semele lay with Zeus, their union producing Dionysus, the ambisexual sybarite of the Greek pantheon. The Thebans disputed Semele's claims to divine insemination, and when she was killed by lightning because of her wish to see Zeus in his true form, her son Dionysus was denied his birthright, the status of a god. Orphaned and forced to wander Greece (like Laius and Oedipus after him), Dionysus returned to Thebes to exact his revenge. His hedonism and demonic charisma infected the city's women, who became his Bacchanalian followers or Maenads.

Among the women was Semele's sister Agave. Agave had a son, the Spartan prince Pentheus. Straining in his display of martial masculinity, he energetically persecuted Dionysus' crazed disciples in an effort to suppress their bisexuality, lustfulness, and savage abandon. But Pentheus' vain war with instinctuality came to a hideously ironic conclusion. According to Euripides' *Bacchae*, intrigued by the Dionysian mysteries in spite of himself and dressed in women's clothing, Pentheus spied on the Maenads. Having mistaken his golden wig for a lion's mane (the paranoid distortion is telling), Agave and the other women murdered him in the glens of Cithaeron, dismembering the body and ripping off Pentheus' head. Hence Thebes' first filicide at a *mother's* hands.

Whereas Oedipus was able to solve the riddle of the Sphinx, the mystery of life, it seems that Pentheus may have succumbed, despite his masculine protest, because of his intolerance of his own instinctuality, specifically his bisexuality. Disavowing desire, he fell prey to what Mark Kanzer (1964) and George Devereux (1953) later described as the emasculating, murderous power of the preoedipal and phallic mother. In her grasp, this first son was effeminized, castrated, and destroyed. But Oedipus escaped her reach only to fall victim to an indifferent (if oedipal) mother and, above all, to an ignorant, weak, authoritarian, and by all accounts homosexual father. He was a father who had much in common with his would-be forebear, Pentheus.

Laius the Father

As a baby, Laius himself had been subjected to abandonment and persecution. His father Labdacus, the ruling Theban king, died when he was a year old, leaving Laius to the care of his mother. When his uncle usurped the throne, Laius was expelled and forced to wander Greece before he could return to Thebes to reclaim his kingdom. In the meantime, he himself seems to have displayed that same constellation of characteristics which modern-day clinicians and researchers associate with father absence. If the anachronisms can be pardoned, Laius' misdeeds and delusions can be taken as evidence of disturbances in gender identity and sexual orientation; problems with impulse control; unmodulated aggressivity; cognitive and intellectual impairment; and pathological narcissism.

First of all, almost all versions of the legend point to the Theban monarch's pederasty, which he is credited with having invented. Pedophilia was, of course, notorious among the Greeks. It found its way into the gymnasium and those rites of passage that sexualized the older male's dominance of the boy and the latter's induction into masculinity, his infusion of manliness through submission.

Philip Slater and others have further underscored the sadomasochism and misogyny implicit in the Greek men's homosexuality, their devaluation of women. Loving boys and men, the Greeks sought to controvert the influence of the pre-Hellenic matriarchy and to escape their embittered mothers and wives.[5] These women, in their turn, retaliated for their husbands' indifference and subjugation by avenging themselves on their boys, sexually and aggressively overwhelming them. The sons responded as their fathers had and fled them for the company of males, where as adults they enacted the abuses suffered passively as their mothers' playthings. Hence Agave's Dionysian filicide, which figures as the first parental horror in the House of Cadmus, may be symbolic of the ambivalence then prevalent between mothers and sons.

Laius' life as a boy with his mother is an uncharted chapter in the legend. But what happened after this, in Laius' adulthood, was well known, chronicled by poets and dramatists, and indicates that he carried common practice beyond the bounds. While visiting Pisa, Laius kidnapped and sodomized Chrysippus, the beautiful illegitimate son of his host, King Pelops. The erotism of the act, the pedophilia itself, was not a crime in the Hellenic scheme of things. But the violation of his protector's hospitality was a serious breach of princely etiquette and human trust—not to mention the miscreant's overbearingness and violence toward the hapless boy. Laius' kidnapping and rape were true transgressions.

They infuriated the father, Pelops. He cursed Laius and, together with the Olympians Zeus and Hera, condemned him to remain for a long time childless and then to be both murdered by the son he eventually conceived and replaced by him in his wife's bed. (The versions vary somewhat.) Thus the famous oracle, sealing the destinies of father and son, did not spring into being as a matter of happenstance. Rather, it bespoke revenge—a retaliation for violations perpetrated by a man so caught up in his sadomasochistic desires that he is oblivious of a boy's needs. Oedipus is fated to avenge Chrysippus, his alter ego.

If Pelops' life history is considered as well, his curse may also be seen as an act of self-vindication; he was himself a childhood victim of aggressive and sexual abuse. Tantalus, his father, had chopped him up and served him for dinner to his guests, the gods, who took pity on the hapless boy. Thrown into a cauldron, his body was knitted again—all save a shoulder, which was eaten by Demeter and replaced by a beautiful prosthesis made of pure ivory. The god Poseidon fell in love with young Pelops, with his shoulder especially—always an object of cannibalistic attraction, according to Shengold—and abducted and used him sexually. Not once did Pelops the man inveigh against his earthly or divine patrons, cruel though they had been to him as a boy. But Laius' betrayal of his graciousness and analogous indiscretions toward his son excited Pelops' vengeful wrath.

Some versions of the myth link Oedipus directly with Chrysippus, the two of them shadowing each other through time. Oedipus also falls in love with the boy and kills his father in a duel for him. In other renditions, the homosexuality is more latent or, better, implicit. Laius does not simply endure years of barrenness but rather, fearful of the oracle's prophecy, of his own accord abjures intercourse with Jocasta. Sexually starved, her wish to be a mother frustrated, she finally intoxicates and then seduces her otherwise abstemious husband, conceiving their fateful son.

Whatever the real and symbolic connections between the victims Oedipus and Chrysippus, Laius did intrude pitilessly into the life of his son and in this sense "raped" and robbed him of innocence. Responding to the prophecy of death with abject, self-serving terror and self-inflating sadism, the father visited upon the child, his heir, an expulsion akin to what he had suffered, but worse by far.

When Oedipus was born at last, Laius ordered the infant's ankles to be pierced with a spike, leaving him with a club foot. It was a stigma that Oedipus carried with him throughout his life and from which he derived his name. Oedipus means "swell-foot" according to classical etymologists or, alternately, he who knows. If the two meanings are combined, perhaps the further implication is that a special sort of insight may be derived from the scars of the cradle—a knowledge of one's origins and of the parents' hidden malevolence.

Pinioned so that he could not crawl (as if a neonate could crawl), the baby boy was left to the desolation and elemental violence of the mountain. If it can be said that Laius is a fabrication of the oedipal imagination, so too is Laius' representation of his son as a misshapen product of his paranoia, indicating a hideous projective identification on the part of the father.

Only the kindness of strangers saved the infant Oedipus. Jocasta's messenger handed the wounded baby to a shepherd, who brought him to King Polybus and Queen Merope of Corinth—Oedipus' adoptive parents. (The parallels with the deprived rich children of our own times and their redemption through benevolent servants and therapists are striking, as are the ultimate meaning, function, and origins of the family romance implicit in the tale.)

It is said repeatedly that there can be no sadism without masochism. What did it mean for a man who loved boys to torture and kill his own son? In this vein, George Devereux has interpreted the attempted infanticide as a self-castration on Laius' part, a sacrifice of manhood bespeaking his primitive desire to be a woman. Even Oedipus' incestuous liaison with Jocasta, Devereux believes, might represent an eroticized access of sorts to Laius' bed and his forsaking affections.

Whatever the masochistic and homosexual submission that may be read into a father's persecution and sacrifice of a son, Laius' first cruelty toward his baby remains basically an act of manifest evil. In a certain sense, it needs no further interpretation, no psychologizing. In its own right the deed serves to climax an intricate allegory, encapsulating a whole complex of delusion and moral failure.

First of all, there is Laius' monumental and multidimensional narcissism, the psychological bedrock of his hubris. Above all, Laius thinks of himself. The oracle has named him as the sole victim of destiny; his personal survival alone is at stake. Thus the blatant selfishness of the would-be murder contrasts with other near or actual sacrifices of children portrayed in folklore and mythology and manifest in wars, where the collective or individual fathers at least make some pretense to a higher purpose.

Such self-absorption compromises clarity of vision, endowing the world with one's own intentionality and omnipotence. Not only is the intended infanticide self-serving. It is misguided, again feeding into the fatal trespass at the core of the tragedy. Laius reacts to the prediction of his inevitable death as if he could, in fact, defy nature and live forever. Oedipus knows better. He responds to the Sphinx's question, "What walks on four legs in the morning, two in the afternoon, three in the evening?" by answering, "Man, in the morning fresh and joyful of hope, in the evening weak and broken." Man must pass through the life cycle, age, and eventually die.

Loveless and prideful, also blind to destiny, Laius fails to understand this intimation of mortality—at least insofar as it applies to him. Yet he becomes just such a deluded creature. In this sense too, he is very different from the son who, unjustly victimized, blinded, and maimed, openly betrayed by his father and his sons, will find solace in his care for others and an informed redemption in old age and death. The tragic irony is that, in endeavoring to deny death, Laius hastens his demise. His egocentricity and brutality make an alien and an enemy of a potentially loving, dutiful son, so that the prophecy of patricide becomes self-fulfilling. One might speculate whether Oedipus would in reality have slain a father known to him.

It is a biological truism that physical life requires death. Psychological parricide is also inevitable. In assuming more and more their independent responsibility, their "paternality of self," children are fated to usurp parental functions and eventually to do away with their parents. Even in social institutions like the Hindu joint family, autocratically governed by elders, the realities of obsolescence, senescence, and death find recognition in ritual disengagements. Once powerful but ageing householders cede their material goods and secular authority for the begging bowl of the wandering holy man.

Greek mythology and drama offer analogous social cautionaries and promises of spiritual release. But the castration implicit in this accession may be too much for some men to bear. For them, the blush and promise, the inevitable brashness, of youth are excruciating reminders of their own frailty and finitude. Then, as now, men have made magical and often tyrannous efforts to undo the passing of the generations by attempting to create an illusion of personal immortality, by acting to make the young subservient reflections or clones of the self or by simply oppressing or destroying them. Laius does all of this. Despite his contrasting virtues, Oedipus shows the effects: profound neglect as an infant, and thus as an adult a sense of discontinuity, lost origins, identity confusion, and these despite his visionary powers.

Along with his profound selfishness, Laius betrays a readiness to jealousy, which is probably a legacy of his own (one might say) oedipal childhood and a by-product of homosexual desires. If the augured murder is the father's as well as the son's, so too is the incest, projected onto the child and future rival. Laius' refusal to satisfy Jocasta sexually, his apparent impotence and infertility and, by inference, his horror of women, seem to call his masculinity into doubt and may have made him especially vulnerable. After all, as Jocasta later tells Oedipus, "How many men, in dreams, have lain with their mothers? No reasonable man is troubled by such things."

But Laius was troubled, profoundly so, not only because he heeded the oracle but possibly, one might imagine, because he remembered his own childish "dreams" and their untimely fulfillment in the death of *his* father and exclusive possession of his mother. And is it her desires and their enactment that he fears, recollecting his mother and then projecting her onto Jocasta? In this sense, Laius' "Laius complex" may represent a transfiguration of his own "oedipal constellation" and its only half-unwanted realization.

Even more primitive oral, and indeed preoedipal, elements may come into play in a possessiveness like that of Laius in the wish of a man to have his woman totally, as if she were the mother of infancy, to devour her and to cast aside all others. Unmediated by the presence of a father, such demandingness can go unrestrained and unchallenged, eventuating in the childishness of an imperious adult. As Freud implied, no doubt recollecting his own childhood, the love of a mother for a son (or any child) is often without parallel. It easily equals in intensity romantic love in its ascendance and, quite probably, surpasses it once infatuation has worn into everyday mutuality. If a father of such a child is insecure in his relation to his wife; if, by virtue of narcissism and lovelessness, he is unable to share and derive pleasure from a mother's joy in her children; if he is possessed of an overweening sense of entitlement—such a father may treat a son (or daughter) as a threat. Having failed to identify with his father, he cannot discover his love for the dyad of mother and child and assume his role as its guardian. Without a father, he is left with an inadequate awareness of temporality; for he does not recognize that his wife will once again be his, just as the typical mother is seen to reassert her loyalty to her husband, his father, when early childhood comes to a close. Depending on his moral sensibility, an unfathered and infantile father may be moved to deprive mother and child of each other. He may demand absolute loyalty and obeisance from the woman, even at the expense of her maternal rights and obligations. Laius, lacking a father and thus a template for the development of conscience, was morally wanting as well.

Another possible current suggests itself here, though it is not so directly evident in the myth itself. This has to do with the rivalry not for the mother but rather for the child and the close bond between them, for what Mahler called the "dual unity." Were Laius a real person rather than a figure of the collective imagination (and how often the analyst errs on the side of literalization), who knows how he would have reacted to Jocasta's birthing or suckling of her son after years of frustrating abstinence, impotence, or infertility? One may speculate: Was the exclusion too much to bear, the last straw that broke him, broke them all? A man's envy of child and mother—and perhaps this word "envy" is more apt than jealousy—may take the form of an indiscriminate spitefulness in which everyone loses. As already noted, the attempted murder of Oedipus represents a rageful self-castration, implying Laius' underlying wish to be a woman and even, I might add, a mother.

Whatever his motives, Laius demanded that Jocasta give up her baby.

Like so many children today, Oedipus was spiritually and actually deserted by *both* mother and father. The abandonment was encompassing, as I have said, an expulsion from the family far exceeding mere "father absence." Were it not for the real-life family romance, Oedipus would not have survived.

Finally, there is Laius' imperious violence, his greatest and most pervasive instance of hubris, according to Licht and other authors. Initially Laius tries to disown direct responsibility for his actions, by making other people and the whims of nature the agents of destruction. Thus he commands Jocasta to hand her baby to the servant for the mountain to dispose of. At first his aggression is supposedly motivated by self-preservation. But even then its excessive cruelty is without even this justification.

Later, in the encounter at the crossing of highways, the cruelty and domination become undeniably gratuitous. Even here, Laius would try to escape responsibility as well as the dangers of direct confrontation. Acting out of pride alone, he orders his charioteer and groom to humiliate and strike the first blows against the stranger-son who stands in his way. He engages the youth directly only when he has no choice; Laius is, throughout, a coward. It is his dastardly aggression that the hero Oedipus must answer, rising to the challenge and at last killing the king, "killing them all."

Phallic little boys act to elicit what appears to be an almost instinctive aggressive behavior from fathers and other adult men. Inviting them to roughhouse, they seek to enact the competitiveness necessary to masculine development. Without this kind of actual aggressive interplay, boys may not know the limits of both their own and their father's durability. Untested, their aggression will intensify and fester into what is experienced as a frightening well of seemingly pure destructiveness. Hence the unconscious violence and projected castrative urges of so many men deprived of "adequate," strong fathers. Hence, perhaps, Laius' own untrammeled hostility, fearfulness, paranoia, and sexual uncertainty.

The well-adapted father and other men rein their power and check their inherent pugnacity. They confine expressions of sadism to teasing. They overpower children only when they must, when the genuine demands of discipline and development call for restraint. Love and instinctual inhibition modulate their aggression. There may even be an instinctive basis to parenting. The mere presence of the young moves many men and women, like Oedipus himself, to rise above the past and above character and to be gentle and take care. Even among animals, it has been established that the foreshortening of the juvenile face and ritualized gestures of submission serve to inhibit attacks from the older males.

Some men, whose conscience is severe and whose drives are particularly pressing, may overcompensate and become excessively guilt-laden—obsessively remote or perhaps depressed—in order to spare their children.[6] But in others, like Laius, defects in instinctual "neutralization" are compounded by moral deficits. These give rise to intemperance and harsh impulsivity and to frank failures in fatherliness, which defy the thrust of adult adaptation. Such men may parade their power to hide their infantile fears and fixations, give vent to their unalloyed hostility, and murder, abuse, ridicule, or otherwise injure their own offspring. The effects here seem almost self-evident.

Oedipus the Son

Yet, precisely what is the impact on Oedipus of his father's anxious and relentless self-absorption and aggression? This proves to be as various and contradictory as human nature is complex. The several versions of the myth each depict, in fact, a different Oedipus—each an incarnation of the possibilities inherent in different individual constitutions.

In the more disheartening renditions, Oedipus reenacts the sins of his malevolent and vindictive father. Oedipus' own homosexual rivalry with and ultimate submission to Laius have already been touched on. In other accounts, he is said to have engaged the king openly in mortal combat for Jocasta's favors, with the implication that the patricide—or at least the regicide—was willful rather than unwitting. Fragments of a lost epic, the *Thebaid,* and Sophocles' last play, *Oedipus at Colonus,* indicate that Oedipus himself cursed his own sons because they slighted him. Lacking the empathy of Antigone, his generous and self-sacrificing daughter, he doomed them to be fratricides (although Homer, Hesiod, and Pindar do not corroborate this identification with the aggressor). And in the end there remains the deed. For this, Oedipus, according to the moral absolute, must be condemned.

Yet there also is the hero of *Oedipus Rex*, with which the modern commentator, like Freud, is more familiar. From the play's beginning to its denouement, Oedipus remains, in the words of the Chorus, "noble, great and powerful," more good than bad, and unswervingly courageous. He is also a man more sinned against than sinning. As Jocasta puts it:

> My child was *doomed* to kill him;
> and my child—
> Poor baby!—it was my child that died first.

This may be an error of fact perhaps, but it is one whose irony is its emotional truth—Oedipus was cast from innocence as from his mother's arms. What he endured apart from her, what wrenching agony and chaos fueled the baby's cries in the wilderness, are beyond the adult's empathy. His ordeal is as mysterious as the emotional storms of infancy, the first elements of failed expectation and miasmic mistrust. The later incest only further undoes the secure relation of mother and child.

In fact, Oedipus rises above fate. He stands at his best as the lofty and poignant opposite of his base father. His tragedy testifies to the resilience of the individual and of that individual's capacity for fidelity, love, and care in the face of fate. Oedipus is a virtuous son. He is unsettled by the vague hints of a drunken friend that Merope and Polybus are not his real parents. He then flees Corinth upon hearing the terrible prophecy, lest he happen to harm those he loves. There are, to be sure, unconscious motives to the contrary in Oedipus' choices. These are evident in his failure to integrate the two pronouncements and his paradoxical decision to eschew the moral safety of his adoptive home. Like so many adopted children, Oedipus is driven. He is haunted by his severed origins, searches for them, and is inexorably drawn to his past.

Perhaps it is Polybus' and Merope's goodness that he has exploited in constructing his own humanity—transmuting their love into personal honor and devotion. As an adult man, Oedipus is as faithful to those with whose care he is entrusted as he was to the parents who tended him. "My children" are his and the play's first words, echoed again as he attempts to unearth the causes of the plague and to discover the murderer. He owes his first duty not to himself but to others:

Thebes ravaged by disease, the "pallid children laden with death who lie unwept in the stony ways." Oedipus has invited their trust not because he simply inherited the city, but because he has won it—by virtue of his adult achievements. He is a caretaker, a healer, a man of knowledge.

One of these accomplishments has to do with his grasp of the mysterious paradoxes of life. His is an intelligence foreign to the father. Oedipus' virtue is informed, his search for truth relentless. In every sense Oedipus, unlike his father, strives to assume the total responsibility for his thoughts and deeds. But here's the rub, Oedipus' first tragic flaw. Lacking a father, Oedipus must father himself. In more senses than one, he is the "fathering son." The precocity forced upon him as an orphan, his consequent pride, and his inability to depend on others (at least, until his guilt does him in) make him refuse any mentorship other than his own, even that of the sage Tiresias, who embodies his fate.

A second flaw lies in Oedipus' monomaniacal thirst for knowledge at all cost to himself and in the arrogance implicit in his uncompromising integrity and ultimate self-immolation. He tortures himself with the "flooding pain of memory never to be gouged out." Oedipus, noble and mighty, perspicacious as he is, does what he chooses. He acts from the heart and would know and see all that he can. There is a certain phallic narcissism, and aggressivity, in all of this. His virtue is dangerous. It is reminiscent at times of Freud—Freud the conquistador, hawk to the hens who once tutored him, as Breuer put it—and of a rationalistic and haughty perfectionism whereby comprehension is believed to conquer all. He too has little regard for those defenses and illusions that protect most men from themselves.

Oedipus' rage, insufficiently modulated and repressed, can overwhelm him. Most of all, however, it is the relentless violence of his guilt that destroys him. His harshness is internal and self-initiated. Conscience and filial duty move Oedipus to flee the safety of his adoptive home. Concern and then guilt, less and less rational, drive his dangerous inquiry. It is his growing, inexplicable and unbearable guilt and the effort to expel it which provoke Oedipus' most uncharitable moments: his persecutory anxiety over Creon; his character assassination of Tiresias; his selfish relief at the news of Polybus' death; the identification implicit in these acts, and in his later condemnation of his sons, with Laius' paranoia and aggression. And it is the searing white light of the final inescapable revelation of himself as parricide which moves him to plunge into his eyes the dead Jocasta's brooches, which long ago he must have undone, loosening her robes in preparation for their incest. Oedipus' self-destruction is monumental. Insight, he learns too late from Tiresias, can be blind. The blindness is a "tight cell of misery blank to light and sound . . . a dark agony beyond all recollection."

But is this really so? Do the crime and the shame belong only to Oedipus?

"Ah, Cithaeron" are the words that conclude Oedipus' self-excoriating utterance. The infanticide is ever present, the original sin. True, Oedipus slew the father and slept with the mother, as must the four-year-old in his imagination and in play. All men, as Jocasta says, have dreamed such things. The son is guilty of dark intentions and bad deeds. But the parents acted of their own volition and not from unwitting impulse alone. They raised their hands in deplorable violence against their child. Certainly Jocasta is condemned. She is an "unspeakable mother" and then a suicide. Had she not killed herself, she might have suffered Oedipus' revenge. But what of Laius?

In Sophocles' first play, not one word is uttered against him. Perhaps his actual death has been punishment enough. But not one word? Must Oedipus, innocent that he was, bear the full culpability? It seems he must. The sins of the fathers are also his, loosed like demons, detached from their sources and transfigured as the child's own. "Ghosts," the dramatist Ibsen called them, "the Furies" or Erinyes, according to the Greeks, who further personified and partly disguised them as angry female figures from the matriarchal past.

Freud and Oedipus Again

Once more the blind spots of Freud, so closely identified with Oedipus, are remarkable. Not only did he omit mention of Laius' crimes in his summary of the myth itself. Once he ceded his seduction theory, Freud also tended to ignore or to exculpate quite actively his patients' and subjects' fathers in the case histories. Repeatedly Freud neglected the familial reality lurking behind psychopathology, ascribing the latter mainly to the workings of fantasy.

As Freud turned his conceptual eye ever inward, he came to see in symptoms the workings of unconscious fantasy. Such fantasy he viewed as essentially predetermined, probably universal, and possibly inherited from the collective past.[7] Hence he illumined psychic reality, a momentous discovery whose great truth is still indisputable. But in theory, if fortunately not in practice, Freud and many analysts after him often tended to overlook the intricacies of the interpersonal climate in which such imaginings take root and grow. If, for example, the imagined genital seductions reported by his late adolescent and adult patients were most often fantastical, they probably served to screen other problematic traits, rumored activities, and actual behavior on the part of parents which excited the pregenital sexuality and aggression of the child. Freud, lacking the hindsight of another half century of observational and clinical contact with children, failed to account for these *age-specific* seductions in his developmental theory.

In his spectacular attack on Freud's motives and integrity, Jeffrey Masson suggests that Freud abandoned his seduction theory in order to curry favor with the Viennese establishment. Freud, Masson contends, sought to win acceptance for psychoanalysis in circles where the hypocrites of the day sought to guard their dirty little secrets—namely, their proclivity for child molestation. Given Freud's character, his abiding highmindedness and defiance of the status quo, along with his yearning at this time for idealized father figures (mostly in the person of Fliess), this seems unlikely. Quite the contrary, other more honorable motives led him to veer away from the darkness in the heart not only of the son but also of the father. Freud, it must be remembered, was struggling with the Theban *agon* just as his own father lay dying. He, like Oedipus, was striking out on his own on the "royal road" to make inquiry of the oracle. Freud sought answers to the riddle of the Sphinx whose insights had eluded the most original of his mentors.

It is clear that all men, even Freud or the legendary Theban king Oedipus (or Pelops, for that matter), *need* their gods and fathers. And Freud, we know, loved his dearly. At times sons and daughters will do almost anything to maintain the defensive and self-sustaining idealizations in which these patriarchs are ensconced. They will assume a remorse that is not theirs; emasculate, blind, and kill themselves; sacrifice or exploit their children. Need and guilt conspire in the exoneration of the father—the need for his protection, the guilt as his internal proxy. Witness, for example, Freud's defense of Fliess in the Emma Eckstein debacle. Freud himself put it this way in his dissection of the religious imperative. The believer

> harks back to the mnemic image of the father whom in his childhood he so greatly overvalued. He exalts the image into a deity and makes it into something contemporary and real. The effective strength of the mnemic image and the persistence of his need for protection jointly sustain his belief in God. (1933:163)

So compelling are these forces that they defy understanding. As we have seen, Kafka wrote of his father's rasping indifference and helpless stupidity. Yet he could not free himself of its absurd consequences, the abiding and irrational remorsefulness that put him, like his protagonists, forever on trial. How could Oedipus, having glimpsed his father's fate, allow himself to see as well into Laius' murderous heart? Rather than embrace the most terrible of revelations, and the despair it would bring with it, he yields to an identification with the aggressor's transgressions. He falls prey to the kind of hysterical identification, introjection of guilt, uncompromising self-prohibition, and propitiatory longing for a father's beneficence which, Freud noted, lie at the core of so much neurotic suffering. One might underscore obsessional neurosis in particular, and those alien but unyielding obligations within the self that are its hallmark. Perhaps this is Oedipus' most apt diagnosis.

Discovering the inner sources of the plague is only the first step in Oedipus' drama and purgation. It is only after he has come to recognize the limits of his responsibility in *Oedipus at Colonus* that he finds inner peace and release from suffering.[8] In the end, self-blinded and self-exiled, he is honored and shepherded by his daughters, especially the devoted Antigone. Ultimately Oedipus, the old man, is redeemed by none other than Theseus, king of Athens and slayer of the Minotaur to whom the young of Crete were offered up for slaughter—Theseus the son of a devoted father, Aegeus, and himself a founding father of the democratic state. In this rendering at least, Theseus figures as the civilized opposite of Laius, the fatherless and primitive autocrat. Although elsewhere the Athenian monarch is portrayed as a selfish, exploitive philanderer, here he is cast as the father that he foundling prince never had. At last, through the king's grace and authority, Oedipus is freed, freed from self-torment and free to die.

Theoretical Implications

Methodological advances in the last twenty-five years have realigned psychoanalytic perspectives on development. Where Freud reconstructed his adult patients' histories on the basis largely of their individual reminiscences, actings-in, and transference phenomena, relying on anecdotal glimpses of children, modern observers have refined his notions of development by way of direct systematic observation. Investigators have actually watched children grow within their families.

Babies, René Spitz emphasized, are the only persons in a family without a past. Soon enough, though, they are fitted with one, that of their parents, into whose representational worlds they are assimilated. Parents respond to children according to predetermined images of what they are and will be in ways that demonstrably influence their behavior and emerging sense of self. Such inputs become evident long before the consolidation of a child's self-boundaries, his or her demarcation of fantasy and reality, and the establishment of character. Thus a parent's needs and inevitably distorted perceptions penetrate to the child's basic core, in the words of Annemarie Weil. Personality does not come into being simply as a product of the dialectics of danger and desire.

In this spirit, other investigators have begun to chart the transactions of parent and child from the neonatal period, through infancy, toddlerhood, and into adolescence. In a variety of training, intervention, and outreach programs, pathology in the parents has been described along with its manifestation in various "dysparenting" phenomena, including asynchrony, incest, and abuse.[9] Such applications of psychoanalytic principles lend dynamic meaning to Freud's conceptualization of the "complemental series." They point to interactions wherein the individual's constitution affects the environment, and vice versa, establishing elaborate feedback patterns of resonances between the two. In other words, this work suggests that each particular child has his or her own significant part to play in the parents' lives. This role is very much a function of the particular child: premature or full term, endowed or damaged, female or male, first or otherwise in the birth order.

This is so, we have also learned, because parents are vulnerable. Prompted by Erikson's conception of the life cycle, a number of investigators have arrived at the notion of adult development. If adults' sensibilities and personalities evolve for different reasons, at a slower rate and with less dramatically, than children's, mature individuals do evince discernible change, for better or worse. Individuals both grow and deteriorate as they respond dynamically to the successive tasks and crises of adult life.

Critical among these tasks are procreation and caretaking. Parenthood has been conceptualized as a developmental challenge or, better, the climax—rather protracted—of a lifelong adaptational progression. Responding to the birth of children and to the high pitch of their developmental crises, parents—both mothers and fathers—may find themselves thrown into states of disequilibrium which awaken the past and thus activate progressive as well as regressive trends. The potential for an outbreak of psychopathology is great, as Freud noted when he emphasized the vicissitudes of adult misfortunes, specifically setbacks in procreative capacity, in compromising adaptive resolutions of neurotic conflict (and good analytic results). Forced to play out major parts in the parental drama, which they may unwittingly have set in motion, children are directly affected by a parent's conflicts and their expression within the family.

Psychoanalytic developmentalists have not surrendered the centrality of unconscious fantasy and intrapsychic conflict to an emphasis on external reality. But they have responded to the insights of object-relations theory in concert with their own research. Thus some analysts have come to view psychic reality and external transactions between people as repositories for each other. Each realm, inner and outer, reflects, enriches, constrains, and shapes the other, while both continue to evolve throughout the life cycle. The correspondences are never exact, of course; the mediating processes of internalization alter externality according to defensive needs and developmental capacities, while other people accommodate to the individual only insofar as their character structures will allow.

There are few constants in this system of reverberating object worlds, and the theorist has created them mainly because it is taxing and perhaps conceptually impossible to do otherwise. If the more balanced view lacks the elegant, often surprising, and dramatic simplicity of the original, more "classical" scheme of things, still it may point to a more open system that is truer to life, and thus more descriptively encompassing and accurate. It is less reductionist, since heuristic conveniences remain poor substitutes for real people.

Against this backdrop, let me summarize the aggressive dimensions of the father-son dialogue. The father's Laius complex or, for the sake of terminological parsimony, his "Laius motif," includes both filicidal and pederastic trends. It is instigated partly in reaction to the child's own developmental demands but seems inherent in the adult himself. It represents a transfiguration of the adult father's childhood oedipal constellation, including both his competition with his father and his identification with the latter's paternal aggression. But it is also a phase- or age-specific response to the succession of generations and to his own predestined demise, the narcissistic blow inherent in our mortality. This may be compounded by conflicts in sexual identity, with hostile, sadistic, and phallic displays serving to defend against homosexual and infantile trends. A delicate balance must be struck between a father's empathy and mature love for his child and his complex expressions of unconscious hostility and selfish desire.

Communications of paternal aggression have both adaptive and maladaptive consequences. Early on, as the work of Herzog, Yogman, and Brazelton shows, fathers virilize sons and organize their own aggression. Intimations of a father's aggressivity serve as dynamic preconditions or releasers of the son's oedipal complex—universally, I believe. The adult man's inevitable intrusion and domination invite a more or less sexualized submission, his oppression and interruptions exciting narcissistic and possessive hostility. Indeed, there is a feedback system of sorts between the adult's Laius and the son's Oedipus constellations.

Clinical Implications

Present in its own right, the would-be imperiousness of the child can itself assume either a pathological and destructive or an adaptive and assertive form of expression, depending on a father's manifest actions and reactions. There are many implications for all levels of clinical intervention to be derived from an awareness of the Laius motif.

First of all, therapeutic work with fathers of child and adolescent patients must be attuned to these phenomena. Noteworthy is the male parent's apparent indifference toward children. Denial and avoidance constitute defenses against potential hostility while at the same time effecting a representational void and thus a distorted expression of psychic murder. The de facto exclusion of fathers from the treatment situation often bespeaks a fearful glimpse on the part of all involved into the realities of paternal aggression. This perception is exacerbated by the clinician's identifications with the child and unconscious rememberances and projections of murderous urges onto the patient's father. The clinician, the child, and the father himself may accede to images propagated by many mothers to the effect that fathers are alternately dangerous, indifferent, incompetent, and irrelevant— "hopeless nonparents."

Second, the problem of father absence has been treated as a fait accompli before which the clinician is helpless. It is instead a dynamic process in which intervention may be possible and beneficial. Related to this issue are the conflicts of divorced fathers. According to Wallerstein and Kelly, there is no way of predicting the postdivorce relationship on the basis of what has taken place in the past. The pain of loss commingles with resentment in the face of old hurts and new burdens. Much can be done to confront the denial, avoidance, and reassertion of lost youth plaguing fathers who are in the process of becoming absent. Nor, as the analyst well knows, will exhortation or instruction suffice.

Let us look at the example of B, a thirty-five-year-old writer who sought treatment in the wake of an unhappy love affair. He had left his older wife and son Eric, when the boy was eighteen months old, for a younger, sexier woman, only to find her withholding and eventually rejecting.

It gradually became apparent that B's feelings of loss and dependency had as much to do with his son as with his girlfriend. He had been intensely involved with the boy as an infant and toddler. His and his former wife's schedules were such that during the day he functioned as the child's primary caregiver, embracing the role wholeheartedly.

But after the parents divorced when Eric was two and a half, B withdrew from the boy.

Fears of femininity and a strong maternal identification, along with a horror of associated homosexual trends that became clear within the transference—all moved B to flee his son and his fatherhood. He had become preoccupied with parading his manly body before the new girlfriend, whose own phallic attributes were explored in the analysis (she also energetically rejected his son). Ignored by his once loving father and relegated by his hardworking mother to the care of babysitters, B's son became increasingly timid and evidently rather schizoid, requiring evaluation and treatment. His learning disabilities, reminiscent of the patient's problems as a child, added to the difficulties and compounded B's disappointment in and guilt toward the son. All the while he was at pains to disavow any hostility toward Eric.

At one point, however, he began to speculate about me and my children, particularly an imagined son, in the context of complaining about his more limited life and about the prospect of growing old. B had long ago surpassed his father, while having identified with the old man's plaintive, embittered, and self-defeating posture in an unconscious atonement for his better lot in life. Now he recalled the father's herniated scar from abdominal surgery and remarked on how small, set against his bulk, his father's penis had once seemed to him when as a late adolescent he caught sight of it in the shower. In contrast, he imagined me to be more powerful, fit, well muscled and "well hung," in addition to being smarter, kinder, and more fatherly. He envied my intact family. He thought that the analyst's son, in contrast to Eric, must be similarly well endowed and a source of pride. Next he remembered holding his pet dog before the vet put her to sleep.

Then with great shock, B uncovered his wish to rid himself of a boy who, once his darling, had become a burden and a disappointment. Failing to solace him with the promise of self-perpetuation, Eric merely reminded B of his limitations and failures as well as his mortality. Avoiding him allowed B to contain the fits of anger he now confessed to when presented by the child's sloppy appearance, slowness, and preoccupation with "little people." In effect, it served to do away with him: out of sight, out of mind, out of existence.

With these insights B was enabled to rediscover some of his love for Eric. Whereas in the past he might not see him for a month or more at a time over vacations, he now rearranged his schedule and living space to accommodate him three days a week, further contending with a new wife's jealousy of her stepson.

A third point about the Laius motif involves work with adults. Therapists and analysts must be aware of the actual, prospective, and potential parenthood of their analysands. Often relatively absent fathers themselves, by virtue of their own long training in midlife, male clinicians have tended to overlook or underestimate the paternal conflicts of their male patients. When these do not emerge in treatment, for example, many clinicians fail to interpret the resistance. Conversely, when a patient does discuss his fatherhood, one reflexive tendency is to relate this material to the transference neurosis and to *filial* pretension and competitiveness. Parental inclinations toward the clinician are further treated as defensive distortions. Take the case of H, a twenty-nine-year-old attorney who was in analysis with my supervisee, Dr. Q. After five sessions a week for over four years, he was finally able to propose to and marry his girlfriend of a year. He had been terrorized by a controlling, explosive, strap-wielding mother whose aggressivity confounded his evident incestuous impulses toward her and pervasively injured his masculinity. "It's tough," H remarked, "when the hand that hits is the hand that loves."

The patient devalued his generally more loving and gentle but inadequate father. He resented the father's lack of self-respect and, with this, his inability to control the mother, who eventually left him when the patient was seventeen. Initially, H had wanted his father to act as a disciplinarian, even to hit him, subsequently trying to play this wish out in an obvious oedipal transference neurosis.

More precise reconstruction unearthed the father's aggressivity. Rather than roughhouse, the elder man played a "flinching game" with his dangerously asthmatic and easily startled son—sadistically and to excess. Perhaps, the patient later mused, this was one of the sources of his compulsion to look over his shoulder while walking down the street. Similarly, the mother's initial timidity, self-doubt, and overprotection were clarified, as he reflected on the motives for her mistreatment. H discovered to his dismay that his mother, devalued and narcissistically deflated by her father and then her uncle, had exacted her revenge. She beat him and commented on how small his penis was.

In his parents' stead, H clung to his maternal great-aunt and great-uncle, who had also reared his mother after her parents died in a car accident. He cherished his enveloping and somewhat alarmist and overly cautious "nannams," with whom he lived when he began analysis. He found the powerful old man authoritarian and therefore awesome, "a real man," and he utterly idealized him. Only with great pain, remonstration, and repeated defensive regressions could the patient allow himself to see the man's defects and indiscretions. More specifically, he became aware of the ways in which such compulsive tyranny and misogyny had been indirectly responsible for his hapless plight at his mother's hands.

His fiancée, later his wife, was experienced as being like his great-aunt, motherly and loving, rather than vicious like his mother. When he wed her, H softened the "challenge to the gods" (his most problematic phobia involved thunder and lightning) by using the great-uncle's wine cup at the wedding.

The analysis was extremely complex, volatile, and arduous. For one thing, H's phallic posture served to defend against a strong maternal, bisexual identification. His defenses revealed an intense parental interest in a younger brother who was born when he was six. Even the analyst became subject to maternal concerns in what the patient called a role reversal.

Prior to his marriage, H developed upper-abdominal gastric and duodenal pains, which he associated to his father's gall bladder condition. Following the ceremony and a Latin American honeymoon, the symptoms shifted and became reminiscent of the ominous signs of his great-uncle's cancer. Now he complained increasingly of lower-left-quadrant gastrointestinal pain. This eventuated in a "spastic colon" that moved him to subject himself first to a sigmoidoscopy and finally a colonoscopy—the latter undertaken without anesthesia because of his history of asthma. When he was able to acknowledge his hypochondria, the patient began to explore the extent of his parental ambitions, his pregnancy fantasies, and the propitiatory homosexual submission obvious in submitting to an invasive procedure that amounted to rape. In his idiosyncratic way, H was getting ready for fatherhood. He was even inuring himself to the baby "shit"—his own—that once appalled him.

Among the many issues to be worked on was the patient's identification with his mother as aggressor. He punctuated his frenzy over the state of his body with bouts of weeping and rage at the violence he had suffered at his mother's hands. He was further terrified that in becoming a father he would act like her (as well as his great-uncle), repeating her cruelties out of envy for the better parenting his children potentially might have had from her. An avid urban botanist, he loved his plants dearly, he said, even though they "stole" his light from him.

After months of analysis, the gastric distress abated and then disappeared, only to be temporarily replaced by a headache. He dwelt on this for a week, concluding his complaints with the following rather poignant Friday session.

"I have a score to settle with my boss and you, just like my mother." He associated to a suicide, a man in the newspaper who was caught stabbing his wife, and to a man on the west coast who set his son on fire during a custody battle. "They're upper class. There are Rastafarians who put kids in the oven to get the devil out of them. But that's just ignorance and superstition. It's crazy we harbor these crazy instincts in us. Horrible. My wife's parents brought back a present. I dislike getting valuable gifts because I'm afraid of worrying about them. I don't want them to get ripped off or up. I remember buying different clothes when I moved out—a way of getting away from her. My mother bought me white socks. They were ridiculous."

"And," Dr. Q interjected, "the gift of a child?"

"I have a lot of concerns about children, and I would need to differentiate from her, from my mother. My mother set up rules, but she wasn't loving—although I guess she was overprotective when we were young. I might—I put a cover on my wife when she went to sleep—I reprimanded her—I'd probably do that too with kids. Having a child is a risky proposition. Anything can happen. With me too. There are no guarantees. It depends on stresses. I'm afraid of running out of patience, getting angry. Like with toilet training for example, if the kid kept making a mess in his pants. I wouldn't succumb to peer pressure, but still I'd get furious. I feel sorry for my friend M with his hyper kid—he takes after the mother, not him. I don't know how he can stand it."

"You're afraid of hurting, killing?"

"Hitting, yes. It might erupt. It's not conscious—something spontaneous. Like the way I keep waking up in the early morning. Frustration.

Like the old foot banging. If the kid was being disobedient. If he played games with me, like wanting toilet training and then he craps in his pants. What are you doing, fucking with me? Or an ugly kid. I joke about gassing kids or sedating them. I'm—it sounds cruel and inhuman. In order to raise a child you have to be understanding and stable. I'm understanding now, but I'm not so sure I'm stable . . . Somewhere along the line I have to decide about the headache. I'll have to go to the doctor."

"You're talking about children being headaches."

"Yeah, but not acting out."

"You're torturing yourself ahead of time because these wishes to hurt the kid you plan to have conflict with your wish to mother babies, to be a better mother than your mother. And they make you feel guilty, so you hurt yourself with a headache."

"Yeah, but you have to recognize there are certain energies to do harm. You can't delude yourself. That's why I was quizzing you yesterday about the kids coming here. It's the parents who screw up the kids. With S [his wife], I don't like the way her mother treats her father. She kept taking over the stories he told about their trip—like he had nothing valuable to say. Like making fun of him. You wanna know a Freudian slip I made last night? Her mother brought back twigs from South America. S said it's like my mother, who collects rocks. I said it's like for her husbands. You know what I mean. She wittles them down and puts them on the mantel piece. The association is between rocks and balls—like the slang. That's why I hate these women. Come to think of it, put the sticks and rocks together and you've got the whole thing, the whole magillah."

"That's another reason why you'd be moved to attack a child. Just like her. To avenge yourself on your mother in displaced fashion and make yourself feel like a big man."

"I wonder, does it matter? What sex it is—a boy or a girl. My mother was put down by her father. I'd get even with a daughter, like she was a little twat. I think the only difference between men and women is a man has a penis. I know you disagree with that stuff about the insides. The estrogen's the mainline. Cut off the balls, and you lose the testosterone and the man turns into a woman . . . [He gives more details about biology.] I always viewed it as the haves and the have-nots. Girls are fucked up because they're the have-nots. I used to think the doctor slipped during circumcision. That was the going joke, later. But I believed it. My mother's behavior robbed me of a feeling of masculinity. She stripped me of it. Even if you had a dick or they cut off your balls, you feel like a woman if your mother acts that way. [Laughs.] Like a whimpering cock, unmasculine. If you get whipped into submission, big deal you have a cock, because you can't use it. I guess I did see women as powerful, and I hated strong women."

"The abuse you fear you would commit has to do with your fighting to be a man rather than a woman."

"Or, better—defective. Castrated. It would be a constant struggle. I can't relax myself. Even today I can't make myself sleep. In order to relax you have to be trusting and realize if you wake up you can defend yourself. You have to let your guard down to sleep. Uncle Melvin could. And S's dad. This aunt of mine and my uncle Sam. That son of a bitch Rachel destroys him. He's a tyrant in her presence. Like he needs to do it. He walks around with a stiff dick."

"And you?"

"Yeah, it's the same, all that Hulk and Superman stuff. Getting angry to feel like a man."

"You felt overwhelmed and abused by your mother and were moved to identify with her cruelty and her femininity."

"It's unconscious. You make it conscious in analysis, but then you have conflict. There's an overhead to saying you want to smack a kid and know it's morally wrong—rather than just acting on it."

"The overhead now being a headache."

"Yeah."

A fourth set of implications has to do with the uses of the transference in suggesting genetic reconstructions. Interpretations of the oedipal dilemma have often been left incomplete by virtue of an exclusive focus on the intrapsychic conflicts of the patient as a child. Such a focus tends to exempt parents from the pressures of psychic life and its systematic scrutiny. Representations of destructive fathers have most often been ascribed to the patient's projections. Images of a father's domination and cruelty have been seen as reflections of the child's own cruel intentions, which serve to externalize and thus to alleviate the tension engendered by intrapsychic conflict and guilt. Transference distortions underscore the unreality of the patient's anticipation of murder and mutilation in the analytic situation. They are used to clarify the internal nature of his conflicts.

This is true enough, of course. But, left at this level, such constructions may serve to further invalidate the patient's intuition into the father's obvious or unconscious wish to kill his offspring. In blinding himself, Oedipus would close his eyes forever to his parent's cruelties—only then, in his dependent weakness, to compromise *his* children's well-being, identifying willy-nilly with Laius' and Jocasta's abdication of parenthood. In some instances, conflicts over oedipal rivalry can provide a whole defense *organization,* in Hoffer's term, screening longings and dangers of a more primitive order. Guilt, constriction, and abiding submission may act as a father's internal proxy, as slavemasters obscuring the recognition of the parent's human frailty, vulnerability to impulse, and unpredictability.

The need for a father's protection is, as Freud wrote (1929), perhaps the most pressing condition of childhood, an imperative around which a great variety of neurotic edifices are constructed. Without it, one, all, is lost. In childhood especially, the ontological upheaval of a life alone is, quite simply, too great to bear. The little boy or girl must feel sustained and secure in his or her idealization of parental guardians. Challenging even the most brittle of these images is a risky undertaking when treating a child, no matter how transparent the parents' deficits or malevolence, and notwithstanding the compromising of various ego functions necessary to buttress such denial.

But as an adult, cognitively equipped and socially and physically independent, a patient should be better able to face the dangers and solitude of being on one's own. This aloneness is also what Oedipus' story, his journey—heroic, sublime, foolhardy, agonizing and relieving by turns—is all about: It is, as Freud implied, what must be the ultimate work of analysis.

Finally, there is the problem of the analyst' own Laius complex and its place in his paternalistic countertransference toward patients. As the analysts Atkins and Grunberger have suggested, it is the underpinnings of their own intergenerational countertransference reactions, often passing unperceived, that prevent many clinicians from contending with these issues. As a result, they fail to analyze their patients' irrational deference to erstwhile and evermore ephemeral figures of authority. No analysis is exhaustive, and we all remain prisoners to some degree of our dependent pasts as well as our unwanted mortal destinies. It is man's fate that Oedipus anticipates and finally welcomes.

I offer a brief case in point of a more subtle countertransference. More obvious examples I leave to the collective "conscience of the analysis." A twenty-eight-year-old male patient, had been in intensive three-day-a-week psychotherapy with me for four years. Having decided on his profession relatively late in life, he then dallied within it. C contented himself with a lackluster and bureaucratically constraining job on the pretext of his vague left-wing convictions, sentiments without, he conceded, a clear ideological base. He wished to help the poor. Reflecting on his "underachieving," after much thought C concluded that he would like to remain an adolescent after all, with both the omnipotentiality and dependency afforded by this status.

C spoke about his aggressive, overbearing mother, with whom he had an unwanted conspiratorial and seductive relationship. She complained to him about her husband "incessantly and inappropriately." His father was a weak, debilitated, passive man who had a stroke when the patient was sixteen. Soon after this happened, he found himself masturbating, as if in triumph, he concluded retrospectively and to his horror. C did remember wrestling with his father as a boy. But he lamented his "old man's" ineffectuality and weak will, and his lack of interest in the patient's considerable high-school academic, athletic, and political successes. As with H, so with C: memories surfaced in which the father's loss of control and his sadism became clear as well. Helping with homework, he exploded at his son. While wrestling, he sometimes hurt the boy.

Basically heterosexual, the patient had fantasies of being enslaved and used erotically by women, "slave fantasies." Explicit homosexual dreams and fantasies involving his father and emerging during treatment gradually revealed the disguised "father hunger" underlying these sexualized but still heterosexual constructions.

The transference also came more and more to assume a frankly homosexual or negative oedipal cast. At first I was seen as a straight, conventional older brother, advocating bourgeois achievements such as marriage, money, and hard work. C "argued his case" to the contrary. He resisted fee increases at the close of the year and often withheld the fee for more than a month. But the fighting, both verbal and silent, was also a provocation with other aims. These became conscious, and the transference shifted from defiance to an idealizing, tender, warm, and increasingly erotic interest in my person. He had been, he remarked, wrestling with an angel.

Working genetically and transferentially, C made great strides. He shed his passive, sleepy demeanor along with a scraggly beard and wrinkled shirts. He seemed suddenly alive, both in and outside his hours. He later described how he no longer sank into the waiting room's soft sofa but chose instead a hard chair with a straight back. More important, C found a better job, one that provided not only more money and power but the opportunity to exercise his commitment to helping the underdog. No longer a grudging underling, he was a boss now, a role that had once connoted being "snakelike." He became less withholding with his girlfriend of eight years and with me, whom he paid promptly and gratefully. Finally, we began to talk more and more about wanting to be a father. With this, he considered the prospect of terminating therapy—that is, once he was certain that the inner strength he had gained was really his own.

I was pleased with the patient's progress. Aware at the same time of pangs about the separation to come, of the fact that in treatment closeness and collaboration portend loss, I privately foresaw another nine to twelve months of work. It was a time, incidentally, when many of my somewhat younger male patients seemed to be approaching termination. Succumbing to the sort of countertranferential enactment described by Theodore Jacobs, I then made an obscure but ultimately telling error.[10] On one month's bill, I failed to count one of the sessions and undercharged my patient. Though, as C said, he had toyed with the idea of cheating, he called the error to my attention. It was the first time he had noticed such a mistake, and it surprised him. Perhaps, he added significantly, the therapist had somehow charged him the lower and long superseded fee (though even then, the therapist told him, the figures would not have totaled the way they did).

C proceeded to describe an uncomfortable weekend visit with his parents. He had felt ashamed of his father, who had exploded foolishly at a waitress. The next day, wandering through a beach club, he and his girlfriend decided to hide in a cabana and make delicious illicit love. For some reason, however, they masturbated each other instead, she "touching" him first, as he put it with an uncharacteristic recourse to euphemism. While she did, he had a fantasy of anal penetration reminiscent of his "old self." He interpreted this "mini" regression as a guilty reaction to his rage and shame at yet another demonstration of his father's fallibility.

Still uneasy because of my mistake with the bill, I was unsatisfied with this conclusion. It was incomplete, facile. I had the sense that the patient was letting me off the hook. If I said nothing and simply agreed with him, everything would continue to go smoothly, perpetuating our mutual-admiration society. "That flaky old father" of his continued to take the fall. I contemplated my lapse and the realities and inner motives behind it. It had been a month in which my scheduling was disrupted more than usual, but this was not the whole story.

Bringing my own intrusion back into the transference, I remarked on the patient's telling distortion in reinstating the old fee. We noted his guilty temptation to cheat, to take advantage of my weakness, and a further error in which the patient called the bill the "check." What the two of us concluded was this: the patient had regressed in the face of my evident imperfection in order to atone for the hostility excited by my vulnerability. C wanted to keep me ensconced in an ideal position whose warming presence he could continue to bask in. He was not really independent yet, C sighed, and "how fragile the human psyche is! I know you make mistakes, you're not perfect. But still!"

Privately, I went on to contemplate my inadvertent gift, the seductiveness as well, and realized the intuitive truth of the patient's attributing the error not to the free hour—perhaps the one in which he had wondered about finishing up—but to the old fee. The gift had been a Trojan horse, a killing with kindness. I did not want this "son" to complete his adolescence after all. I did not want him to make me obsolete and leave me. So I would surreptitiously diminish and thus undermine him in order to remain his rescuer and hero. I had prided myself on my patient's growth in independence and masculinity. But unconsciously I had invited the man's regression and homosexual submission. And in true sadomasochistic fashion, I had led *him* into temptation. He could to get away with murder while I remained the innocent, unwitting victim.

There is always choice, along with analysis and the prevailing zeitgeist, and in fact a certain parental instinctiveness. Victims like Laius need not victimize. Even though they are creatures of character, adults have discretion at their disposal. After all, even infrahuman primates have access to wellsprings of love which, with felicitous circumstance, flow forth and submerge inherent hostility toward youthful usurpers.

As in the beginning, so in the end there remains the deed. For this, according to the categorical imperative, Oedipus the parricide, like his filicidal and pederastic father before him, must be condemned. I have attempted to interpret the Oedipus myth as a metaphor for the sinister and sometimes tragic "confusion of tongues," in Ferenczi's words, that can take place between fathers and sons. My objective has not been to discharge the individual of responsibility for the darker ambitions of childhood, his Oedipus complex. Ultimately such faults are still in ourselves. Quite the contrary, positing the Laius complex adds to the great weight we must all bear. As adults, another constellation of deadly desire and terror is at work within us, affecting our lives and those in our care.

6

The Riddle of Little Hans

In this book I have emphasized the fateful consequences of paternal insufficiency. During the second and third year of life, a critical period in the articulation of self-constancy and gender identity, a lack of actual or felt fathering leaves a boy at risk on various fronts: his masculinity and selfhood uncertain; his elemental knowledge of sex differences befuddled; his fears of fusion and emasculation pronounced.

But the development of sexual identity does not end there. There is, after all, the ensuing oedipal crisis and the organization of not only gender but sexual identity in its fuller elaboration. At this point—in the representational realm more than in actuality—paternal deprivation or dysfunction makes for a more conflictual dilemma. Faced with the seeming exclusivity of phallic narcissistic strivings and the parental ambitions inherent in his residual maternal identifications, a boy gropes not only for a heterosexual but also for a procreative identity. The unavailability of the father as a subject for identification further confounds the boy's efforts to answer the riddle of the Sphinx. To be a man means to be barren; to make a baby portends castration; males do not "have" children.

It is in grasping and identifying with the father's fatherly role that a boy can more fully reconcile two opposing strains in his sexual identity. For only then are sexual union and the self-completion and fecundity it yields possible within the confines of his masculinity. Potentially perverse trends—and the partial objects and partial identifications they eroticize—also become subsumed by genital fantasies and strivings.

In seeking out shared data on the many aspects of oedipal development—a common text—I turn to Freud's psychoanalytic parable, the case of Little Hans. In fact, much is known about Little Hans—later identified as Herbert Graf, stage director of the Metropolitan Opera and intendant of the Geneva Opera, as well as about his father Max, a musicologist and member of Freud's Wednesday group (see Seides, 1987; Graf, 1941, 1942). But here I will deal only with the narrative data, with a clinical legacy, that is, available to all working analysts. A choice like this steers clear of the Scylla of forced evidence and the Charybdis of violated confidentiality in tendering clinical vignettes of one's own. Available to the reader in the same form as to the author, such a narrative invites alternative readings and constructive disagreement.

Students of psychoanalysis are familiar with "Analysis of a Phobia in a Five-Year-Old Boy" (1909a), which Freud used so brilliantly to embody the general propositions on infantile sexuality set forth earlier in the *Three Essays* (1905c). Little Hans figured as a case in point of the castration complex suffered by the boy as he attempts to negotiate his oedipal passage—his positive oedipal complex, in more modern parlance. Freud stressed Hans's wish to replace his father in his mother's bed, his ambivalence toward the man he both loved and hated, and his fear of retaliation at the father's hand.

The neurosis (a phobia in which Hans's conflicts were displaced, projected, and externalized, engendering a fear of biting and falling horses) was set in motion by the birth of his sister, Hannah. His mother's screams, the bloody vessels, and, notably for our purposes, Hans's confusion about the anatomical implications of the event set his castration fear in motion. He succumbed first to an agoraphobia of sorts and, subsequently, to the zoophobia detailed by Freud. Once Hans's father, supervised, as it were, by the Professor, made Hans aware of his own intentions, of the imagined danger accompanying them, and of the anatomical differences, he was relieved of the symptomatology.

But Freud himself, alluding to yet another thread in the story, noted that Hans's ignorance of the procreative function of a man remained to be addressed. It is this strain that I will pursue here, Hans's ambisexuality. Speculating further, I will attempt to reconstruct from its many derivatives a particular fantasy, which may well have contributed to the genesis of the phobia and which was still in evidence at the close of his treatment. Hans, in my view, was not offered sufficient opportunity during the oedipal phase to reorganize his disparate libidinal aims, fragmented object images, and various identifications into a heterosexual paternal identity. Because of a failure to embrace a specifically fatherly identification, this first child-patient ultimately resorted to what we now would label a negative oedipal position as a compromise solution. With this, Hans's symptomatic improvement was effected by a sort of transference cure, or so it seems from the case material at our disposal.

The Clinical Narrative

Hans is introduced as a prototypical phallic boy of five years, enamored of his own "widdler" or "wee-wee maker" and intrigued by those of others. His age-appropriate struggle to grasp and accept the genital distinction between male and female is chronicled repeatedly.

The narrators, Hans's father and Freud, tell us little of the boy's mother apart from her son's glimpses of her mysterious pubic region. The ambiguity of her responses to the little boy's questions about her genitals is highlighted as if somehow she were denying her apparent castration. Early on she responds to her son's query, "Mommy, have you got a widdler, too?" with an answer and a question, "Of course, why?"

"I was only just thinking," he replies. Hans's infantile idiom is as confusing as his mother's response. Does widdler or wee-wee maker mean just that, or does it refer only to a penis? No doubt Hans's mother is not asserting that she is in possession of a male organ. Rather, this is Hans's, the father's, and even Freud's phallocentric inference.

Hans confuses a cow's udder with a penis. Pondering the boy's confusion about this quintessentially female beast, Freud emphasizes that this organ "plays an apt part as an intermediate image, being in its nature a mamma and in its shape and position, that of a penis" (7). He then leaves the hermaphroditic motif behind, lacking as yet a theoretical framework in which to place it.

At the time, what would only later be referred to as the Oedipus complex meant the "positive" Oedipus. And so Freud concentrates instead on the external danger, namely, the mother's warning that should Hans dare to masturbate, Dr. A. will be sent for to cut off the

boy's penis. It is a threat with prophetic but by no means self-evident-
ramifications, and Hans's immediate reaction must be kept in mind in
interpreting the plumber fantasies at the close of the case. Asked what
he would widdle with then, he responds, "My bottom," thereby betraying what Freud later described as Little Hans's underlying cloacal
fantasies of reproduction.

Baffled because he cannot see or feel what his mother possesses,
Hans exclaims that he thought she was so big that she should have a
widdler like a horse's. (Freud tells us to keep this analogy in mind.)
But where is this widdler to be found? It is in the context of this search
that the "great" and pathogenic event in Hans's young life occurs—the
birth of his sister, Hannah, when he was three and a half—though he
would not fall ill until over a year later. Freud describes Hans's impressions of the delivery: his mother's coughing, the doctor's bag
in the front hall—perhaps the same doctor with whose gelding shears
he was threatened—and the blood-filled vessels. Pointing to the bed-
pan, the boy observes, "But blood does not come out of my widdler"
(10).

Dissatisfied by references to the stork and his parents' other attempts
to evade his inquiries, Hans attempts repeatedly to piece together the
bits of information and sensorimotor experience that have come his
way about the bodily reality of procreation. He senses that sex differences are also at issue in making babies. Hans is confronted by little
Hannah's unobscured vulva and again becomes preoccupied by the
absence as well as the presence of male genitals. All the while he seems
to intuit that there must be something more to the feminine anatomy,
for simultaneously the little boy begins to play out birth fantasies,
which intimate his dawning intuition into a woman's recesses. The boy
talks of the storeroom and, fetus-like, enters a bathroom, exclaiming
that he is widdling—urethral enactments and imaginings that further
reveal an intuition into the male and female roles in procreation.
Finally, at four and a half, Hans laughs at the small size of Hannah's
widdler as if deriding her femininity. Yet it is at this point that the
father relays to Freud the outbreak of the boy's phobia.

With hindsight, the modern analyst—Silverman (1980), for instance—would stress the identification with his baby sister and
preoedipal longings in the early stages of Hans's symptom neurosis. In
January 1908, when the case history proper begins, he wishes, some-

what ambiguously, to stay home and "coax," to cuddle with his mother. The specificity of oedipal conflict and symbolic representation, however, soon gives greater shape and specificity to his angst. Now he becomes afraid that a horse will bite him—a reference to earlier cautionaries and to outcroppings of his castration anxiety. Freud stresses the boy's masturbatory urges and activity and, according to the old anxiety theory, the conversion of repressed longings into anger.

At first, the Professor, himself a tyro in the treatment of children, attempts to have the father, now his therapeutic proxy as well as a journalistic observer, resolve matters cognitively. He is instructed to inform his son that his mother and all other female beings have *no widdler at all.* In the wake of partial enlightenment, his castration fear temporarily allayed, Hans improves.

A second significant event occurs, however, one that Joseph Slap (1961) called to our attention fifty years later. In early March, the father records perfunctorily that "after another week which he has had to spend indoors because he has had his tonsils out, the phobia has grown very much worse again" (29).

Remarking on the operation's pathogenic impact, Slap underscores the representation of the realistic trauma of his surgery in the subsequent phobia. Hans's ever more specific fear of white horses with black muzzles might be traced to the common costume of surgeons at the time, black masks and white gowns. In fact, it is not implausible that the infamous and ubiquitous Dr. A may have indeed been involved either in the diagnosis or in the procedure, lending still more substance to the mother's early warnings. Slap goes on to highlight the concretized paternal castration threat inherent in this ill-timed intervention.

Also I would speculate that Hans might have made an additional association between his operation and his impressions of his mother's delivery of Hannah. There are, for instance, his previous interpretations of his mother's groans and retching as *coughing,* as well as his focus on the blood-filled pans. Veiled references to menstruation may even have been suggested in the comment that blood did not emerge from his genitals. Febrile states preceding the surgery, Hans's passive position before and after it, and the aftereffects of the anaesthesia would have confused the already tenuous distinctions between reality and fantasy to be drawn by a phobia-prone five-year-old. How might the boy interpret the surgical intrusion into one of his orifices, the cutting off of the two "balls" contained within its inner recesses, the blood, the swelling, and so forth?

To borrow from Bruno Bettelheim, one might infer that the surgery was suffered as a sort of "symbolic wound," a ritual cutting not only threatening retaliation but offering the promise of invagination, effeminization, and the assumption of childbearing powers. Hans may well have come to imagine that his mother had been impregnated in some similarly violent manner, as his later fantasies indicate (the Grete play, for instance), or that somehow she had been given to exchange her penis for a baby. He may have construed his tonsillectomy as a variation on these primal scenes, one in which he himself was actually or symbolically impregnated or delivered of a baby. One day perhaps his penis, like his mother's, would be cut off as he himself prepared to give birth to an infant. Perhaps, then, the operation whetted and partially gratified this little boy's conflictual desires to become a mother—his inarticulate and dreaded wishes to unman himself and submit to castration as the price to be paid for the woman's "painful prerogative." Now this is, as I said, speculation. Yet there is ample evidence in the case history of Hans's ambisexuality and identifications with both mother and father.

Hans's earlier fantasy of the phallic woman, which foundered on the shoals of his abrupt "enlightenment," had already indicated hermaphroditic promptings—her anatomical bisexuality mirroring his own. When he was apprised of the mutual exclusiveness of phallic aspirations and maternal power, he may have further succumbed to an intense *intra*systemic conflict, a crisis in sexual identity brought to a head by a juxtaposition in time and symbolic equivalences between his mother's delivery of Hannah and his own tonsillectomy.

The ensuing analysis of the phobia reveals an array of paradoxes in which male and female qualities and the modalities of intrusion and inceptivity are condensed. For instance, the father interprets Hans's notion, quite rightly but remarkably nonetheless, that, like a horse, his widdler *bites*. The metaphor is telling, possibly betraying unconscious interchanges in the dialogue between father and son. Counteroedipal feelings and intention permeate his father's conduct of the "analysis," for better and worse. In all events and in this particular instance, the notion of biting to depict the boy's genital sensations inadvertently implies that not only has Hans's penis been stimulated but that, in his or his father's fantasy, the organ has taken on an incorporative mode akin to that of the vagina, or the mouth for that matter. Penises, after all, expell or eject; they do not take in; they do not bite.

Even more suggestive is Hans's famous giraffe dream: "In the night there was a big giraffe in the room and a crumpled one and the big one crawled out because I took the crumpled one away from it. Then it stopped crawling out and I sat down on top of the crumpled one" (37). Hans's father, aided by Freud, discerns in this wish fulfillment a typical incestuous fantasy. Yet might it not relate as well to the image of delivery—the crumpled giraffe representing not only the so-called defective, penisless female, but also the ill-formed (fecal) baby in childbirth? Hans says as much, and he may strive to steal the infant from the mother even as he would wrest her from the father's dominion.

Similarly, Hans's wish for a gun seems an obvious phallic equivalent. But this too takes on added meaning by virtue of Hans's confusion of the German words for "shooting" and "shitting." He wants his penis, like his anus or a mother's vagina, to make something—to produce. Hans also wants red raspberry syrup, possibly suggesting that he too would like to menstruate and be a childbearing woman—a possibility that finds further confirmation later, when we learn about its use as a laxative. Not only has intercourse taken place in the night in this boy's world, but childbirth as well. Yes, Hans is fascinated by projectiles, digits, and limbs, but also by spaces. In his manifest fantasies, entrances and enclosures are barred by policemen, prohibiting incestuous access and, with it, the vicarious assumption of procreative power. The horse's whiteness is, incidentally, his mother's as well as his father's. Both figure as self-protective and potentially vindictive authority when it comes to trespassing on their territory and sexual and procreative prerogatives. And both are love objects.

In any case, his father's interpretations of these phallic urges and rivalries fail to dispel Hans's fear. And Freud's one encounter with Hans and his ingenious interventions make, it seems, for a transient improvement. For one thing, they overlook Hans's growing fascination with and fondness for his father. More and more, his rivalry and identifications seem to center on the mother as well—his father's bedmate and Hannah's parent.

In fact, the derivatives of Hans's childbirth fantasies come to assume an increasingly negative oedipal cast. He becomes less afraid of horses biting him than of their falling and spilling the contents of their carts, as repeatedly he enters the parental bedroom, apparently drawn there by his attraction to both father and mother. Hans's incestuous and parental ambitions are further complicated by more passive desires, which are evident in his fantasy of "standing by the cart and the cart driving off quickly and my standing on it and wanting to get onto the board and my driving off in the cart" (47).

At this point, the fear of horses with muzzles reemerges, which the father rightly interprets as a reference to his own moustache, but one which, following Slap, also harkens back to the penetrating, invasive surgeons. Hans was supine and passive then, anesthetized and transported (in a cart of sorts), violated, perhaps in his unconscious fantasies sexually transformed or at least mysteriously altered.

Hans's childbearing wishes intensify, overshadowing his boyish castration anxiety. He becomes afraid of horses falling and making a row with their feet. Furniture vans obsess him. Big, fat horses are further sources of anxiety. He imitates the pawing and the row, as if identifying with the woman in intercourse or childbirth. Nor is it simply that he fears the birth of another sibling rival, for Hans pointedly compares the horses on the streets with himself seated on the potty to make "Lumpf," when he himself makes a row with his feet. And he does so within the context of commenting on his father's "lovely" whiteness. Increasingly, the modern reader is struck by the boy's identification with his mother both as the sexual partner of the father, to whose intrusion she submits, and as the woman who, also on her back, bears children.

It is now revealed that Hans has been subjected to repeated anal stimulation in the form of enemas given him by his parents. The father himself, the reader infers, is preoccupied with his own bowel movements, inviting identification in this regard. Hans, having seen his mother on the toilet, wonders all the while, too, about her complex excretory functions. Hans associates to pregnancy and childbirth. Thus he confirms, Freud remarks, the latter's findings about children's cloacal theories and the production of fecal babies. But Freud does not address the relation of these childish conceptions to phallic themes within the Oedipus constellation.

The connections begin to become clearer. Hans tells his father the first of two plumber fantasies, which probably derive from his birth theories and his mysterious wishes to submit to mutilation and, further, to penetration by a man as a means to parental power: "Daddy, I thought something was in the bath (like little Hannah) and then the plumber came and unscrewed it. Then he took a big borer and stuck it into my stomach" (65). Hans's father interprets his fear of retaliation for a wish to be in bed with his mother, the erotic personage who gives him his bath. Similarly, discerning the transference, Freud proceeds to emphasize the big penis with which the potentially castrating father drove him from the bed.

Both interpretations miss the point. Along with references to the actual surgery and the invasive analysis, the "thought" most probably betrays Hans's identification with the position of a woman in the primal scene (or the baby in utero). We have Freud's comment on Hans's notion about his father's procreative role: "With your big penis you bored [gave birth to] me and put me in my mother's womb" (128).

As if intuitively, somewhat later the father does touch on Hans's identification with the *producing* mother. He underlines the fact that Little Hans has often seen horses defecating and concludes that "the bus horse that falls down and makes a row with its feet is no doubt a lumf falling and making a noise" (66). Hans's fear of defecation, and of heavily loaded carts, is traced to his fear of a heavily loaded stomach or abdomen and to his sibling rivalry. But that Hans would *himself* like to be so encumbered and deliver himself of more vital concoctions— this unconscious fantasy escapes the father's awareness. So do the boy's intuitive glimpses of the origin of babies in an instinctual encounter and of the mother's sexual role in all this.

Had Hans's case followed that of his fellow protagonist, the Wolf Man (1918a), Freud would have had the developmental theory and language with which to render such clinical inferences. He would also have had a frame of reference in which to consider the boy's musings on the mother's power over life and death and the threat posed by her even in an incestuous meeting of reengulfment.

Misunderstood, Hans regresses and betrays his awe of a vitally omnipotent but potentially engulfing mother when he expresses his terror that, in giving him a bath, she might let go of him, allowing his head to sink into the water. It is not the big penis but the big bath that concerns him at this point, an allusion to an enveloping and dangerous womb. Once again, the father speaks to the periphery of Hans's perception of girls and women and his urge to be with and thus identify with them, when he stresses only the boy's death wishes, fears of retaliation, and sibling rivalry.

The riddle continues. With his glimmers of his mother's black pubic region, Hans draws equations between "lumfs," "lumfees," and "wumpfees," or children. Though he too has anal powers, making babies appears to be a woman's prerogative. Unlike him, she may even be able to retract when she has extruded, to reincorporate the child she has made and delivered into the world.

Getting erotically involved with him has risks of its own, then, independent of the threat posed by his jealous father. These become all the more intense because of yet another yearning and dread—the boy's desire to be a baby in the womb. And there may even be a certain secret spitefulness in Hans's apparent sibling rivalry, a wish to destroy what the mother alone has succeeded in making—a baby, who is not only Hans's competitor for attention but the envy of his would-be creativity.

More and more aware of his mother's pregnancy, Hans would like to take something in and make something more of it. Hans remains, as earlier, more attuned to womb-like equivalents—baths, boxes, and babies—than to penises. At times he endows his father with maternal capacities—for instance, when he suggests that the stork came, unlocked the door, and put Hannah in the father's bed while his mother was asleep. Only when confronted does he correct himself, asserting that the stork put the infant in the mother's bed.

The father emphasizes his son's wish to possess her rather than his less discrete longings to be more fully, and variously, at one with his mother, to be mother and child, in a regressive revival of fantasies involving their erstwhile dual unity. Hans remonstrates that he is quite fond of Hannah and looks forward to nurturing her as well as babies of his own making. (Freud remarks here on his failure to inform his proxy of the child's cloacal birth fantasies.) It is in the context of these transparent wishes to rear her that Hans endows Hannah with a whip, implying that she, like the phallic mother, can have a penis. In this act of apparent generosity, he reveals his compelling wishes himself to be a baby and a mommy, yet to retain his phallus and masculinity.

Reasserting his virility, Hans once again verges on a solution to the riddle of the Sphinx: "Once I really did it. Once I had a weapon with the horse and it fell down and made a row with his feet" (79). Attempting to grant himself a role, a phallic-sadistic one, in the sexual making of babies, Hans gropes toward an understanding of paternity. He continues by saying that he would like to "beat" mommy and thereby make a baby. Again, his father fails to pick up on his son's reproductive aspirations, just as he has neglected to educate him about the male part in procreation.

So again his father's emphasis on heterosexual incestuous prohibitions has fallen short of the mark. Hans's fear of horses with carriages, symbolizing sexual union, increases, and once more he retreats indoors. Freud the narrator underscores an obscure sadistic desire for his mother and an impulse for revenge against his father. But he too fails to put all of it together in the form of a coherent and organizing fantasy.

Later in the month, his father reports one more "primal scene fantasy" in which questions about the maternal phallus, the origin of babies, and the link between birth and the tonsillectomy are condensed:

> At lunch time I was told that Hans had been playing all morning with an India-rubber doll which he called Grete. He had pushed a small pen knife [like a scalpel] in through the opening into which a little tin squeaker had originally been attached, and had then torn apart the doll's legs so as to let the knife drop out. He had said to the nursemaid, pointing between the doll's legs, "Look, there's its widdler . . . I tore its legs apart; you know why? Because there was a knife inside it belonging to mommy. I put it in at the place where the button squeaks and then I tore apart its legs and it came out there." (84)

Is the knife a phallus, a surgeon's knife, a baby, or all of the above? Do penises get cut off and turn into babies after penetration and sufficient gestation? And with whom has Hans identified in this drama? While focusing on his mother's knife, presumably her penis, Hans also proclaims that both his father and he laid eggs out of which a chicken emerged, thereby approximating her incorporative and generative power.

Freud concludes that by means of a "brilliant symptomatic act" Hans was saying, "Look, this is how I imagine birth takes place"—not only birth, one might add, but conception. In fact, the boy again speaks of his wishes to make children and tend them—to have a baby himself. To his father's suggestion that he would like to have a little girl, he responds, "Yes, he is going to have one and call her Hannah, too."

His father asks, "But why isn't mommy to have a little girl?"

"Because I want to have a little girl, for once!"

"But you can't have a little girl."

"Oh yes," Hans counters, "boys have girls and girls have boys" (righting the sexual imbalance and uniting maternal and feminine aspirations).

"Boys don't have children—only women, only mommies have children," his father asserts again and again, as he becomes increasingly defensive. He omits the male role—his own, Hans's—in creating babies.

"But why shouldn't I?"

"Because God's arranged it like that."

"But why don't you have one? Oh yes, you'll have one, alright, just you wait . . ." Hans pauses and then asks, "Does Hannah belong to me or to mommy?"

His father answers, "To mommy."

"Not to me? Why not to me and mommy?"

Freud concludes, "So long as the child is in ignorance of the female genitals, there is a naturally vital gap in his comprehension of sexual matters" (87–88). More in the way of sex education is indicated, it seems. At last the parents tell him the facts about women and pregnancy: children grow inside the mommy and are brought into the world by being pressed out of her like lumpf. All this, they add gratuitously, involves a "great deal of pain." Once again, theirs is but a half truth; they neglect to tell him of the father's part and satisfaction in this whole process.

Yet again the father errs in interpreting Hans's butting him a day or so later only as an expression of competition, rather than a sensorimotor, if sadistic, enactment of intercourse. Hans persists, telling his father that he would parent him. But the authoritative disavowal is too great. His inchoate theories of insemination ignored, Hans can only resort to the fantasy that babies are born from the behind, a compromise seemingly borne out by the bits of revelation offered by his parents.

At last, Hans's father suggests to him that Hans would like to be a daddy. Immediately excited, Hans picks up on the cue:

"Yes, how does it work?!"

"How does what work?" the father fumbles.

"You say daddies don't have babies. But how does it work—my wanting to be a daddy?"

His father's explanations omit the vital connecting link that might have helped resolve the boy's ambisexual conflict: penetration, ejaculation, insemination. Rather than educate, as he did earlier when the mother's genitals were at issue, he interprets: "You'd like to be a daddy and married to a mommy—you'd like to be as big as me and have a moustache and you'd like mommy to have a baby." Hans seems to intuit a tacit injunction—the knowledge of the tree of life is God's alone, God the father's. Paternity lies beyond his cognitive grasp, and so he tempers his instinctual ambitions: "And Daddy, when I'm married, I'll only have one if I want to—when I'm married" (92).

All the while, he has reiterated his parental aspirations, seizing on having children in addition to oedipal possession in the suggestion that his progeny, not his wife, will always remain in bed with him. When his father asks him later why he was always thinking of his children, Hans responds, "Because I should like to have them."

"The startling contradiction," in Freud's words, betrays Hans's intense conflict between wishing to produce babies and the dreaded outcome that is stressed throughout as a consequence of all *parental*, maternal and paternal, ambition—castration, from within or without.

The synthesis of a fatherly ideal denied him, Hans proclaims that he really was the mother of the children at Gmunden. His maternal fantasies are amplified in the absence of possible paternal powers: "When I couldn't get all the children into bed, I put some of the children on the sofa, and some in the pram and if there were still some left over, I took them up to the attic and put them in a box. And if there were any more, I put them in the other box" (94). Oedipal access beyond him, his paternal future cloudy, his masculine anatomy irrefutable and seemingly barren, Hans again makes recourse to a negative oedipal fantasy. When his father asks him, "Who did you think you got the children from?" Hans responds, "Why from me" (94).

Simultaneously, he now becomes even more preoccupied with babies and behinds. He used to call the doors of the custom house "holes" but now refers to them specifically as "behind holes." In counterpoint, he proclaims his masculinity. When Hans's father comments on his playing with merely imaginary children, he responds, "I was their mommy before; now I'm their daddy" (96). His penis has grown. He makes of his father a grandfather. Freud infers that "things were moving toward a satisfactory conclusion, but little Oedipus had found a happier solution than that prescribed by destiny. Instead of putting his father out of the way, he had granted him the same happiness that he desired himself: He made him a grandfather and married him to his own mother too" (97).

The interpretation, however, omits the submission underlying Hans's new optimism. This is not the final but merely the penultimate transference fantasy. The next day Hans describes his vision of taking his children to the bathroom, cleaning their behinds, and "doing everything one does with children," just as he himself had been treated by his parents. He is now freer to venture forth into forbidden territory and to confront horses and buses head on, yet he points to the bus and exclaims, "Look, a stork boxcart!" The symptomatic improvement owes itself basically to Hans's *negative* oedipal resolution to his many competing wishes and fears. This is most evident in the fantasy that climaxes his treatment, one that derives from the father's and surgeon's psychic and physical examinations and intrusions:

> The plumber came, and first he took away my behind with a pair of scissor-pincers and then he gave me another. And then the same with my widdler. He said, "Let me see your widdler," which he also removed, giving him a bigger widdler and a bigger behind . . . [His father concludes] "Yes, like daddy's, because you like to be like daddy." "Yes, and I'd like to have a moustache like yours, and hairs like yours." (97–98)

Hans's earlier fantasy is reinterpreted by Freud in the following manner: "The big bath meant the behind; the borer or screwdriver was, as explained at the time, a penis. The two fantasies are identical. Moreover new light is thrown on Hans's fear of the big bath. He dislikes his behind being too small for the big bath" (98).

But what does this bigger behind stand for in the light of all the previous symbolism associated with it? Is it not also a would-be anal womb, rivaling the encompassing organ of his mother? And is Hans's not a fantasy of being in possession of ambisexual powers? More important, why emphasize the widdler and bypass the behind? That is, why ignore the submissive currents—the passive route to phallic power so typical of the homosexual quest? Indeed, Hans's construction has much in common with those pederastic rites of passages (described by Lidz and Lidz, 1987; Stoller, 1985) in which boys surrender to adult males in order to be anointed as men while the collective fatherhood lays claim to birth-giving powers. These rites take place long before puberty, and with boys who do not become actively homosexual.

The postscript gives more clues regarding the neurosis, pointing to all the etiologic factors emphasized by Greenacre and others (Gillespie, 1940; Bak, 1968) in the genesis of perversions. Hans was about four years old when he was moved out of the parental bedroom into a room of his own. Hence he may have been privy to primal-scene experiences and to his mother's nearly naked body, a circumstance that prover-bially promotes a lasting bisexual identification.

A further suggestion is that there was a close, if ambivalent, rela-tionship with his mother. Until the boy's illness, his father was only a sporadic presence in his life—notably during vacations at Gmunden—a presence inadequate to offset Hans's immersion in his mother's being and her femininity. With his intervention into the boy's psychic life, however, the father then became all too present—forceful, intrusive, and stimulating to a fault. Hans would suffer invasion, have his father wholly or not at all, while being discouraged from actively compre-hending or identifying with his paternity.

Finally, as Hans enters a remission, Freud refers to the phobia as the "nonsense that is past . . . nonetheless an unresolved residue remains behind . . . Hans keeps cudgelling his brains . . . to discover what a father has to do with his child, since it is the mother who brings it into the world" (100). Freud concludes, "Yes, the doctor, the plumber, did take away his penis, but only to give a bigger one in exchange for it." Provocatively he adds, "Each step forward leaves an unresolved residue behind."

Implications

I have emphasized Hans's identification with his mother and specu-lated about his fantastic interpretation of his tonsillectomy not only as a paternal castration threat, but as a symbolic act of impregnation and birth. The patchwork nature of the enlightenment offered him and the parent-therapist's apparent inhibitions regarding the reciprocal pro-creative functions of father and mother seem to have left the boy adrift. Wanting babies and a penis at the same time, he resorted to a negative oedipal compromise in which he would suffer penetration and castration to produce life not as "daddy" but in the manner of a woman. Had his wish to be a father been clarified, along with the mechanics of paternity, he might have progressed beyond the allevia-tion of symptoms and arrived at a more adaptive, progressive resolu-tion of a central conflict within the oedipal constellation—that is, between the wish to assert his emergent masculinity and the desire to participate in the generational cycle, to make babies. What Hans re-peatedly strove for was a representation of the father as a producer, male procreator, and nurturer by which to offset the intersystemic conflicts born of oedipal rivalry and the essentially intrasystemic conflicts clustering about the wish of a phallic oedipal boy to give birth and to be a woman.

A careful reading of the "Analysis of a Phobia in a Five-Year-Old-Boy" reveals the clinical importance of *identification* with the father qua father to a resolution of sexual identity. These psychoanalytic concepts were not yet available to Freud. He himself would only name the Oedipus complex a year later, and more time elapsed before he was equipped to elaborate clinically and theoretically on both its nega-tive and its positive sides (1918a, 1923). It would also be some time before he would expound on the "phallic woman" (1927) and the interweaving of early defensive distortions in object representations (A. Freud, 1936) as a consequence of uncertainty in one's own gender identity. And it would be yet another half century before students of Little Hans would be proffered Jacob Arlow's concept of an organizing unconscious fantasy (1969), in which elements of real experience and inner oedipal and preoedipal conflict become woven into a dramatic tapestry, a personal narrative whose threads can determine the course of a life.

Then there is Peter Blos's delineation (1985) of the persistence and neurosogenic impact of the negative Oedipus motif on the eve of adulthood, long after the resolution or repression of the positive. With these developments, and with our current appreciation of fatherhood, a boy like Hans might have been even better understood and his heterosexuality truly secured.

Yet another postscript regarding the real Little Hans: All indications are that Herbert Graf had a pretty successful life. He married, fathered two children, worked creatively, and nurtured many professional lives (Holland, 1985:246–281). His parents fared less well, divorcing (as Freud noted) when he was still a young man. His father Max, initially one of Freud's most zealous acolytes, later shunned and rejected the Professor (Seides, 1987). Not only this but he was critical of his son's noisy "primal scene" staging in productions at the Met. To this the son is said to have responded, "My father is responsible for me, perhaps, but not I for him."

We can never know what went on psychically in Herbert/Hans's life as an adult: his dreams, fantasies, erotic experiences, everyday symptomatology. Negative oedipal resolutions, in any event, do not usually manifest themselves in overt sexual symptomatology, which usually results from more profound preoedipal and narcissistic hungers. Rather, conflicts at the oedipal level tend to find more neurotic modes of expression in symptoms and character traits. Nonetheless, it may well be that the case history is as much about Max Graf's intrapsychic life as about his son's: *his* wish to mother the child better than this wife; *his* ambivalence in deferring to and later rebelling against a father figure in the person of Freud; *his* uncertainty about ceding his own paternal authority to his son. We will never know, but the speculation is intriguing. Our cases and our legacy of clinical myths contain many hidden characters and mysterious dialogues.

7

Beyond the Phallic Illusion

When I began to study fathers, the realities of parenthood were not in the forefront of my concerns. I was more impressed with the mystery of what Lawrence Kubie was to call, in one of his last published writings (1974), "the drive to become both sexes." An old adversary of Karen Horney's, Kubie is said to have fainted when he delivered the paper, which represented a partial and unacknowledged accession to her views on reciprocal relations between the sexes, to his colleagues at the New York Psychoanalytic Society.

In everyday life, I further surmised, men might find a resolution of the conflict between their efforts to maintain their masculinity and their anxiety-laden wishes to be mothers. And this without succumbing to the transvestite's delusion; or mutilating their genitals in the primitive rites of passage described by Bettelheim (1954); or subjecting their psyches to the Tantric mystery and its arduous course of erotic training (Kakar, 1982b); or striving for the creative artist's inspiration, an aesthetic and hermetic self-insemination (Kris, 1952). They could do simply and acceptably enough by becoming fathers—men who make, tend, and ideally delight in growing children—and, I would now add, by becoming lovers.

Spearheaded by Spitz and Mahler, developmental research elaborated on Freud's notions about hallucinatory wish fullfilment and demonstrated the gradual unfolding of the infant's diffuse sensuous reactivity into, first, inchoate longings to possess what is no longer present and, subsequently, into discrete wishes for objects. These gain representation and enduring substance as a function of visual, symbolic, and semantic capacities.

Wishes for objects bring an individual full circle. Inevitably the desire for an object will imply union with it, partially reviving outmoded primary identifications. The little boy hungers for the mother whom he once, primevally, experienced as indistinct from his nascent sensed self. Failing to possess her when he *first* begins to grasp the triangular relation of mother, father, and self, he would fill the void by way of two diverging identificatory routes.

First, the male toddler assumes attributes of his father's perceived gender in stereotypical or, better, sensorimotor fashion. In what Piagetians call a vertical decalage, he begins by enacting the masculinity that distinguishes him from his mother and provides a template for the unfolding of phallic strivings. Having virilized himself through actions associated with the father's person and thereby feeling male in his body, he then subjectively likens himself to his father and defines himself as male, like the man.

At the same time, more covertly and eventually unconsciously, the young boy also comes to replace the mother as an unreachable object with a *secondary* and increasingly selective series of identifications with her person, her mothering, and her femininity. Because he, not she, has been passive with regard to her ministrations, he draws psychic equations between being with her and being passive, between being with her and becoming like her, between being passive and being feminine. He longs for such states and qualities but strives to defy these longings by being forever active and, in this activity, male.

In this context, the penis does indeed become a vehicle with which to regain what is at least retrospectively felt to be a paradise lost—the postpartum womb of life before "psychological birth." Seemingly contradictory desires to use one's penis, to be a woman, and to be a babe-in-arms constitute a paradoxical unity at the hidden core of a boy's and man's heterosexual impulses and identity.

If analysts had not demurred from inquiring into the details of coital experience, rationalizing their timidity on technical grounds, they might have discovered *in vivo* this commingling of aims—a concatenation that Ferenczi (1924) called an *amphimixis* of the genital and pregenital. And they might have analyzed some of the typical defensive

strategies invoked by timorous lovers masquerading as phallic con-
querors, maneuvers aimed at pulling back from an immersion in sexual
passion.

Typically, however, clinicians have tended to accept rather easily
their male patients' facile descriptions of intercourse as an act of
penetration in which the status of a man's erection and its performance
are stressed and evaluated. In so doing, the therapist often becomes
complicit in the phallic illusion. Tumescence and entry are but penultimate achievements, after all. They usher in but fall short of (and,
when concentrated on, may serve as masturbatory equivalents that
guard against) the subjective crossing over of sexual boundaries and
the pervasive release and ego regression that occur at the height of
orgasm, the "little death." (Ejaculating one's germplasm entails the
death of the self as a differentiated, sentient being.)

With Aristophanes as his purported spokesman, Plato put it this way
in the *Symposium*. Humans began life as spherical creatures with eight
limbs, two faces, and two genital organs facing in the opposite direction. These beings were so mighty that they posed a threat to the
Olympians. When they attacked the gods, Zeus retaliated against their
hubris not by destroying them but by cutting them in two. From then
on, the two parts of human beings, each desiring the other half, "came
together, and throwing their arms about one another, entwined in
mutual embraces, longing to grow into one: they were on the point of
dying from hunger and self-neglect, because they did not like to do
anything apart." They were in the process of destroying themselves
when Zeus took pity on them and turned their genitals around to the
front so that they could at least embrace in intercourse. Thus they
"might be satisfied, and rest, and go their ways to the business of life:
so ancient is the desire of one another which is implanted in us,
reuniting our original nature, making one of two, and healing the state
of man" (145–146).

The Narcissistic Defense

The clinical literature has tended to set in relief those frank regressions
from the phallic position to be seen in severe psychopathology, along
with the more hidden abdications of masculinity and acts of sexualized
submission underlying neurosis. The hypertrophy of martial masculin-

ity and the sadistic and narcissistic fixations typical of many men in our culture have been less well studied and conceptualized.

These are the individuals who are basically afraid of intimacy with women, fearful of being united with them. They are "in and out like a shot," as the patient I shall describe put it. They are also frightened by the prospect of fatherhood, which perforce calls for nurturance, taps their regressive empathy, and arouses fears of effeminacy and infantilism. When they do produce children, they absent themselves or else tyrannize, exploit, and in one way or another sacrifice their own young in the service of self-aggrandizement.

A number of etiological factors may conspire in a boy's entrenchment in a phallic narcissistic holding position, with its ensuing caricature of oedipal development. Yet all in some way or another have to do with the unavailability early on of the father as a libidinal object and a figure for internalization and identification in this regard. A father may be absent, emotionally or otherwise, deferring to a powerful mother who fills up her son's life and invades the inner reaches of his emerging identity. Or, quite the contrary, he may be a brutal oppressor who invites an identification with men merely as aggressors. Or he may be so inhibited and ineffectual that his little boy must provide for himself—through the enactments of fantasy—age-specific but exaggerated versions of a father principle. Mothers may disparage or fear men, further shortchanging the actual relationship.

In all events, the manhood thus achieved is a screen, a self-encasing sheath, an artificially aggressivized, brittle, cardboard creation. It is unserviceable in negotiating the successive tasks of adult life, most important among them husbanding and parenthood.

Good Sex

My supervisee's patient H, described earlier, was in the fourth year of analysis as he contemplated marriage and fatherhood. He initially presented an infantile, pan-phobic, and severely obsessional picture. It was further characterized by a devastating castration anxiety, which was at times quite conscious. H's fears for his bodily intactness had roots in his failure to separate from an overpowering and demeaning mother, in his intense and projected oral rage toward her, in his generally unmodulated and frightening aggression, in marked homosexual fears that at times assumed paranoid proportions, and in a variety of narcissistic lacks and overcompensations.

When he began treatment, his sexual and work functioning were profoundly compromised. H's earlier difficulties infused his positive oedipal strivings with equally unnerving destructive aggression and fears of retaliation. The revival of both preoedipal and oedipal struggles in adolescence was compounded by the traumas of his parents' divorce and his great-uncle's death.

He had been fired from one job and was intimidated by his female boss at a new one when he began treatment. Nor had he had intercourse in a year. (He had masturbated only once as an adolescent, though he later became reasonably sexually active.)

H idealized his dead great-uncle, who had reared his mother after her parents' death. The old patriarch had seemed strong and manly, and H recoiled from any perception that might tarnish his perfect image. Nor did the patient mind fearing the uncle and the thunderbolts that, Jove-like, were connected with his representation (electrical storms, Moses and the burning bush, the Hulk from television).

Indeed, he bowed to these phobias because, as he said repeatedly, he desperately needed role models whose fortitude and magnificence he could draw upon to feel both empowered and protected. H's father had always disappointed him, and he disparaged the fat, sloppy, loving, garrulous, and affable man as "gassy, dirty and weak," unable to stand up to his wife. As a boy he had both loved and unconsciously hated this volatile strap-wielding but beautiful mother, who had overwhelmed him in toddlerhood and again in adolescence. She had emasculated his father as well, finally leaving him for another man. This second husband also fell prey to what proved to be her vindictiveness toward males.

H had lived with a great-aunt and uncle since his parents' divorce when he was eighteen—two years before the great-uncle's death. He complained that the old woman made him even more nervous, especially after her husband died. She fueled the fires of his phobias and hypochondria with her own incessant worries about his safety and health. Still, "Nanams" had been more motherly than her harsh niece. Better a Jewish mother than none at all.

Significantly, H lamented his own father's failure to discipline him and the evident role reversal in his parents' relation to each other and to their children. What he partly meant was that his father had failed him as a guardian and mentor. Nor had he acted to excite and then to modulate the patient's phallic aggressivity. Speaking of his mother, he told Dr. Q that "it's tough when the hand that loves is also the hand that hits."

During his first two and a half years of analysis, H idealized Dr. Q variously as "stud," family man, and professor. With his bald oedipal fantasies about the "stable of women" parading through the analyst's office, he played rough within the transference, like Jacob with an angel of his own making. Rediscovering his competitiveness, he drank in manliness of a more primitive mode. As a result, H made great strides at work and school, eventually graduating at the top of his class in the law school he had entered after two years of analysis. He moved out of his aunt's house and, in his words, bedded women—"big ones" like his mother, not "shrimps" like an earlier girlfriend. That girl he had enjoyed lifting up, as if wielding her on his erect penis, envisioning himself as Superman.

Indeed, H remembered dreaming as a child of flying home from the schoolyard, like the legendary comic-strip hero, in so doing compensating for the cruel fact that he was transported to school in a bus for the handicapped. His seemingly protective mother had been responsible for this arrangement, equating her asthmatic son with the crippled children for whom the bus was a necessity. Another time, he recollected, when he was three, she had pointed to his exposed penis and remarked to a friend how small it was. In the transference, the patient and his analyst became superheroes, friendly foes like Robin Hood and Little John. This imagined combat reminded H of a photograph of himself arm wrestling with his potent uncle, who could easily escape the "clutches of females."

Many of H's symptoms subsided in the heat of what, on the surface at least, initially seemed to be a stark transference neurosis. But, alas, he found himself increasingly "driven and hyper." Unable to stay still, he paraded his stuff. He was forever on the go. The narcissistic and aggressive strains in H's character, unleashed by his identification with an idealized male analyst and serving his strivings for independence and success, remained to be dealt with.

Nor was this new state of mind altogether adaptive—not when it came to the other people in the patient's life, particularly the women.

So impatient did H become now that he made even his girlfriend, Sharon, who was fast finding her way into his affections in spite of himself, sleep on a cot next to his bed so that she would not crowd him out.

In part, he was afraid of punishment for finding a woman who loved him. Having intercourse in his sublet apartment, he was afraid that the landlord or perhaps a neighbor would become enraged and castrate him. When Dr. Q interpreted both the projection and the real-life genesis of the threat in his mother's violence, H responded: "It's 99 percent probable you're right, but what about the 1 percent?"

More than this, the uninterrupted intimacy was in itself terrifying. As Hans Loewald long ago suggested, the threat of paternal castration serves to fend off reabsorption. Cloacal fantasies abounded as H became more and more interested in his girlfriend. And the patient, who had propped his feet on the analytic couch in the position of women during delivery, confessed that he was afraid that her womanliness was catching, that her secretions would somehow contaminate him. When her sexual demands threatened him, he verbally abused her to hide his fears.

Gradually, however, H acknowledged his love of Sharon and his fascination with oral sex. In the past, masturbation fantasies had involved a sequence wherein cunnilingus was followed by a reassuring near-rape. Fitfully, he spoke of playing with her pillow-like breasts, of his urge to melt into her, of being taken aback by his relish in the smells that used to repulse him. Even more tentatively, he admitted that on occasion, ejaculating, he had "squealed like a fuckin' baby." With all this good sex, fatherly ambitions also began to emerge. H started thinking about making babies with Sharon.

I will now excerpt H's words over approximately two weeks of sessions from this period.

Your doorknob gave me a shock [an old bugaboo about electricity]. It made me furious. I wouldn't be so angry if I had struck back when I was a kid. If I had a kid, I sometimes think I'd smash his brains too. You gotta be tough. [The problems of abuse and H's identification with the aggressing parent were also important subjects of analysis, the mother's violence having been screened by the threat of castration at God's (the father's), hands] Maybe that is what's warranted in my old age to get it out of my system. Women are like cats, they turn on you.

In the next session:

My gay neighbors disturbed me last night, pounding all night in the closet [sic]. I still haven't gotten over those fears about the gays completely. [Later.] I'm rebellious. I didn't work on Saturday and stayed with Sharon. We're getting closer. She cried after intercourse. It scared me—I still don't stay in for long. She wants to marry me. But I got no models of good marriage. Maybe I'll get married next year. I imagine telling my uncle, "I don't want to bend over backward no more—to submit." You know, nobody had control over my mother, not even my father. Maybe that's why I don't trust people. I think how her father and then my uncle intimidated her, but so what . . . You gotta have somebody to look up to. I used to put you in the godly role . . . Being stubborn is masculine. I wanna be Superman. With my coat behind me, I felt like Superman with his cape. [He was deeply offended by the movie *Superman II*, specifically when Superman cedes his super-human powers to make love to Lois Lane.] Women are supposed to be gentle, passive. Female activity turns me off. Again I think about having kids. I'm a baby inside and it scares me. Sharon's breasts are so big. I sometimes think I like playing with them better than anything. How can you be a father if you're weak? A kid'll see right through you.

Another hour:

I read an article about fathers—they can be better parents than mothers. I realize I like kids a lot. Sometimes I think my treating Sharon mean is a big coverup. I don't want to show her my fears. I'm real soft inside and care for her, and I get so scared for her [weeps]. I don't really think you should be involved with someone and not care for them. I'm thinking about kids a lot, like my [much younger] cousin. I was mad she liked Sharon better.

[Later.] Sometimes I wonder whether I'll have children. I checked my old coin collection and trains to see whether they're still there. One day I may have a son. [Pause.] My father wasn't good mechanically like my uncle, and he was subservient. I wonder what traits make a good father? Mine never showed me how to make the football spiral. The best fathers do everything . . . Still, he was always there when I was sick. And he hit a stickball a mile [an activity he had criticized him for until earlier].

If I had a son, what kind of father would I be? I could have conflicts. All that shit. Older toddlers are interesting, but then teens are pains again and turn around and stab you in the back. It's anticlimactic. [Pause.] You know, I remember how excited I was when my brother Jason was born [at six years]. And then teaching him things—she, er he, was a cute little doll. They say I really loved him.

[Later.] It seems like bullshit reasons to me, but they say men have kids to prove their masculinity and also relive their own childhoods . . . Still, I can't imagine why a guy would want to be kidless. Even Joe, this big guy [at work, an ex-football player], he's all caught up in his sons and daughters. It blows my mind. [Pauses, weeps.] That's what I mean about analysis! How can I go to the interview like this?

In a later session:

If I had a son, I'd name him after my uncle . . . but I'm scared he'd be defective, maybe . . . a daughter I'd like to shove back— like a booby prize . . . Still, my friend's daughter is pretty cute. I don't know, it's all so scary . . . When I think how much I really feel for women. You know, Bill really cares for his daughter— more than Uncle Nick did, he was less involved. My father—he cared for us a lot, though my mother put him down all the time. . . .

A later session:

Sharon's [irregular] periods bother me. I haven't had sex with her for two weeks. She felt so big inside the last time—it's scary, like there's a lot going on. I was reading an article about having kids when a woman's over thirty. I'm thinking a lot about kids. It can't be all biological. I'm thinking something—I don't want to say anything before I'm ready. I guess the bottom line is I don't know what I want.

[Later.] I found these sex magazines unappealing [for the first time] . . . It's not deep at all. How do *you* do it, having a family and working? I don't know . . . I just don't want to pass on my fears to my kids. I guess I think you have to be perfect to be a father. But there's no perfection. There are no role models—not even you any more—and it pisses me off. I want things boom, boom, boom, not the complications. I don't want the gray stuff, but it's there.

A later session:

I had oral sex with S—I like it. And screwing her again, I thought how big she felt. But it wasn't too bad. [Earlier he had compared his penis in intercourse to "a pretzel in the Lincoln Tunnel."] But I had this fear the rubber might come off . . . I'm thinking about giving her a very special present on her [thirtieth] birthday [a proposal, I later learned], but save that for another time.

Particulars and Universals

Every analytic case is just as interesting in its particulars as in its more general import. Obviously, a few excerpts cannot do justice to the complexity of this man. And even these brief extracts point to his idiosyncrasies, further modified and exaggerated by the impact of the particular analytic process—and the analyst. To generalize about maleness and its development becomes difficult indeed.

One is struck, as it were, by the patient's mother. With her strap, obsessive cleanliness, and sharp tongue, her remarks leveled at her boy's autonomy and masculinity, she caricatured in real life the universal male fantasies of the phallic, vaginally abusive, and verbally castrating mother. With a mother like this, one might well wonder, how could the patient achieve heterosexual functioning to the extent that he did?

In this vein, H's father comes to mind as another strong influence, perhaps the hidden hero in the patient's psychic drama, having been upstaged by the obvious and severe masculinity embodied by his revered great-uncle. Probably it was paternal nurturance that quietly redeemed this man—his father's motherliness, in fact—sowing seeds to be watered in the transference and flowering first in the form of a latter-day phallic machismo and, more gradually and fitfully, in H's unfolding capacities for genital love and potential fatherliness. His father's failures centered on his understimulation of H's aggression and on his inadequacies as a husband.

Apart from particulars, a patient like H may provide some universal truths or suggestions about the psychic life of men in general. His development as a young adult (albeit one in treatment) seems to suggest that encounters with women in late adolescence and early adulthood tend to revive a succession of phallic and paternal *motives* from the course of phallic oedipal development. It is frightening but ultimately thrilling for a young man, a sexual tyro, to experience the capaciousness and potential fertility of woman rather than merely to conquer her. As he experiences her womanliness in the erotic sphere, consolidating his genital stance, he revives his awe at a woman's pro-creative powers and, through the sex act, further imagines her womb. With these encounters, both real and illusory, a young man attends to a woman's thoughts about getting married and having babies, and he begins to discover his own generative yearnings and, as it were, his paternal instincts.

Ultimately, as this patient himself suggests, with some cavils, the promise of procreation in intimacy is rewarding. Participating in the succession of generations, a man finds that his masculinity in the deepest sense is indeed memorialized. And, in loving and caring, he recovers through a reversal of voice the passive pleasures of a childhood lost and inevitably lacking.

During the year and a half following these sessions, H was able to marry Sharon, though not without some regression, atonement, and propitiation. His tendency to see her as more maternal than sexual gave way to a fuller representation of the whole woman. He and his analyst now worked on the preoedipal maternal transference. As H became more tolerant of his own feminine side, this came to replace the first paradigm, in which Dr. Q had been subject variously to H's rivalry, competitiveness, idealization, and, throughout, his father hunger.

Much was to be learned about H's sufferings at his real mother's abusive hands. Memories of being slapped in early adolescence opened pathways to an earlier childhood in which he had either been hit for being dirty or else seemingly overprotected, his stabs at manhood and independence derogated or disallowed. In the process H came to recognize that he had tried to fortify his imperiled manhood by exaggerating and stereotyping it and by projecting a pure culture of maleness onto the therapist.

His rage and hostility within the transference became more heartfelt, no longer reflecting pretenses to phallic bravado, as he himself put it: "It's real. I'm not strutting stuff." Mexican food on his honeymoon, for example, set in motion gastric symptoms. For some time he became preoccupied with feces. Only later, after he found himself smearing chocolate on Dr. Q's office door, did H recognize that in becoming "inflamed" he had been at once unconsciously defying his mother, propitiating the gods (composite images including his exalted uncle), and filling himself up (becoming pregnant) in the expectation that he would be a better mother than she. His wife's love and warmth and the genuine understanding tendered through analytic interpretation set in relief his mother's intolerance for his masculinity and, ironically, her impatience with his infantile neediness.

H could at last acknowledge his joy in cooking, food shopping, and housekeeping without seeing himself as a sissy. He no longer needed to buy impressive gifts to prove himself but chose instead symbolic fruits and vegetables to present to his wife. More secure in his own masculinity, he even ceded the idealization of his electrifying uncle. He felt freer in lovemaking and, to his surprise, found himself burrowing into his wife's soft enfolding contours. He might just be a decent parent after all, he conceded, since he did enjoy cuddling, rocking, and cooing to babies. He was more patient than his mother. He began to see her, himself, and his future children as part of the generational cycle—as limited, frail people. His mother, he realized, had suffered at *her* parents' hands.

Periodically, of course, regression and resistance served to deflect his focus from such insights. In the midst of this painful growing up, on the Monday following his wedding H asked Dr. Q to remind him that "my no-nonsense macho attitude is a *lot* of nonsense . . . I feel things and I like loving."

In this chapter we have looked a little more closely at the postadolescent male's experience of his sexual and reproductive potential. The phallic illusion, regressively clung to in an effort to "disidentify from mother," as Ralph Greenson (1968) put it, shortchanges the man's future genital as well as generative functioning. The teleology of male sexuality, its phylogenetic function, is obvious, especially among infra-human primates and in simple societies: reproduction of the species. Its ontogeny is not so explicit in a contemporary world where birth control, in freeing us, has also obscured the purposefulness of pleas-ure—in re-creation, pro-creation.

It is only on the eve of adulthood that a male gets a clear picture of the genital aspects of masculinity. As biological maturity is presaged in the rumblings of preadolescence, a boy is precipitated into an anal and quasi-homosexual regression. Disguised or open homosexual activity and masturbation serve as rehearsals for acts of heterosexuality. The teenager reassures himself repeatedly of the intactness of his body, his person, his penis and testicles, and his masculinity at the height of orgasm because in part—unconsciously—he wants the dreaded ef-feminization, emasculation, and dissolution. Preparing for the genital-ity that is now possible but still frightening, the adolescent's mastur-bation, in its frequency and form, is aimed at reiterating his phallic wholeness. At the same time, though, his masturbation *fantasies* and homoerotic wishes cannot help betraying the maternal identifications still alive in him. Again and again, a boy must rework the path toward manhood in the face of motherhood's great allure—in the face of his wish to be a woman.

Indeed, more attention probably needs to be paid to a boy's first involuntary and then his induced ejaculations, to the sensations, fan-tasies of body wastes, and fears of damage and sterility that accompany them. In contrast to menarche, a boy's emissions, harbingers of his capacity for procreation, are not ritually heralded but occur as private, often secret events. Nor do most boys anticipate their later caretaking functions, typically girding their loins in the phallic, combative cama-raderie that characterizes the social life of the male adolescent.

The typical first experiences of actual intercourse described by young men, their triumphs over body parts, reveal that theirs is most often not an image of sexual man as a sensual being. In sex too the aggres-sivity of desire—the strivings for phallic conquest and anal-sadistic control—guards against a dwelling in libidinal arousal and, with it, a loss of self in the presence of woman.

At no time is the interdigitation of the psychosexual and psychoso-cial strains of identity more poignant than in adolescence. The teenager wants to assure himself that he can perform as an adult man in arenas as seemingly discrepant as work and sex; he needs to verify that he can remain in fact the person he believes himself to be, wherever he is and whatever he is doing. It is probably only after achieving a sense of integrity in late adolescence that a young man can tolerate the loss of self inherent in a fully realized erotic encounter. Moving from self-absorption to self-possession, the postadolescent youth becomes capable of yielding willingly, losing himself, and falling and being in love. Finding a woman with whom he can consider or at least imagine creating a mutually generative and caring life, a woman he loves, a man can at last discover his genuine sexuality and thus rediscover both the femininity and the fatherliness bound up with it.

8

Young Love

Before proceeding to describe falling in love as the final phase in the development of male sexual identity, I should first define romantic and erotic love from a psychoanalytic perspective. My emphasis here will be primarily on the affective components in passionate love and, secondarily, on the drive derivatives, dynamics, genetic antecedents, cognitive factors, structural and developmental prerequisites of the experience—some of which I have touched on earlier. In so doing, I will cite philosophers and poets of love from a variety of cultures and eras to fill a void in clinical psychoanalysis: a careful examination of the phenomenology of passion. In other words, paraphrasing Cherubino in *The Marriage of Figaro*, "What does love *feel* like?" (Much of what I say here pertains to young women as well, but, in this volume on men, the accent is on the conflictual emotions evoked in males.)

Perhaps it is the fact that our analytic patients often seek us out because of inhibitions in love and work, but rarely does the psychoanalyst have an opportunity to observe romantic love in full flower. So I counted myself lucky indeed to receive a closely detailed narrative from a colleague about a twenty-eight-year-old investment banker, V, and how he fell hopelessly in love. Having first sought help to deal with compulsions, affective inhibitions, mild perverse trends, self-sabotage in an otherwise relentless pursuit of material ambitions, and a general malaise, V had been in analysis for two and a half years when he met Rachel at a company picnic. He had had several lovers since college, but never had this young man been so taken by a woman. Gifted as a writer of fiction and poetry, avocations devalued by his parents, V was particularly well equipped to articulate his new state of feeling and mind, sometimes at the expense of his immersion in the experience itself.

He found Rachel's touch "at once electrifying and calming." When they had intercourse, after a premature ejaculation on his first attempt, V described her vagina in more oxymorons. It was like "living velvet ivory," and he "slipped into its possessive warmth" as if he had always belonged there. Sexual union and orgasm were rivaled only by the hour or so of postcoital bliss, during which the lovers revealed their innermost secrets. Between meetings, his longing for Rachel was delicious and unbearable, and V found himself frozen at streetcorners or doors to meeting rooms, fixed on her image. Perhaps, the young man reflected, analysis had primed him to fall in love.

Despite these heights of ecstasy and periods of suspended repose, however, as the love affair progressed into its sixth month V inexplicably found himself avoiding the pleasures of intercourse. The two were living together most of the time now, but a barrier seemed to have interposed itself between them, like the sword dividing Tristan from Isolde. A dream then brought to light one level of V's dreaded desires. In it, he dove with other children into a "great gulf." He emerged uncertain of his body—of what lay beneath the neck—and found himself crossing his old school's soccer field (pun intended, he indicated in his associations), but making his way not to the boys' but to the girls' "changing" room.

In his associations to the dream, the patient talked of the eerie feeling he had come to notice after penetration. When he let himself go, sensing with his body and not seeing in his mind's eye, he felt wedded to his love. It was as if their pubic hair and bones were enmeshed. R's breasts seemed to seep into his own chest, to penetrate *him* and yet to become his own possession. Upon climaxing, he found himself in an altered state, "weirdly" longing to take in her moistened vagina with his penis but fighting off unnamed fears and becoming physically chilled and anxious. Finally, as he associated to the act of intercourse, V remarked on his long-standing inability to weep, to his surprise equating the watering of his eyes with the lubrication of a woman's genitals. The dream further reminded him of a memory involving water and potential drowning. V now understood that he wanted to be as beautiful and bountiful as his lover. He yearned to incorporate her. He wished to be a woman. Contemplating the illusion of their interpenetration in the safety of analytic reflection with a male therapist, he wondered whether he would reemerge from Rachel as a man—ambitious and powerful and, one day, rich.

Perhaps his analyst "knew" women in much the same way as V did. Had not the self-revealing hero of Janet Malcolm's *Psychoanalysis: The Impossible Profession,* the workmanlike amalgam portrayed by her as the typical psychoanalyst, had not Dr. Aaron Green confessed the source of his failure to speak or write more? To do so, he lamented, would be symbolically to fulfill a treasured but shameful wish—to parade himself as a beautiful woman, and this before the gaze of other analysts, who presumably "saw into people's souls." Not only his sex but his selfhood seemed at risk. Even as V played with exchanging sexual identities with Rachel, he resisted what he felt to be her smothering envelopment. Sunday mornings, with the respite they provided, ironically proved the most disquieting. As Rachel lay in bed, having encircled herself and V with all her things—clothes, papers, magazines, cats, Sunday food and drink—he felt closed in. So he would drag himself away, preferring weights at the local health club or some last-minute job from the office to the unbounded lovemaking that such leisurely interludes afforded and that, during his frenetically scheduled week, he otherwise craved. There was some danger, V sensed, as if invited into Rachel's welcoming arms he might never escape intact and get about "my father's business." He needed to resist her hold and define himself.

With the analysis of V's uncertainty about his sexual identity and fears of engulfment, he again "lost [him]self in Rachel." But other matters troubled V. He began to complain bitterly of the demands made on his time by his junior position in a high-pressure profession. Whereas in the past V had tried obsessively to comply with each and every task, now he found himself becoming careless. He grew more casual about his hours and efforts, and his bosses, demanding an almost filial devotion, were stung by his ill-concealed diffidence. Eventually, rather regretfully, they suggested that he seek a position elsewhere.

In part, further analysis revealed, V's failure at work bespoke a typical acting out of oedipal guilt. He dared not try to have it all—professional success along with a loving woman—because of the murderous aggression toward and identification with his father which these conquests implied and the castration they invited as retaliation. And so he had unconsciously worked to undermine at least one of his triumphs. V's father hunger—with its preoedipal roots and resonances—had also moved him to place obstacles in love's path. He sought the very punishment he feared and ironically, he noted, the further illusion of security, the felt structure, that its "hard" presence afforded him.

At three, he recalled, left with a maiden aunt in Florida for several months while his father established a new residence, taking the patient's mother away with him, V had fallen into an unguarded pool and nearly drowned. As he associated to it, the incident yielded a screen memory for the pitfalls of erotic entanglement in the absence of sustaining father love and reliable inner authority. His seductive mother and her sister had suffused V with a sense of unending entitlement, so that he felt constantly at risk with women. And in an unusual way: he was fearful of deluding himself into thinking that he was indeed "his majesty the baby," as Freud had put it, V said, in "On Narcissism"—an infant afloat in "oceans of boundless love," tiny in being so important, potentially lost in being cherished. He needed to feel the restraining anchor of an authoritarian, external male presence, one like that of his tyrannical but remote and narcissistic father, if he were to be self-assured enough to let himself go with a woman. Otherwise he was afraid to feel love.

Thus, in a subsequent elaboration of the memory, V found himself wondering whether he had been pushed into the pool by an older boy and rescued by his uncle (the mother's other sibling), who then punished the perpetrator. He felt unprotected from himself, from his own inability to deny himself pleasure. In so many words, he required the safe mooring offered by what Roy Schafer has called the "loving and beloved superego" in order to venture forth into the seas he yearned to explore.

The next challenge came when V secured an even better job, and Rachel continued to love him. After a brief flurry, once again they made love infrequently—"maybe weekly," he said pointedly, like "an old married couple." Instead of acting out in work, his actions serving to discharge and obscure his inner tensions, V brought his conflict closer to home. He now enlivened his lovelife by manufacturing dramas aimed at provoking his analyst (a man in his fifties, like his father) to take him to task. Rachel and this "stern" older male, who tore him from her bed in the early morning hours (an appointment time he had requested) or who deprived her by taking the money the couple needed for their revels, became rivals for his heart—a heart now in full oedipal conflict, positive and negative. V's loyalty to Rachel seemed to vie with his duty to the analyst and his longing to depend forever on his beneficence. Like Tristan with King Mark, V kept creeping back to pay reluctant homage and, often belatedly, his bill. Ironically, the conflict heightened his love; V found that his passion for Rachel grew even as he felt more bound to his analyst.

Neither of the genetic reference points that had proved so meaningful—oedipal or preoedipal—could quite account for the sense of ultimate peril and the moral drama injected again and again by V into his passion, as if to keep the flame alive. Something by way of an age-specific agenda, a young-adult life crisis, seemed to be at work. But the nature of the conflict and its underlying imperatives remained to be defined.

Psychoanalytic Contributions

Psychoanalysis was designed by Freud to be a psychology of love. Yet it has had more to say about the childish precursors of what is called—rather reductionistically—mature genitality than about eros in adult life. Not all sexuality is infantile sexuality, after all, though our analytic literature makes it seem so.

Rarely describing in detail the adult patient's current erotic experiences, analysts have pretty much taken heterosexuality for granted. Instead we dwell on the pathways toward its achievement and on the fixations surviving into adulthood as perversions, inversions, and symptoms compromising its full expression. We avoid identifying what it is that is sexy about sex. Either passionate love is confounded with the marriage bond and the long-standing affection of the couple, or else it is viewed skeptically as an immature and maladaptive variant of the real (adult) thing. How ironic these oversights are, since romantic bliss and erotic consummation are what adult patients so often crave and what we as practitioners must try to help them attain.

Responding to this void, a number of psychoanalysts have written books on love in the last few years.[1] Omitted from the 1968 edition, "love" has at last been inserted into the 1990 *Glossary of Psychoanalytic*

Terms, with its passionate and sexual form described as a special subset of the larger case. Still, psychoanalysts have generally and repeatedly betrayed their faint-heartedness in approaching a subject arguably at the very heart of their inquiry. Whatever the lackluster denouement to their relationship as husband and wife, Sigmund Freud's voluminous letters to his fiancée Martha figure among the most poignant exemplars of passionate feeling in the western world. Nonetheless, Freud's later and more official pronouncements on love tell a different story, in different terms.

In what was to become canon, Freud came to search out the infantile prototypes of adult passions. All passionate feeling was tied to sexuality, first of all—to the evolving sequence of body zones and modes through which libido expressed itself—and, second, to the persons or objects who first gratified its various modes of expression. The loves of the adult man or woman were viewed basically as transfigurations—more or less inhibited by later moral and realistic constraints—of these primal instinctual encounters. Thus all love might be reduced to a sort of transference love (Freud, 1915a; Bergmann, 1986), parental images imposing themselves on and rediscovered in the present.

Freud saw in love certain "economic problems." In *Three Essays on Sexuality* (1905c) he hypothesized the bifurcation of libido into two currents—the sensual *(sinnlichkeit)* and the affectionate *(zaertlichkeit)* and emphasized the tension generated by their coexistence and inevitable opposition. It was only with adolescence that the two diverging trends could be reconciled (1921). From early on the child struggled to safeguard his guardians from feeling the full brunt of his intense and imperious desires for them. This made for persistent fixations on the primitive pleasures and persons of the past and for inevitable frustrations and intrapsychic tension and prohibition, the nature of which was clarified with the structural model (1923).

Incestuous in origin, "forced upon us by nature" but "repugnant to morality" (Freud, 1900), the child's amorous wishes were inherently fraught with dynamic conflict. Freud's case histories are all of them infantile love stories, therefore tales of unrequited love. Engendering guilt and frustration, more often than not repressed, giving rise to anxiety, inhibitions, and symptoms—the loves that Freud describes are quintessentially neurotic. There are no heights of ecstasy here, no deep fulfillment, no reaching beyond the moment for the ineffable. In fact, moving as these woebegone accounts are, Freud seems merely to assume the existence of the sort of love in which a measure of libidinal gratification is possible and never makes its experiential qualities and, through the analysis of these, its determinants explicit. In other words, passionate, erotic, romantic love can only be inferred in Freud's writings from its negatives (see also Balint, 1948).

Freud was no stranger to passion, we know, and some of what he had to say about love echoes its more poetic interpreters. For example, stressing its origins in self-love, he noted that object love in adolescence and adulthood tended to deplete or otherwise weaken the self, touching on themes evident in twelfth-century poems on the subject (1914b). In pondering the development of a capacity for passion in late adolescence, he alluded to the exaltations and sublimation of feeling described by the Romantic poets: "The depth to which anyone is in love, as contrasted with his purely sensual desire, may be measured by the size of the share taken by the aim-inhibited instincts of affection" (1921: 112). Yet Freud himself never elucidated the specifics of love's phenomenology.

From the very start, analysts have focused mostly on the content of the love relationship—the dynamics, the unconscious fantasies, the points of fixation, the infantile objects—rather than the form and quality of romantic feeling. Ironically enough, they have left affect out of their understanding of love. Unlike their approach to symptoms, when it comes to love analysts have not proceeded "from the surface." In addition to its genetic and dynamic determinants and, to a lesser degree, its structure, early theorists also attempted to explain love in terms of its teleology. Following Freud's lead in *Three Essays*, Sandor Ferenczi, Wilhelm Reich, and especially Karl Abraham constructed a theory of genitality, the attainment of which came to be seen as the sine qua non of mature sexual and overall ego functioning. Ferenczi came closest to real life when he described what he called an amphimixis, a coalescing of pregenital aims in sexual union, with all these component instincts subsumed in genital pleasure and penetration. This, in its turn, subserved the reproductive aim of the individual and the preservation of the species. With his interest in both epigenesis and character, Abraham posited the genital type as the highest of characterological levels in his hierarchy—an ideal type omitted by Freud in his own personality classification.

Once more, particularly in the heyday of id psychology, the focus was on libidinal impulses rather than feelings, albeit this time on the functions of sexual love. More important, again the experience of sensual love eluded careful observation. Eroticism was confounded with the overarching purposes served by sex—integration of the drive organization as far as the individual was concerned and survival for the species. Making love came to mean making a family, as it had a millenium earlier in the western world, that is, before the aesthetic "invention" of romance.

A number of later contributors questioned the link between genital gratification and the bond of love. Michael Balint (1948, 1956), for example, saw the attainment of what he deemed a "genital identification" and consequent "equanimity" as prerequisites for mature love. But he then proceeded to the ironic conclusion that, for such an ideal, individual passion might well become an unnecessary hindrance. Rather than tame and adaptive, genital love might imperil an individual's well-being with the haunting threat of regression, a return to a state of primitive and illusory union wherein reality testing was swept away. We have learned to love—Balint implied (Bergmann, 1987)— and could now learn to live without it.

In a similar vein, W. A. Binstock (1973) later stressed the crossing over of gender boundaries in heterosexual encounters. But he went on to warn of the perils posed by lovers' longings for and illusions of *Liebestod,* love death, with its dependent and bisexual ramifications. Lovers, he suggested, reach their highest plateau when they can contemplate life without the other and give up more concrete expressions of their bisexual and symbiotic yearnings.

Nathaniel Ross (1970) called into question the facile equation of orgasmic capacity and psychosocial maturity. He pointed to the fact that borderline and psychotic patients often reveal a great capacity for genital pleasure, whereas higher-functioning neurotics, who are capable of devotion to people and forebearance, might tend toward sexual inhibition. Others also took a less than sunny view of sexual love, likening its longings to those seen in mourning and melancholia and the unattainable object of such yearnings to lost love objects of the infantile past (Arlow, 1980; Bak, 1973). Thus, while they proved closer to the poets in emphasizing just how unruly and dangerous the passions of lovers are, the rationalism of these later theorists, wending its way back to roots in the pre-Romantic Enlightenment, moved them to pull back. They too withdrew from immersing themselves in a scrutiny of their subject. Such love, they continued, can be deceptive and disruptive. Some even seemed to verge on the Sophoclean ideal articulated in Plato's *Republic*—a life free from Aphrodite's savage enslavement.

In recent years analysts have returned to the Romantic, and romantic, view of love, in the spirit of Wordsworth's "Prelude."[2] They grant a legitimate place to the "spontaneous overflow of powerful feelings" that occurs in love as in poetic inspiration. Several of these authors have looked more carefully at what real and fictional lovers have had to say about what they feel. Beginning with Martin Bergmann in 1971, analysts have stressed the interpenetration of self and other in passionate love. With this meeting there also emerges an interplay of idealization and identification. Thus falling in love makes for an expansion, rather than a depletion, of the sense of self and for an awareness of the complex nature of the beloved.

The crossing of boundaries in mature love harkens back to the "dual unity" of mother and child described by Mahler and her coworkers (1975). Yet it also involves much more than a revival of this symbiosis. What is called forth in love is not a primitive fusion, effacing self and object representations alike, but a union of two more defined and sexually differentiated persons (see Kakar and Ross, 1987). So love's crossing over is also a transcendence of the limits of gender, reminiscent of Plato's androgynes, a completion of an inevitably incomplete self made possible, ironically, by the bedrock integrity of that self (as Binstock had suggested). When this is missing, according to Otto Kernberg (1977), the lover is either fled from or is confounded with an aspect of the self, becoming its narcissistic extension in a variation on what Stendhal in 1842 dubbed "vanity love."

Mature romantic love, in Kernberg's analysis, also requires transgression, a symbolic sally at least across generational barriers into the forbidden domain of sensuality, the arena of the primal scene. There the lover rediscovers and revels in the once hidden sexuality of the parents and that of the imaginative oedipal child she or he once was. In such sexual love, arising at the close of adolescence and ushering in young adulthood, though sometimes lost thereafter, there are certain genetic preconditions and emotional consequences. Freud to the contrary, each love affair, amounting to a forbidden encounter, may drain otherwise inexhaustible reservoirs of incest. Symbolic violations of the taboo ease the conflict and expose the defenses it calls up for what they are. Like most analysts, however, even Kernberg fails to spell out the uses of adult love for further development. With a few exceptions, there is scant reflection on love itself. The poets' musings, patients' voices, and the descriptions of sex to be found even in books like the Kinsey survey or the Hite reports on men and women, with all their methodological problems, are absent or muted in these generalized accounts and theories.

Fear of Feeling

Why have analysts so persistently, perhaps phobically, avoided confronting the passions expressed in adult sex and love? Most of the speculations about this glaring omission center on Freud biography (see Bergmann, 1987). Eissler (1951), for example, traced Freud's reticence to the trauma that ensued upon his falling in love with Gisela Fluss when he was sixteen. Bergmann points out that Freud believed passionate love to be shortlived, because his own infatuation with Martha waned after their wedding.

In this vein, Harold Blum (1991) has refuted Swales's contention that Freud had an affair with his sister-in-law, Minna, while vacationing in Italy. According to Blum, Freud remained chaste and monogamous, making his way to Rome while she went to the sanitarium for reasons other than having an abortion, as Swales inferred. In fact, it was on this very trip that Freud first saw Michelangelo's *Moses* at San Pietro, beginning his lifelong fascination and identification with the Hebrew patriarch. Likening the statue to one in a niche of the Catholic church in Moravia to which his seductive nursemaid took him as a boy, Blum has remarked on the sensual currents in Freud's flirtation with Christianity.

Like Moses, I would add, Freud eventually repudiated the temptations of the Golden Calf, the Bacchanalian icons and sensuous metaphors of what was for him a more concrete, decadent, hedonistic religion—a regressive revival of the idol worship and pantheism abjured by the Jews. Behind the Christianity that Freud repudiated lurked the illicit and unconsciously incestuous sensuality proffered by the banished caretaker and seductress. Like Moses too, Freud went it alone. He may have replaced the temptations of Minna's body with a more lofty mission and an idea, more or less disembodied, so that he and psychoanalysis were thereafter lost to love—unsublimated love, that is, love on earth.

Still, why the enduring reluctance of analysts after him? In his preface to the famed 1914 article on the statue, published pseudonymously, Freud offers more clues about the sources of his and his discipline's abiding uneasiness with passionate feeling. When it comes to a work of art, Freud tells us, he cannot derive pleasure without first understanding it; by such understanding, he means conscious reflection and conceptualization. In all matters of the heart, Freud seems to imply, causal explanation is to precede rather than follow from aesthetic experiencing, careful description, and exegesis of the "text" in and of itself. Thus music eludes Freud's ken and his interest—music, perhaps the elemental form of romantic expression, envied by poets doomed to sing love's praises in mere words.

Analysts after Freud have been mistrustful of affect without ideation. Indeed, the essence of analytic technique as Freud first conceived it was to replace other modes of expression with "word presentations" and, in making the unconscious conscious, to subject the primary process to the sway of reason and discretion (1900). Later, with his structural model, he declared, "Where id is, there shall ego be" (1923).

From the psychoanalytic vantage, as from that of the social order, the desire for another person inevitably threatens the status quo, the institutions and laws that regulate interactions among people, and so ideologies of all stripes have been loth to give it free rein. While impelling some of its highest attainments, the emotions of love threaten the rule of mind, disturbing psychoanalysts as it has so many philosophers who have pondered it since Plato. Indeed, affect theory in general has found but a tenuous footing amidst the instinctual drives and psychic structures of our model, and analysts have had to be guided by observations and theories outside their orbit. Similarly, with the elucidation of romantic love, analytic thinkers have had to begin by turning to pursuits other than their own.

Love Stories and Theories

For many people, in midlife certainly, neurotic and mundane entanglements subdue feeling or abort romance before it can flower. Lovers themselves have little libido left over for analytic transferences and rarely seek or stick out treatment. The conflicts evoked in the trans-ference may also interfere with the individual's ability to fall in love outside the analytic situation once in it. And, in the countertransfer-ence, once again envy may rear its ugly head. Muted, mostly middle-aged or older, undemonstrative by training and disposition, not a few analysts begrudge patients their passions—especially the younger ones. Reflexively, and with a certain surreptitious narcissism, they tend to refer these back to the transference and their own person, as if giving true love the lie.

So most of the accounts of love that come the way of clinicians are retrospective or subject to dulling scrutiny and self-consciousness. Because of this paucity of data from practice, analysts have been forced to turn to characters like Anna Karenina and Vronsky, enduring in the literary imagination, for more multifaceted and dynamic portraits of love's complexities. Besides, "applied analysis" has been with us from the start. Without an *Oedipus Rex*, we may wonder, would there have been, ten years after he reflected on the play, an oedipal complex?

In this spirit we may consider some of the great love stories of classical western, Sanskrit, and Perso-Islamic literature, along with some of the more modern poets and philosophers of love. Now and then I will venture even farther back in time to the Greeks or the poetry of Virgil—to eras predating the elaboration of romantic love as a distinct form. My aim is not to psychoanalyze the poets of love but to learn from them as theorists of love, to seek out certain recurrent themes in the passions they depict. There is a male bias in my gener-alizations, derived as they are mostly from authors who are men. Yet a good deal of what they have to say about feelings of love cuts across sexual differences and individual variations. My focus is also on the emotions evoked in heterosexual encounters, though several of the major contributors—such as Auden or Barthes—were homosexuals.

When it comes to erotic love, as opposed to procreation, there is no such thing as safe sex. Danger, the great love stories tell us, is an integral aspect of sexual love. Such passion is by nature perilous, in the words of the poets, its bliss tragic and filled with "anguish most sharp." From the time romantic love was, as some say, discovered or at least cata-logued as such by poets around the twelfth century, love's celebrators have also told of its inevitable terrors. According to Shakespeare's 129th sonnet: "All this the world knows; yet none knows well / To shun this heaven that leads men to this hell."

The lover, according to poets as diverse as the twelfth-century Persian Nizami or the Jansenist Racine, finds himself in an altered state, one of heightened sensibility and intense pleasure. Love is like a waking dream, according to John Donne. Much as Freud suggested in his narcissism paper (1914b), it has been seen as a sort of sublime madness, wresting the individual from the safety and self-satisfaction of his filial, social, and moral anchorage. In so doing, the feverish incorporation of the beloved's promised replenishment offers exhilaration and an immortality not unlike union with the Godhead. In the words of Teilhard de Chardin: lovers seek "one another in the light and darkness of the soul; the pull is toward mutual sensibility and completion, in which preoccupation with preserving the species gradually dissolves in the greater intoxication of two people creating the world" (1972). Like addicts, such lovers dread the return to normal consciousness.

This is not to say that the lover's state is one of unalloyed joy. Quite the contrary, such sensual and emotional excitement trenches all too quickly on pain—as Freud implied in "The Economic Problem of Masochism." (One analyst, William Evans, 1953, went so far as to suggest that love stories merely provide a pretext for masochistic gratification.) Indeed, as Keats repeatedly rendered it, romantic love is fraught from the start with suffering. This is so partly because, while elevating the self through union with the other, love paradoxically threatens to infantilize, debase, and deplete a self because it is no longer whole.

Especially in absence of what has become one's "better half," the lover experiences an excruciating incompleteness. But even when reciprocated by an ideal lover, no love can wholly be requited because of the intangibility and inaccessibility of the beloved's spirit, because his or her innermost thoughts and feelings remain essentially unknowable. An intrepid Cupid might at last snare his Psyche only to find that her soul—now indistinguishable from his own—eludes him after all. Kept from the beloved, soldiers and courtiers like Shakespeare's Antony and Romeo, Virgil's Aeneas, Beroul's Tristan, or Nizami's Quays all become fools for love—abject, infantile, effeminate, entirely lost to themselves. Thus, more recently, W. H. Auden speaks of Tristan's and Isolde's urge to be one when they are doomed to add up to two (1973), and Octavio Paz of the penetrable body and the impenetrable consciousness (Kernberg, 1977). Ultimately the lover recognizes that "this state where there is no twoness in response to joy or sorrow" (Bhav-abhuti) is but another instance of what the Hindus call *maya*, another mortal illusion. In our less fanciful terms, two persons have two personalities.

Nor, as the courtiers of Aquitaine and others after them averred, could true love exist naturally within the institution of marriage, whose sexuality serves the teleology of reproduction. Tender, pleasant, but by its very nature inhibited, socialized and familiar lovemaking falls short of the mark. In contrast, free from constraining paternalistic sanctions and obligations, outside kinship and genealogical systems of deference, risky and uncertain, first love, unrequited love, or an adulterous liaison paradoxically proves to be more pure. In these contexts, each moment of ecstasy (from Greek *ekstasis,* out of place) amounts to an orgasmic little death, a transport of pleasure foreshadowing the final love death, the *Liebestod* concluding so many of the world's paradigmatic love stories of all cultures, according to Denis de Rougemont (1956). The stories of Tristan and Isolde, Aida and Radames, Romeo and Juliet, and Layla and Majnun are filled with dread, haunted from the start by their tragic conclusion.

In love as in religion, the mystical union does not come easily in a secular world, often demanding the ultimate sacrifice—martyrdom, the immolation of one self in the immortality of the two. Challenging the economic and feudal order (in derivatives of what analysts infer to be the oedipal level) and yielding up individuality (within the preoedipal dyad), the romantic lover of fiction is a revolutionary and a mystic who invites death in the act of passion.

Thus two interwoven elements in love as it has been fictionalized and conceptualized have to do with the lovers' implied emotional violence toward the powers that be—their defiance of the guardians of social order who erect barriers to its consummation—and the willingness of each to risk all in a quest for union with the beloved. As one patient of mine put it, "Damn them all—the experience is so exquisite that it's worth the hurt and loss." There are some—Jean-Paul Sartre, for instance, Theodore Reik, or Robert J. Stoller—who have accented the lovers' hateful, vindictive, embittered feelings and urges to avenge old hurts through domination on the lover's part. Sullerot (1979) sees even in a woman's shows of selfless enslavement her effort to control absolutely a man's emotions—his pleasure, excitement, expressions of guilt. And hell, of course, has no fury like a woman scorned—to which the wrath of Dido, Phaedra, Medea, and other spurned lovers provides testimony.

Certainly there are destructive aims in the imperious desires that lovers feel for each other—in their urges to conquer and consume, to possess and devour. The affective corollaries of Freud's hypothetical *Sinnlichkeit* are undeniable, and love can, as Freud himself suggested (1915a), turn quickly enough to hate, particularly when frustrated. With two sets of drives, moreover, libidinal and aggressive, both of whose derivatives find the same object, it is inevitable that a lover should want both to join and to destroy his or her lover. In the words of Roland Barthes: "I want to possess, fiercely, but I also know how to give, actively . . . I see the other with double vision; sometimes as object, sometimes as subject; I hesitate between my tyranny and oblation. I am condemned to be a saint or a monster; unable to be one, unwilling to be the other" (1978). Or to quote one patient, a woman who had recently broken with her lover of a year: "I had a dream that I was going down on Billy. I love this, as you know—always did with men. I was sucking harder and harder, and Billy was going wild with pleasure. And then suddenly he was hurting, too, and asking me to stop." Asked what came to mind, she replied "power." Indeed, in real life, it is this sort of ambivalence that most often brings romance to a close.

Nonetheless, with exceptions here and there—Isolde poised with her slain uncle's sword above the beautiful Tristan in his bath—the stories of true love are remarkably devoid of frank acts of aggression on the lovers' part toward each other. The violence is directed toward or by them to oppressors outside the dyad. In this regard, certain sex differences do come into play. Rather than abuse his lady, the male hero will flee instead, betraying her for other women or for king and country. In contrast, a woman finds herself ingesting the man whose heart she has won or cursing him when he abandons her for another. But, for the most part, hostile feelings are banished from the dyad, whose preservation is safeguarded by the play of idealization and identification and the overriding sense of cherishing and perpetual longing. These processes and imperatives further secure the affectionate ties that keep desire from being self-serving.

Nor is romantic love all *sturm und drang*. The burning torments of

unrequited or unconsummated love, the sharp stabs of jealous possession and the high pitch of supreme joy—the *hoechste Lust* of Wagner's
Isolde—describe but one of its incarnations. However intense or multiple the lovers' orgasms may be, they occupy only moments in the
relationship. Love is characterized as well by a near religious intimacy,
by postcoital discourses of sentiment occurring on "tolerant and en-
chanted slopes," where, Auden tells us, Venus sends grave visions of
supernatural sympathy, universal love, and hope. In such contempla-
tive and tender states of mind, the lover's sentiment toward the beloved
is captured best in the words of Augustine as "I want you to be."

Where the love is hollow or unreal, of course, where vanity and
disillusionment prevail, feelings of depression and disgust follow sexual
union. Even where this love proves "true," sadness enters the picture
in the form of "postcoitum triste," expressing the sense of loss in
intercourse and a lover's inevitable ambivalence about having given
himself (or herself) so utterly to another.

Even when they succeed in escaping society's intrusions on their
intimacy, the lovers themselves—especially the men—fear entrapment.
So they act to attenuate it. Tolstoy's Vronsky, Shakespeare's Antony,
Beroul's Tristan, Krishna of Jayadeva's Sanskrit poetry, the paradigmatic sufi Majnun of Nizami's epic, Virgil's Aeneas—all warriors
turned lovers—at one time or another try to escape the hold of their
beloved's beauty. They do so variously and with varying degrees of
success, calling upon martial duty or else lapsing into peccadilloes with
other, lesser women in order essentially to reestablish their freedom,
virility, and responsibility. Sometimes, too, love is felt to grow stale or
the beloved's faults are reviled, with boredom and contempt exaggerated and exploited to defend against the prepotency of desire and the
grip of longing.

Thus it is really Anna Karenina's mesmerizing and womanly beauty,
not her flaws, that her once cavalier lover resents in their exile. The
real danger for Vronsky, a man without a father, lies in the rupture of
those tenuous filial and fraternal lifelines from woman and mother to
masculine selfhood and professional advancement. And where the
fatherless Vronsky fails to save himself from love, incidentally, the
scion and patriarch Aeneas succeeds in wresting himself from Dido's
hold, revisiting his beloved father Anchises as a shade, honoring his
own son, and pursuing his destiny as the founding father of Rome.

Only with Anchises' death is Aeneas able to begin the affair in the first place. Eventually he casts off the woman's robes in which Dido giddily dresses him because of principles inherited from his father and duty owed to his son.

Here, then, are some of the affects and sustained emotional states associated with falling and being in love: a sense of abiding danger; pleasure and ecstasy; divine madness; exquisite pain; protracted suffering; defiance; suicidal despair; a measure of inherent hostility and hatred; intense feelings of desire; a cherishing of the beloved, accompanied by gratitude and surprise in response to his or her very existence. Appetitive states and consummatory acts give rise to intense excitement, passions whose pitch is unequaled in almost any other activity (except possibly war or religious entrancement). These alternate with periods of equally remarkable repose when the lovers, having satisfied their longings for the moment, become intimate in alert inactivity (Wolff, 1965), gazing upon each other and exploring their innermost thoughts and feelings.

As Michael Balint noted, both states—passionate and intimate—compromise the lovers' reality testing. Either the longed-for lover comes to envelop the universe with his or her presence, or this world becomes "garbed with beauty to his taste" such that its dangers and demands fade into the background. In such a frame of mind, when the ordinary exigencies of real life are subsumed in love's spiritual heights and sensual demands, it becomes difficult to go about one's business. Feeling trapped, distracted, and controlled by their passion, lovers resent loving and being loved; inevitably they become ambivalent and try to wriggle free. And so romantic love is also dogged by the sense that it cannot last. It is a "quick bright thing" all too soon "devoured by the jaws of death"—"fire and powder[that] as they kiss, consume." When not destroyed from the outside, passion burns itself out (as Freud himself stressed).

For these reasons, perhaps, many of literature's protagonists have been relatively young lovers. Romantic heroines and heroes are repeatedly depicted as girls and boys poised on the brink of adulthood, taken by the ideal other as by sensual self-discovery before they come into their own as adult women and men. The girls forsake their family ties while the boys abandon their internal ones—failing to adhere to duties or to pursue ambitions. In their physical and intellectual prime, these young lovers yield to instinctual tides that might have served worldly ambition but end up sweeping them beyond social convention, leaving them to their own fatal devices. So they are undone and left alone in a wilderness of their own making.

Yet there are notable exceptions here and there, especially in the stories of adulterers rendered impolitic and childish by their quest for rejuvenation: Anna abandoning her motherhood, Antony unmanned by the bewitching Cleopatra, Phaedra possessed by yearning for her priggish stepson Hippolytus, whom she likens to the philandering Theseus when he was young. Certainly these figures are as passionate and heroic as Tristan and Isolde, Abelard and Heloise, or Romeo and Juliet. Where passionate love is rekindled later in life, the lover suffers a second adolescence, with spouse, family, and other sources of adult duty representing parental figures and injunctions not easily disregarded. Love at midlife both rejuvenates a lover and makes him or her incautious. Conflict and the potential for tragedy are immediately apparent. No longer is it the previous generation that is challenged by the lovers—it is the children, and all others they should care for, who are forgotten as lovers devour the lotus root and drink the waters of Lethe.

Thus the fictive tales of doomed young love, perhaps at any actual age, are, as Freud also lamented, mostly *short* stories. As Turgenev's actual short story by this name reveals, "First Love"—and how ambiguous and disheartening this tale is—is charged with both self-discovery and regression, often reaching psychosexual climaxes not repeated in life. Past and present, illusion and reality, find a new synthesis in the sensual romantic encounter. After all those years of onanistic imagining, the adolescent can identify at last with parents in their sexual role and marvel at the fact that intercourse is possible, indeed real. As Vladimir Nabokov put it in *Speak, Memory,* recalling his first sexual encounter, "I parted the fabric of fancy, I tasted reality."

A Psychoanalytic Definition

From depictions outside psychoanalysis, it becomes clear that romantic love cannot be reduced to one or more instinctual impulses. Nor can this phenomenon be conceptualized as a single affect whose underlying determinants are various. Instead passionate love must be seen essen-

tially as a complex and sustained affective disposition, structurally
rather like a mood (Jacobson, 1971) in its amalgamation of emotion,
fantasy, and perception, but specifically object-directed and instinctu-
ally impelled. The state of love is characterized by the concatenation
of desire and longing, which are the affective derivatives of Freud's
sensual and tender libidinal currents. The lover's paradoxical aim is to
possess or devour a specific person while simultaneously preserving his
or her own existence. ("You can have your cake and eat it too," as Bob
Dylan puts it in his song "Lay, Lady, Lay.") Try as the lover might to
simplify matters, contradictory emotions and sensations, which point
to revived but also current conflicts, inevitably accompany falling and
being in love.

With some notable exceptions—unrequited love, for instance, or
certain religious ecstasies—romantic love eventually becomes erotic
love. It is tied to and expressed in genital sexuality, either in fantasy
or, better, in reality. In fact, for the most part, romantic love progresses
in stages, each altering and deepening the constellation of feelings that
compose it.

The first stage, exemplified in the young Freud's letters to Martha,
is that of unconsummated love. For some—the French troubadors, for
instance—this represents its highest form. For others, to echo Samuel
Coleridge in his critique of *Romeo and Juliet* (1817), such love is mere
"fancy," a state in which the lover is not comprehended as a whole
individual with idiosyncratic emotional needs, sensual preferences, and
spiritual ambitions to which the lover must attune, but rather as an
infantile or split object—as an idea or ideal. With an actual sexual
meeting, "imagination" put into practice replaces the two-dimensional
fantasy. The lover is *known* as a real and variegated person, with sexual
and other responses of his or her own. Subject to a higher level of
idealization (Kernberg, 1974), the beloved is still experienced as much
more than real.

Being in love is thus more than a repetition. Eroticism of this kind
is a quest reminiscent of, but not reducible to, earlier object relationships involving both sensuality and attachment. It represents, if you
will, a search for intersubjective communion, for "mutual transcendence," in Kernberg's words. In the wake of infatuation and passion,
ambivalence and then forgiveness, compassion and gratitude are entertained, and the intimacy of the lovers becomes invested with feelings

of empathy and mutuality. It is now that love's tender current eddies in to quell a self-protective hostility.

Romantic love is not simply synonymous with what is called *genital primacy,* since it also involves an illusory or psychic reaching after the "soul" of the beloved. The capacity for genital feeling and a capacity for orgasm in intercourse are necessary but not sufficient conditions. Ideational and symbolic elements come into play, and, as in artistic creativity, the romantic lover requires a capacity for metaphor. Immediate sensation, though vital, is deliberately endowed by a lover with meanings beyond the momentary gratification of desire.

In states of love, then, both concrete sensations and the emotions called up are subject to intellectual reflection. The romantic lover feels deeply and simultaneously thinks about what he is feeling. His capacity to ponder his desires suggests both a measure of realism about himself and his lover and the ability, as if hypothetically, to make of them much more than they are. Romantic love is a feeling that is simply not accessible to the intellectually immature individual. Rash as they are, lovers' emotions are not merely regressive but fall within the province of the sophisticated adult—hence the limitations of the genetic reductionism of so many of the analytic efforts to explain it.

Romantic love is marked by periods of passionate excitement—exquisite fulfillment, intense frustration, rage, and epiphanies, like the orgasm, when opposites can merge in an explosion of undefined yearning and sensation. Thus passion's particular emotional stamp and the various oxymorons used to depict it—"tragic bliss," "sweet sorrow," and such. At the same time, however, this form of love has its more quiescent periods, interludes of libidinal satiety yet of sustained and suspended interest in the other—intervals, that is, of the highest form of intimacy. Whereas uniting has been the objective of love's more passionate phases, there are times when the lover wants to be known as an individual and to learn about the other as a distinct person (or object).

There is an integral quality in these emotional polarities—passionate intensity and intimate repose. The love object endures both levels of exaltation and proves to be the same person in either slate. Indeed, memories of the one experience serve to enrich the other. Idealization in concert with identification contribute to the altered state of consciousness occurring when one is in love. Even the environment may be invested with the vitality of the lovers. Yet no matter how stimulated and alive the lover may feel, this state of mind is not to be equated with simple happiness. It is charged with feelings of sadness, anxiety, and inevitable loss, all bespeaking the impossibility, danger, and death-defying abandon of the union.

Indeed, love does not easily endure within the confines of most adult lives; dyadic exchanges of love cannot be sustained in a workaday world; love is blind; its time is limited. The easing of self boundaries, heightened appetitive states, acceptance of vulnerability, illusions that love conquers all, and immersion in feeling all compromise reality testing and the capacity for adaptation. Such concerns conspire with the conflictual meanings that love inevitably comes to assume, because of its resonance with the infantile neurosis and its objects, to tip the balance once more toward the side of emotional inhibition.

Defenses and consequent compromises are evoked to contend with the dangers, both imagined and real, inherent in this condition. The individual returns, both grudgingly and thankfully, to "normal consciousness." In our culture, if not in those where marriage has a more frankly economic impetus, romantic love opens its doors to admit third persons and is reorganized into what analysts have commonly called mature love.

Within this context, suspending daily concerns and making use of fantasy, established partners can periodically act to renew their erotic love. Yet these encounters may not include certain critical preconditions having to do with danger, obstacles in love's path, or a sense of transgression and transcendence. Without them, it becomes difficult to sustain the passionate intensity that is warranted by the situation itself and therefore has a life of its own.

Some Developmental Preconditions

Reacting to the irrationality of romantic love, most analysts have underscored its regressive aspects. But elaboration of its phenomenology reveals just how delicate an achievement it is—sexually, interpersonally, and imaginatively.

As many have stressed, eroticism does require the ultimate subordination of pregenital aims and pleasures to genital gratification. Now there is sex, and there is sex—as descriptive surveys like the Hite report reveal (1976, 1981). If a man and woman are successfully to express a more high-minded love in sexual activity, they must be conversant with their own and their partner's anatomy and responsiveness. A man, in particular, must have the control to hold his erection and delay his orgasm until either a woman reaches her climax or he recognizes the need for other forms of stimulation. Both partners must exercise empathy in reacting erotically to the flush of excitement in the other person without exploiting this as a defensive screen to obscure their own arousal because of the conflicts associated with it.

In other words, in romantic unions, sexual pleasures are shared ones. And the lovers must be comfortable enough with their bodies to reveal all during forepleasure and intercourse and then to stay close, to settle into each other, to cuddle and converse afterwards. Failure along the way can engender disappointments, mistrust, and narcissistic wounds that accumulate to destroy the passion.

Successful sex presupposes an early age-specific sensuousness in the infantile and preoedipal exchanges of parent and child, a reasonable resolution of oedipal conflict, and a pleasurable masturbatory history during puberty and early adolescence. If a mother loves her child sufficiently, she can teach him or her to enjoy rather than to hide the physical self and its secretions, to reveal these wishes and sensations in the expectation of their being accepted and understood and of receiving pleasure from others. Earlier I suggested that the father plays significant roles in consolidating the body images of both boys and girls in ways that allow a lover to tolerate the illusions of sexual dissolution, expansion, and transformation that accompany orgasm. For the girl, he presents himself as an available object, who can invite her to give up her mother and thereby define herself—an object later transferred to the person of the lover, who once again takes her away from home. For a boy, he provides a subject for identification, an inner resource that is sufficiently present to guide his erotic experiments with becoming a lover.

As far as oedipal development is concerned, not only must the stress fall on the positive and heterosexual denouement to the conflict, but the child must have struck a balance between repression and expression. With the unfolding of the oedipal complex, autoeroticism is enriched by fantasy and becomes masturbation proper. The initial objects of this fantasy must eventually fade into the unconscious if a child is to feel free enough to indulge in dreamy self-stimulation accompanied by images of love objects less close to home. Acts of incest or visual and tactile overstimulation during and just after the oedipal period, along with a disturbed sexual relationship between the parents, can make for the sort of frank fixations that have an inhibiting effect on children. No longer free to fantasize, because they are sexually unprotected, such children must redouble their efforts to anaesthetize and constrict themselves—to the point that their adult capacities for romantic and erotic love, even for sexual sensation, all calling up incestuous yearnings, are out of the question.

The reverie-like masturbation of the oedipal child is not the real thing—however taken adults may be by a little boy's or girls' precocious sensuality and declarations of love. Such arousal does not typically eventuate in orgasm, much less in mutual satisfaction. Surveys from Kinsey's (1948) to Masters and Johnson's (1966) or Hite's (1976, 1981) have suggested that for both men and women, though particularly for men, a healthy history of masturbation to orgasm, self-exploration, and either homo- or hetero-erotic pubescent sexplay prepare the way for more fully realized heterosexual encounters later in adolescence. A prior personal knowledge of orgasm—or at least the male's of ejaculation—alone or in the company of another person facilitates the sensual and interpersonal refinement of what otherwise eludes consciousness as the mere discharge of tensions. Some individuals need to learn about sexuality in less charged experimental sex before concentrating their energies on true love. Others, in the manner of Juliet, can rush virginally into their first lover's arms and adapt to their own and the other's desires.

Sex differences again come into play here. In the Hite surveys, 99 percent of men masturbated in contrast to 82 percent of women. The adolescent boy needs to overcome his castration anxiety, repetitively assuring himself of his bodily integrity in the wake of orgasm. He must masturbate. In contrast, teenaged girls more often find themselves constrained by inhibitions—by the male-imposed myths and restrictions attaching until recently to female sexuality. Often it is only after her first intercourse that a young woman will feel free to pleasure herself, an activity in which she may reclaim her vagina as her own.

For love to pass beyond narcissistically impelled infatuation to a more wholehearted form of idealization, the lover must have cultivated the ability for devotion to another person. In analytic jargon, object constancy—the ability to sustain the object's integrated image in its absence or during states of ambivalence (Fraiberg, 1969)—must be secured early on. Indeed, it must be well enough in place to weather the revival of quasi-symbiotic trends during orgasm and at other moments in loving. So the lover must have had a satisfactory phase-specific symbiosis and separation-individuation (Mahler et al., 1975) along with the periods in infancy described by Stern (1985) during which objects apart from the self are perceived as having their own contours and life—periods described by Wolff (1965) as intervals of alert inactivity.

In fact, however, the romantic lover must have passed well beyond these early stages in the evolution of object relations—subsequent milestones overlooked by most analysts writing on the subject. Early on, by conversing "to" them, mothers help toddlers begin to talk about their feelings. These interchanges provide the basis for friendships in later childhood, when the child learns how to find gratification simply in making himself known and in knowing another person as best he can—knowing more and more about details of that person's life and identifying with these particulars. The onrush of the drives in adolescence further infuse these friendships—cutting across the genders now—with intensity, urgency, a sense of priority. The capacity for friendship is, then, another developmental precondition for love.

A capacity for love also requires a certain level of intellectual development. All lovers aspire to the music of immortal souls beyond the "muddy vesture of decay," as Lorenzo muses to Jessica in Shakespeare's *Merchant of Venice*. Groping for words to communicate feeling to the other, all are poets. Granting poetic license, love requires a capacity for metaphor, in which all manner of emotional longings find satisfaction in a sexual union with the beloved, which, in its turn, takes on spiritual meanings, which, in their turn, the lover tries to articulate. The capacity for concrete sensual pleasure must be there but, with it, the ability to dwell on the illusions of mystical union accompanying eroticism. When the one order of feeling—concrete sensation or spiritual questing—predominates to the exclusion of the other, the value of the real person of the beloved suffers, and love can founder. Young men who are afraid of feeling or who lack the language to express it, adhering to the ideal of a "man of few words," may find themselves bereft.

Thus, from the cognitive point of view as from that of the drives, it follows that romantic love is a late adolescent phenomenon. Impossible

urges to reunite with the mother in toddlerhood, unrequited incestuous yearnings later on, fantasy and unfulfilled onanistic preoccupations, prepare the way for love's imaginative aspirations and inevitable
deprivations. Still, representational thought, symbolic communication,
and an interest in the world are rudimentary prerequisites. Beyond this,
it is formal operations and the inclination to proceed beyond immediate sensation by making the most of it—the proclivity to think about
thinking (Inhelder and Piaget, 1958) and feeling—which provide the
epistemological backdrop for the exaltations of the romantic lover.

Falling in love also gives expression to the turmoil of late adolescence
and young adulthood. With this come certain developmental consequences. Perhaps most important in terms of psychic structure, passionate love demands a moral or ethical accommodation—a reorganization of the superego so that it can countenance forbidden wishes as
well as feeling states. The discovery of the need to be loved and to love
erotically makes us more tolerant and more aware of ourselves and
others. In the next chapter I shall explore the moral individuation that
derives specifically from dislocations of the tie to the father and of the
ego ideal which are set in motion when a man falls in love with a
woman for the first time.

Finally, not all loves are revivals and not all lovers are "revenants."
They are also irreducible—new people, unique. They bring distinct
personal histories, teach new knowledge, expand experience in unex-
pected ways. The lover must be prepared, sure enough of his or her
own psychosocial identity, to take them in.

Why for so many individuals romantic love does not often survive
late adolescence is another question. At no time thereafter does a
responsible individual have the leisure and energy to expend on love,
so pressing are the demands of what the Hindus call the householder
phase of life. We tend to become more pragmatic and concrete in our
thinking as we get older, less inclined to the metaphoric abstractions
of the lover. Yet, emotionally and perhaps biologically, we need our
passion, to defend against life's stresses. So we are at least episodically
moved to create conditions within or outside a marriage for its expression. In midlife, loving makes one young again.

In this chapter, I have attempted to conceptualize passionate love from
a psychoanalytic perspective. Having noted psychoanalysis' longstand-
ing reluctance to confront adult love, I have turned elsewhere for more

detailed descriptions of its phenomenology. With these in mind, such love can be defined as a complex and somewhat conflictual affective disposition, rather like a mood, evoked by the image of another person and characterized by periods of passionate excitement and intimate repose.

A variety of both pleasurable and unpleasurable affects are entertained in romantic love, which derive from its both sensory and illusory wellsprings, from the opportunities it affords for sensual satisfaction and spiritual overreaching. These affects are activated in response to states of desire and satiety and as modes of communication with and knowledge of the other. They are accompanied and facilitated by the capacity for genital primacy and cognitive components in love—specifically the lover's capacity to express himself or herself in genital orgasm and then to create and dwell in metaphors about the lover's sexual encounters. Whatever its infantile precursors and however regressive it can be at times, love emerges perforce as a late adolescent or young adult phenomenon.

At this juncture, the prepotency of romantic love moves the individual to disengage from the injunctions and desexualized idealizations of his parental images and to reorganize the superego constructs based on these—to create his or her own ethic. Thus, while there may be other routes to maturity, embracing the feeling of being in love with a woman helps a man grow up. Just how this may occur is the subject of the final pages of *What Men Want.*

9

The Uses of Love

In the last chapter I constructed a psychoanalytic explication of passionate love. I suggested that falling in love is a phenomenon seen only with adolescent development. Erotic desire and romantic sentiment require the maturation of genital sexuality, along with the cognitive capacity to contemplate the reality of one's self and one's lover. It is these developmental achievements that permit the lover to perceive the spiritual implications of erotic union with and disengagements from the beloved. In other words, only with the substantial evolution of his sense of sexual and ego identity is a young man prepared to immerse himself in the sensual and metaphorical intensities that are the lover's lot.

The relatively pure culture of formal operations, the teenager's erotic urgency, and the nature of the adolescent passage as a "psychosocial moratorium" afford and indeed demand the leisure necessary for such reflection. And it is this—the obligatory hesitancy on the threshold of adulthood, the self-consciousness that attends a young man's coming of age—that makes romance a quintessential experience of youth.

The feeling of first love may be revived later in life, rekindled in second honeymoons or second adolescences. Indeed, some people only fall in love in midlife after their parents' deaths have freed them from the grip of incestuous conflicts. But if a man fails to fall in love before consolidating his adult work identity, it seems that he has not truly lived his young life. Something is bound to be missing—maybe not irretrievably, but missing for the time being.

Just what the lack might be was a question that remained to be answered. It is one that I will now approach with some thoughts on the finishing off of a man's manhood before he assumes his adult status as a worker, provider and caretaker for the next generation. Having articulated the developmental preconditions for a man's love of a woman, I will now try to identify the developmental or, better, adaptational consequences of a full-fledged erotic and romantic relationship.

When Love Fades

Consider Mr. V once again, the patient described earlier. Not all love stories have happy endings. But the truisms can be true. For a young man like V, it is better to have loved and lost than never to have loved at all.

Rachel's and V's passion eventually wilted over time in the harsh daylight of workaday life. V had been drawn to Rachel because she was beautiful and surprising. Funny and loving, she excited the poet in him. But there was also something more familiar about her. For all the discovery, abandon, and ribaldry, Rachel shared his and his father's love of money and the things it could buy. Herein lay their undoing. As time went on, R's monetary and other mundane demands of V grew, along with her disappointment in him. His analysis diminished their material resources, and his allegiance to it irked her. Promising future provider that he was, he was just beginning his professional life. V lacked the funds and, less tangibly, the confidence of, for instance, Rachel's older brother, with whom she "always had a special thing." And his bouts of diffidence and remoteness got on her nerves.

Rachel was herself none too satisfied with her own mediocre entry-level job. She tended, as some do, to take out her narcissistic frustrations on the person closest to her. Besides, V's own self-absorption and ambition made him an inconsistent listener, especially as they began to take each other more for granted. Then there were the envious friends all too ready to drink in, with disingenuous ears, Rachel's faultfinding in the man who had swept her away from everything, including them. These self-interested listeners were her alternatives to analysis, which she did not believe in anyway.

Aggression, as Otto Kernberg has put it (1991), began to win out over love in the relationship of the couple. Its sources lay in the childhood attachments and conflicts of both partners, in the envy and backbiting of the social group, and in their own increasing needs to guard the territory of their besieged selves. If Rachel had been just a little bit "better," less like V or his father in their crasser materialism, perhaps she could have affected her lover with her generosity and affection. If they had been able to sustain the lovers' quest for the "mutual transcendence" of which Kernberg speaks elsewhere, they might have been able to secure their love from the force of their inevitable narcissism and sadism. As it was, they were moved to protect themselves through escalating acts of cruelty. Individual self-interestedness undid what Martin Bergmann calls the joint "narcissism of the couple" and tore the envelope of their relationship.

Because V was in analysis, expensive though it might be both financially and emotionally, he had greater opportunity to reconsider his angry flights from love into himself. As his analysis progressed, he could admit a wrong and take action to correct his course. Rachel was not so lucky or so inclined. Acknowledging an error was usually seen as a fatal flaw, about which she could do nothing. Or it was felt as a crushing blow and enraged her. Fearful of owning her own aggression, she projected it. Rachel became vigilant for the smallest slight on V's part. As she badgered V for "more," more of everything, he withdrew. Stung by the habitual diffidence with which this particular young man greeted demands that he could not or would not meet, like his bosses before her, she also eventually "fired" him. Rachel broke off the relationship and a year later married a richer and slightly older man. Less soulful than V, the latter remonstrated to his analyst, this good-time Charlie not only had Rachel but also owned the very same shiny black Volvo station wagon that V had himself long coveted.

Thus V's erotic questings and his potential moral revolution foundered short of victory. Rejected, mourning his first love in the aftermath of their passion, the patient wondered what he had gained from that passion, which he had tasted and then lost. Reverting to some of his old ways, womanizing a little for a while, hurting a few women in the process, and making more money, nonetheless he recognized that he had "opened myself up—but to somebody just a little bit like me, the money-minded me . . . Still I feel more for women now, use them less and I don't need to conceal myself quite so much. I want to be known and to know without prying." Despite the cost in loss and

loneliness, V would never again settle for conquest. He wanted more—
to feel more, to care, to "take in."

The next lover with whom V settled in was sweet and sexy—his
"other self." Easing into life with her as the termination of the analysis
approached, he found himself gentled and, oddly he thought, thinking
not about himself or her, for that matter, but "about being a couple."

Their fate—what would happen to their love and where Mr. V would
end up on his ethical trajectory without father or analyst to propel
him—were matters about which the analyst would never know. In all
events, the revolution in process, if not exactly silent, was a quiet one.

First Loves and the Morality of Childhood

Why are the strains of love so consuming? Why is it that the young
lover will expend so much time and energy on his amorous yearnings
and their objects? What is he searching for? Mesmerizing and exhila-
rating, love at this point in life is also scary. It can be so disconcerting,
in fact, that it moved one teenaged patient of mine, Eddie, to exclaim
to his first love on a moonlit hillside: "You're so beautiful you should
put a paper bag over your head!"

Not only did this boy retreat from the specter of incest in the
prospect of sex. He also sensed that in finding his beloved he had
reached a point of no return in his developmental journey. Love in
real life was luring him from the safer directives of childhood. It was
bringing him face to face with the carnal, ambiguous, complex, unprotected, and lonely choices made by an adult. Loving this girl, Eddie
intimated to himself, he would never be the same. She too would
change, especially in the heat of their desire. He would awaken her.
His growing sense of what is sensual in women, of their desires, also
gave him pause, toppling other defensive illusions left over from his
postoedipal boyhood. But still Eddie sensed that, as a man, he would
be transformed in some even more elemental way. He would be
changed by the one he loved.

For many years, listening to adolescent and young adult male patients like Eddie—on the brink, in the throes or in the aftermath of
passionate love—I had the anecdotal sense that, successful or not, such
an experience served to mellow them. Where love had been missing
from a young man's life, he remained somehow callow, rigid, intolerant

of lapses and longings in himself and others. These impressions were different from others that seized my attention. They did not have the same force as a women's need for male admirers, for instance, or the threat of emasculation when a man first falls in love or a father's filicidal impulses (themes I have dealt with in previous chapters). And it was only after I had thought more about the nature of the psychological process in passionate love that I could begin to isolate some of the subtle characterological transformations that had taken place.

The timing is variable, ranging from the late teens to the late twenties, from the conclusion of secondary education to the close of a professional apprenticeship. But at some point in their schooling for adult life, most young men put aside their work ambitions for a time. They prepare, if not to take a mate, at least to "know" and to love a woman. They are primed for love. But they arrive at its threshold with many unresolved infantile conflicts and with different and incomplete character structures. These limitations will determine a young man's ability to accommodate to the challenges posed by passionate feeling and intimacy.

Obviously the ability to fall in love with a woman requires that men have some control over more deep-seated ambivalence toward their mothers. The capacity to love any woman is dependent on introjections of good-enough oedipal as well as preoedipal mothers.

With V, for instance, the fear of seduction and engulfment, of ultimately painful overstimulation by a woman, induced him to pull back from Rachel. In the heat of desire, he tended to reduce her whole person to its sexual components, which, in rather fancy metaphorical terms, he could set in relief, contain, and manage. In his case it was not so much guilt that deterred him. A more narcissistic fear of feeling led V to position himself as an observer of the other and to see her as the sum of her parts. Enjoying his poetry of the body at first, flattered in being so admired, Rachel, like any woman who has real-life agenda and complex needs, came to resent her objectification at V's hands.

Most noteworthy for my purposes, however, are the variabilities discernible in the content and structure of existing ego ideals in men who already trust and desire women enough to love them. The surface possibilities range from the frank narcissism of the more nakedly self-serving opportunist (for whom self-fulfillment is the highest good), to the somewhat more impersonal goal-directedness of the achiever, to the prudery and crankiness of the more duty-bound, ascetic, and pathologically self-abnegating adolescent.

On this note I will turn to Eddie in greater detail. Referred by his father, an analyst, Eddie had come to intensive psychotherapy to contend with the symptom neurosis that compromised his enjoyment of his academic abilities and achievements. Particularly troubling were his performance anxiety when he had to stand up and hold forth before a crowd; his guilt and shame over frequent masturbation to masochistic/exhibitionistic fantasies (mostly of public humiliation at the hands of a powerful woman with other women looking on); and his shyness with real girls.

Eddie was reluctant to deface a pure love or succumb to "lust," as he put it. More moralistically than V, he too sought to attenuate women's power over him. He needed to stay responsible and good and to fulfill what his father wanted for him—academic excellence and community service. Hence the "paper bag."

At first glance, Eddie's moral excesses stand in contrast to V's deficiencies. Yet deep down the two were soulmates. Self-avowed "prince," even V unconsciously saw himself as his Machiavellian father's dutiful subject. His most narcissistic defenses also served to maintain him in a position of inner and secret surrender to him. (V's major transference organizer early on had been a wish to devour his analyst's penis and testicles and, in the process, to pay homage to the analyst's phallic power.) For the deferential Eddie and the self-serving V, their conscience and ideals were not yet their own. On the brink of love, both Eddie and V found themselves submitting to the representation of a patriarchic father.

Nor, for that matter, was the altruistic Eddie any less self-aggrandizing in his innermost heart of hearts than V. Self-styled martyr, paragon of renunciation, teenaged Eddie was, by his own unfolding admission, trying to be good so that he might be great. Although proud to be a Jew, he confessed that he had always harbored "a Jesus Christ fantasy." Eddie strove to sacrifice for the good of others in ways that everyone could see. His Lord and Father would send him to his martyrdom. And this homosexual surrender proved to be the basic scenario underlying

his conscious masturbation fantasy, one in which his father was disguised, predictably, as a phallic woman. Yet in the process of being
martyred—naked, abject, penetrated yet serene—Eddie would also be
admired by both the madonnas and the whores of the land. He would
even gain the upper hand in the competition with his peers, who were
more crude and less proper than he. Women would favor him because
he was so good and thus better than most men. In this wishful self-
image, Eddie revealed the paradoxical unconscious fantasy behind the
morality of most unfinished young men, whatever the variety of surface
configurations this fantasy might assume. Surrender to the dictates of
God the Father, abjure the tender flesh, spurn women, and the sky's
the limit.

Virtue is sometimes rewarded. Young Eddie proved to be luckier in
life than V. Or perhaps his basic character moved him to make better
choices.

Beth, his first love and the lady of the paper bag, was two years older.
Already in college as he concluded his senior year in high school, she
was hardly the innocent virgin he had once thought her—and all good
girls—to be. When Eddie at last gave in to this delightful girl's demands—that, yes, he "use" her for his pleasure—he found himself
enveloped in a veritable world of sex. Beth welcomed Eddie's caresses
with the ferocity and grace of those sex goddesses he had only read
about. She seemed to love every part of him. In so loving, she demonstrated that nothing was bad about the body or its wants. Indeed,
carrying care into the bedroom, Beth taught him that "what matters
most is how people feel, that they feel good, feel loved . . . not what's
right, necessarily, but what's good. And feeling good isn't being bad."

Confounding subject and object as lovers are apt to do, Eddie
continued: "Apropos of that Christ image, I've found another voice of
authority besides 'God, My Father.' I guess what I want now, to be
now too, er, uh . . . isn't the Virgin Mary but Mary Magdalen . . . Not
to be innocent or upright, but to know life, to love life and be merci-
ful—even to myself." With some trepidation he then revealed how his
masturbation fantasy, invoked mostly during Beth's absences, had
changed. In this version Eddie was able to turn the tables on his
tormentor and indulge a bolder exhibitionism. Clad in almost nothing,
the bulge of his phallus evident but still mysterious, he would beat her
up and start to take her, to the delight of the women looking on. Now

and then he placed Beth among them—Beth, admiring him in his imagination as she did his body in the flesh.

Male Morals and Feminine Ethics

In order to understand more of the mysteries of first love, I will draw from Peter Blos's commentaries on the relationships of sons and fathers and the formation of the ego ideal and on Edith Jacobson's contributions to the theory of the superego. Then I will turn to the work of Nancy Chodorow and Carol Gilligan on women and moral development.

Blos has provided a superb overview of the ontogeny of the ego ideal in "The Genealogy of the Ego Ideal" (1974). In this essay he summarizes the intellectual history of the concept, from Freud's initial equation of the ego ideal with a Kohutian-like grandiose self to our current appreciation of this system as a more internal and sublimated set of what have become relatively impersonal values and autonomous guidelines. The ego ideal has its origins in primitive self-aggrandizement and, as Freud initially remarked, in certain primal homosexual ties to the father. And it must undergo successively more complex transformations en route to its status as an agency devoted to what is good in life. According to Blos, the process extends into late adolescence.

In her classic *Self and the Object World* (1964), Jacobson suggests that the developing ego ideal draws on long-standing selective identifications with idealized caretakers as well as on wishful self-images. This value system conjoins with the critical faculty, which is derived from both parental injunctions and aggressive impulses turned on the self. Together they form the agency of superego. Energized by self-love and self-hatred alike, the superego becomes an integrated functional system that provides directives and injunctions and metes out internal rewards as well as punishments. Only with adolescence does the ego ideal disengage to some degree from the more primitive and reflexive structure of the superego. At this point it begins to approach the rational, realistic, discretionary capacities that theorists call "ego functions."

What Blos and Jacobson construe is a progression from a primitive system of self-aggrandizement, punitive moralizing, the search for approval, and unprocessed parental edicts to individualized ethical principles of conduct, which can accommodate the needs and desires of both oneself and others. Though they may not consider explicitly the crucible in which the final transformation takes place (romantic love, in my view), both writers conclude that it is only with late adolescence that the process comes to completion.

These notions proceed beyond Freud's phallocentric view of moral development. In perspective, this development is concluded at six years of age with the male sex leading the way. Freud invited the lasting enmity of the women's movement when he asserted that, as a consequence of their disparate oedipal passages, girls were possessed of a superego that was "never so inexorable, so impersonal, so independent of its emotional origins as we require it to be in men . . . They show less sense of justice than men, they are less ready to submit to the great exigencies of life . . . they are more often influenced in their judgments by feelings of affection or hostility" (1925:257). No one, Freud averred, could fail to remark on women's ethical inferiority.

Underlying Freud's formulation was his stress on castration. A girl, he said, seeks to compensate for "the fact of being castrated" by seeking her father and his penis as substitutes for the missing member. She will do almost anything to attract and hold onto the men in whom those objects come to be personified. In contrast, a boy identifies with his castrating father to circumvent his rage and revenge and to escape the girl's fate. Morally malleable, a woman becomes as putty in a man's hands. In Freud's view, guilt, the highest in the hierarchy of inhibiting dangers, is derived from castration anxiety, one notch lower on the list but still higher than the dangers of losing the object and its love, which are a woman's greatest (and her more infantile) fears. The superego evolves, he implied, from what Anna Freud would later term an identification with the aggressor (1936).

Jacobson also stressed a little girl's penis envy, her feelings of inferiority and fear of mortification. But she saw in this sense of shame a spur to precocious development rather than a source of inadequacy. Because she is forced to struggle with her genital disappointment, the girl must seek redress in the construction of a precocious ego ideal. She repudiates her sexual feelings and genital impulses. Far from being morally deficient, the corruptible wanton of the clever seducer, as Freud believed, a girl is initially more prudish by nature than her male counterpart. Stifling her sensuality, she strives to be good, clean, ascetic—attributes she equates with being feminine. That is, until the upheavals of adolescence awaken a young woman's erotic desires and demand further accommodations on the part of her asexual ideal. Altering psychoanalytic assumptions about sex differences in superego development, Jacobson simultaneously extended this process to include periods preceding and following the oedipal phase.

But there is still more to the story. In Jacobson's as in Blos's scheme, the impact of the one sex upon the other in directly influencing their value systems is not addressed. Indeed, the coming together in adolescence of boy and girl as sexual man and woman is not even touched on. Real sex and true love, so often neglected by psychoanalysts, are missing once again from their developmental overviews.

In this regard, a comment of Freud's is intriguing. In the same paragraph in which he lays his claim to male moral superiority, Freud goes on to assert that "all human individuals, as a result of their bisexual disposition, combine in themselves both masculine and feminine characteristics, so that pure masculinity and femininity remain theoretical constructions of uncertain content" (1925:258). To be sure, he says this by way of apology for the fact that many men fail to live up to the ideal superego he has posited for them. Yet a further implication may be that men and women can learn to take from one another. They can instruct one another on how to behave, on what is right and what wrong, on what to condemn and what to forgive—and these both in others and in oneself.

The basic ethical assumption of the Freudian worldview follows from its amalgamation of Protestant individualism and the absolutism of Jewish law. It holds that adherence to unyielding principles as categorical imperatives represents the sine qua non of moral integrity. Autonomy in one's devotion to justice at all costs is the supreme virtue, the highest of moral accomplishments.

In surveying cognitive development, Piaget also asserted male moral supremacy. He underscored the preoccupation with "rules of the game" which is observable in boys as they begin to advance intellectually. Men's concern with what is legal is more typical of their sex. This orientation represents a greater "decentering" and potential impartiality than the pragmatic and subjective perspective of the girl in rendering judgments or dealing with others. In fact, Piaget hardly considered girls' values at all, save for an aside here and there. In his as in Freud's views, they are treated as exceptions to the rule (Piaget, 1932).

Thus a distinctly paternalistic bias underlies many of psychology's as well as psychoanalysis's assumptions about what is most mature in people. And these notions have come into question as increasing numbers of women have risen to prominence in these fields. Above all, it was Nancy Chodorow and Carol Gilligan who legitimized empathy and personal flexibility and who linked these qualities to a distinctly female interpretation of human relations. A woman's ethical perspective, they aver (Gilligan especially), is different but probably no less "developed" than the attainment of those unwavering moral precepts that ideally guide a man's choices in life.

Sociologist that she is, Chodorow has a teleological slant on sex differences. Women are responsible for childcare, and this social function, more than their anatomy, mandates certain persistent feminine characteristics and values. Females define themselves in relation to other people more than males do. A girl's gender identity is the repository of the ongoing, mutual identifications of mother and daughter— who are, after all, more alike than different, certainly with regard to their sex. Boys define themselves simultaneously both as male and as separate from the mother. They assert their gender role at the expense of "their primary love and sense of empathic tie." As psychoanalysts including myself have also suggested, acting different tends to mean being male. Whereas maleness is defined through individuation, femaleness takes form in a state of attachment. Proximity and then intimacy threaten masculinity whereas femininity is imperiled by separation and solitude.

Thus Chodorow posits that empathy is inherent in the feminine definition of self. Because they are more porous and elastic, a woman's ego boundaries are not perforce weaker than a man's. Her mother's daughter, herself prewired for symbiosis with her own baby, a woman experiences herself as continuous with her objects. She can embrace another's needs and feelings as her own and regress to "preoedipal relational modes" without threatening her selfhood.

A woman's social embeddedness is a potential liability. Development itself, defined as a process of increasing individuation, challenges her sexual as well as her self-identity. The temptation to slip back into the comfort of known attachments is ever present and, with it, the potential for arrest, regression, and oppression. Whereas the emotional flooding of romantic love threatens to engulf a man's sense of independence and to wash away his manhood, it is the prospect of loss that gives his female partner pause. Giving up her ties to her family of origin—and to her mother most of all—in giving herself to a man, a woman then risks losing him as well.

Gilligan takes a rather more sanguine view of what is feminine in a woman's values than Chodorow does. She points to the adaptational strength inherent in a woman's more "relational" attitude toward life. It is true that her sensitivity to others can compromise a woman's sense of personal conviction and integrity. But she also brings to interpersonal conflicts a capacity for care that helps modulate the "hurt" that can occur in adhering strictly to principle. Drawing on Erikson's notion of ego virtues, Gilligan thus offers an implicit challenge to the sequence of moral stages postulated by Lawrence Kohlberg as well as those schematized by Piaget and Loevinger—all of which stress a progression toward autonomy and abstraction: "Recognizing the dual contexts of justice and care, [women] realize that judgment depends on the way in which the problem is framed" (1982:167).

This residue of personal relativism allows women to temper the "morality of rights," which assumes equality, with an "ethic of responsibility," which is cognizant of differences in individual needs. Women demonstrate concern for other people's real feelings as well as for their hypothetical prerogatives. Because of this, they can better approximate the ideal of generosity, which, Piaget himself asserted, may represent the most advanced moral stage of all. Ultimately, though she also omits the transactions between the sexes that bring characterstics of one to the other, Gilligan takes a longer-range view on ethical development than any before her:

> From the different dynamics of separation and attachment in their gender identity formation through the divergence of identity and intimacy that marks their experience in their adolescent years, male and female voices typically speak of the importance of different truths, the former of the role of separation as it defines and empowers the self, the latter of the ongoing process of attachment that creates and sustains the human community. (156)

Chodorow's and Gilligan's notions are subject to many caveats—some raised by feminists, others by psychoanalysis. Despite questions about its generalizability, however, the work of Gilligan and Chodorow succeeds in positing a dialectic in the juxtaposition of male and female moral inclinations. As their bodies and souls interpenetrate, a young man and woman—at least today, in America—may also come to identify with the values, ideals, and injunctions of each other. By reviving his earliest union with his mother, a woman as lover and intimate also offers herself to a man as a subject for moral identification. She may reawaken his capacities for empathy and immersion and help him to become more of a "people person." But just how might this internal change take place?

The Sea Change

In mythic love stories, battles, and feuds, "kinsman's swords" punctuate the romantic absorption of lovers like Tristan, Romeo, and Islam's Majnun. Yet the lover-hero, like the patients Eddie or V, does not simply defy the paternal prerogative, the patron's dominion over all women of the land, *le droit du seigneur*. His is not merely a transgression, symbolic or blatant, of the positive oedipal taboo. It is also a betrayal of the heart, his and his father's heart.

In these tales—unlike the stories of sons like Moses or Christ who abjure the flesh to become patriarchs in their own right—fathers and sons lament their shared loss. They agonize about the chilly nakedness that comes when sons forsake their comradeship and ungird their loins to make love to a woman. Seen metaphorically, such exchanges serve to externalize and thereby to portray a snapping of the intrapsychic ties of the long-lasting negative oedipal constellation or, in Blos's terms, simply the young man's "negative complex": his abiding love, oedipal and otherwise, for his tender father. The adolescent's longing to retain or restore this "isogender" attachment, Blos continues, perhaps more than any preoedipal or incestuous tie to the mother, may be the major precipitant in adult neurosis. This late fixation must be overcome if a man is to "become *his own* man."

Nor is this a simple task. By this late point in development, the representation of the father has become a layered construction that conceals many hidden features and serves a variety of functions. These are exposed once again in adult love, which, like any intense transference-influenced phenomenon, reopens a man's psyche. As with the transference neurosis, so with love-passions melt psychic structures.

They thaw and dissolve into the volatile relational dynamisms that they were originally.

Like the identity crisis, which in Erikson's scheme typically precedes the age of intimacy, falling in love makes for another recapitulatory regression and, to some degree, a reworking of solutions to preoedipal and oedipal conflicts. To borrow from Freud's 1926 speculations, the oscillating orgasmic passions and genuine compunctions of this phase may very well be "sucked back," as it were, into the unconscious. The passionate encounters of late adolescence and young adulthood may even add to the cast of characters from childhood fantasy. They certainly expose those already in existence for what they really are.

Losing the reassurance of fatherly presence, a representation that has been introjected but not fully integrated as one's own, means not only finding a mother in a new woman but losing this mother as well. For one thing, an incestuous mother—to the extent that she is reincarnated in the adult lover—has forsaken her role as nurturer and guardian against the drives. (Hence Eddie's initial hesitation.)

More to the point here, in fantasy the provident father's is a beckoning love. He promises rescue and redemption. He invites a boy from the cradle first into the world of manly initiative, but then on toward the grave (as in *Oedipus at Colonnus*). There at last the illusion of some hovering paternal welcome, of "God the Father," is summoned to discharge the wanderer of the very responsibilities that this insistent paternal authority has enjoined him to assume in the first place.

Thus the representation of a fatherly protector offers throughout development to take over for the mother of infancy while safeguarding the selfhood and (for the male) the masculinity that her abiding allure threatens to undo. The image of the protective father is a "compromise formation" that has been formed in the face of intrasystemic conflicts set in motion by progressive and regressive tensions. In other words, subject to preoedipal maternal transferences, the postoedipal father representation has simultaneously become, of all things, a disguised source of ongoing anaclitic reassurance. To give this father up, as in passionate heterosexual love, may mean to abandon all hope.

Falling in love imperils a man's ideals, which apparently offer sustenance of a higher order. Falling for a woman challenges the young man's existing ego ideal, which is still closely modeled after a man's idealized images of his father and on which a young man has come to depend for a sense of inspiration, well-being, and purpose.

The father's spoken word has long been introjected as the voice of conscience. His injunctions have been internalized and transfigured as the critical faculty, which is heir to a father's prohibitions and demands and the son's identifications with him in that disciplinary role. Whatever the early maternal prohibitions that entered into the construction of a man's superego, and thereafter remain silent within it, with the laying down of the personality's tripartite structure, conscience assumes a distinctly male tone. It speaks to a man in a deep voice, simultaneously admonishing him and awakening his consciousness (to borrow from Lewin). Telling him what and what not to do, its forcefulness and direction move him to move on, away from the mother, and thus to reassure himself that he is a man.

To love romantically and erotically is to opt for less conventional and reliable personas, values, actions, and states of mind. Far from comfortably affirming existing superego functions (including ideals and prohibitions), as some analysts would have it, to love deeply is, at least for a time, to replace paternal idealizations with those more maternal and frankly libidinal in origin and nature—sexier, forbidden, but no less sublime.

The idealization of a woman beloved calls upon the magic of the forbidden oedipal and the omnipotent preoedipal mother. The glorification of a woman originates in the preverbal or sensorimotor unconscious and in the oral and symbiotic precursors of sexual love. Thus a man's sexual love for a woman, even at her most idealized, is inevitably disorganizing. It promises less in the way of moral and social direction than his devotion to his father and the orienting principles associated with him.

Heterosexual passion plays havoc with self-esteem. Erotic love requires that the lover pay homage to Aphrodite after all. It demands that he forsake his duties and that he accept what is instinctual in himself. It grants him a measure of personal knowledge of his own creation in the secretions of the primal scene.

At the same time, these idealizations and the aspirations to which they give rise, primitive as their sources are, are impelled more by libido than by aggression, suffused with love more than hate. As a young man's capacity for love deepens, so does that of his superego. "The loving and beloved superego" begins to hold sway over the hates and condemnations of the critical faculty. Tempering the castrating moralisms of his critical faculty, he gradually becomes easier on himself. He becomes less morally sadistic with both himself and others.

To refer again to Blos's work, the ego ideal and critical faculty have to be essentially in place (partly internalized) if a teenager or young man is to undertake the risks involved in any such inquiry into the heart. Love does require compunction and care for the other, implicit values beyond the ken of the sociopath or crude narcissist. But passionate love carries a man beyond known moral expectations, and these "amoral" transports and emotional adventures are an intrinsic part of the mood itself.

Let me put this another way. In the language of the French neoclassicists, a sense of honor must exist in the first place if it is to be defied by passion. The lover must have a cherished father representation and, more impersonally, a superego to be forsaken. Yet romantic love is neither filial nor initially high-minded in itself, and the synthesis does not come so readily as some former notions would have it. For a man to love a woman means to overthrow God, king, father, and, at the postoedipal and internal level, many of the strictures of his existing superego. And this upheaval makes his ego functioning vulnerable to a rush of instinctual and external excitations, pressures that he now has the cognitive and ethical wherewithal to observe and, at times, lament.

Lost to his own inner lights and thrown into the sort of dynamic disequilibrium that characterizes any developmental challenge, the young lover must find the means to assimilate and then to accommodate to his new experience with the world of love. At first he regresses in part to those earliest modes of relatedness in which identification with and attachment to the object occur simultaneously. Bereft of his patriarchic father, he finds himself emulating the mother reincarnated in his lover. So a young man takes in her female sexuality as, at a more differentiated level, he comes to embrace her personal and ultimately her moral style.

In the psychic loosening that comes with heterosexual surrender, paternal transferences, superego projections, and narcissistic transferences are directed at the person of the woman beloved. Like Romeo, the lover now finds his self-esteem in her eye, in her "look[ing] but soft on him." The "peril of her eye," the lover's disapproval and potential rejection, becomes his greatest fear.

Over time, he invests his heterosexual partner with his oedipal father's erstwhile authority. If this transferential transformation proceeds too far, the process can go awry. It can squelch a man's desire for a woman who has become at once a prohibitor, an aim-inhibitor, and a homosexual object—a father in disguise. (This is one reason why even the most powerful men invest their wives with such power, deferring to them in domestic and other personal matters while desexualizing them as women.) Up to a point, however, the projection of the ego ideal onto the beloved prompts a young man actively to assimilate his lover's specifically feminine values.

It is his assimilation of a woman's whole aura, ethical and otherwise, that leads to a further accommodation—to the sort of autoplastic change that is the hallmark of internalization. Already embedded in her womanly matrix, partly regressed and thus "imprinted" to her, the male lover identifies with the female beloved's acceptance of embeddedness itself. Interpersonally attuned, he can then embrace her ethic of care, altering his self-ideals and self-representation accordingly. Back in the arms of a woman, but no longer a naked babe without powers of discernment and selective identification, he begins to entertain and experiment with her feminine modes of making judgments.

When the relationship ends, as most first loves do, or when it simply becomes more discontinuous (as Kernberg notes) and he must separate from her now and then, this man carries his womanly lover within him. In dialogues of one, he converses with her in "a different voice" about the revelations that their love has brought. And so her voice begins to mute the more patriarchal voice of conscience, which their passion had silenced altogether for awhile.

What love brings, then, is an ethical accommodation and further individuation—a reorganization of the ego ideal and critical faculty so that conscience can countenance and even value hitherto forbidden wishes and feelings in oneself and in others. More receptive now, the young man gradually comprehends, accepts, and identifies with the desires and priorities, often more easily eroticized and personalized, of the woman he loves. He may also come to offset his seemingly abstract but secretly self-serving principles of justice with a more feminine code of conduct—interpersonal, forgiving, compassionate. Without realizing it, he has selectively identified with the ethic of care that once secured his own mother's ministrations.

A youthful lover thereby disengages from his parents' more obvious edicts and injunctions. His rigid moralisms can now give way to a more flexible ethical system. The discovery of love in himself and of a goodness beyond morality gentles a man's conscience, making him more aware and tolerant of himself and others. And this expansion of the self and of his sexual and moral boundaries helps to prepare the way for the tolerance required by the challenges that lie ahead in life. More relaxed and receptive, the man who has been a lover will better handle the pressures of work and the transactional compromises it requires as well as the demands of fatherhood. In Erikson's words, he has replaced "the morality of childhood with the ethics of the adult."

The characterological consolidation and individuation as described by Blos, Jacobson, Erikson, and Gilligan ideally takes place only in late adolescence. I doubt that it can happen unless one has been a lover. Many people do not accomplish this when they are supposed to, of course. They may never fully develop as heterosexual men and women. Or, with luck, they may reserve for their middle years the passions that by all rights should belong to youth. Coincidentally, that is one reason why it is probably best to speak of adult adaptation rather than development. Our individual lives usually play havoc with our anticipation of orderly stages and sequences. It is never the way it is supposed to be.

A Modest Conclusion

In its infancy in the days of my intellectual apprenticeship and early research, the sexual revolution has progressed over the generational span reflected in this book. Gender stereotypes have fallen away in academic circles, toppling the myth of men's superiority and our culture's oversimplifications of the male condition. Under the sway of feminism, psychologists and psychoanalysts take it for granted now that males are no more active by nature than the complementary sex; that, envying women their womanhood, men have to contend with the feminine facets of their nature; and that the resolution of gender conflict is as essential to the development of masculinity as it is for the consolidation of femininity.

In another context, professionals have been made aware of the ever-present danger of child abuse and their legal responsibility to confront it. Analysts now routinely analyze not only parricidal but also infanticidal impulses in what Sandor Ferenczi called the "confusion of tongues between parent and child."

In the light of these developments I would like to raise a few questions before bringing this book to a close. First, just how divergent are men and women in terms of their wishes, capacities, favored perceptual and expressive modalities, values, and patterns of relatedness? Are gender differences any more remarkable and telling than the individual variations in these regards? Does it even make sense to write a book about *men,* men in general and in contrast to women?

Researchers and clinicians have changed their minds about gender differences many times over the years. They are forever contradicting themselves. Eleanor Maccoby finally concluded that the only definitive sex difference, from an exclusively empirical point of view, has to do with men's propensity to act aggressively. Other supposed divergences and dichotomies—such as the male's greater quantitative capacities in contrast to women's for verbal talent—have proved to be, if not exactly spurious, then at least relative.

In contrast, other developmentalists have stressed women's distinct feminine style, one rooted in their earliest experiences as little girls. Some have suggested that sex differences predate the baby's expulsion from the womb and are not byproducts of socialization alone. Studies of fetal androgenization have shown that male brains begin to unfold as such as a result of the introduction *in utero* of androgens. As "heredity goes on" and the sex hormones continue to emerge later in the life cycle, affecting physiology and anatomy, the biology of gender keeps on influencing the psychology of the individual. In this view, males and females are prewired to think and express themselves differently, and these predilections are observable in the clinical setting. As noted by practitioners sensitive to issues of gender, men and women emphasize sex-specific preoccupations and emotional imperatives in distinct ways.

As I reflect on these competing assertions as well as on my own work over the years, I have found myself becoming more of a historical, cultural, and developmental relativist than I would have thought possible a generation ago. These days, particular variants interest me as much as universals or ideals. Indeed, I find there are discernible sex-linked characteristics to be seen at any given moment in historical and life-historical time. Yet these take on different significance at different times.

For example, womb envy has proven to be no less a factor in the inner life of men than penis envy is in the psychology of women. Emerging from the unconscious of our adult patients in analysis, observable in children, both phenomena are undeniable. But in the days when women were constrained from participating actively in a misogynistic world, their oppression as adults made for an equation between being free and powerful and having the penis they once wanted. Their plight as adults made for a regressive revival and exaggeration of conflicts that might have been resolved years earlier or simply might have receded into the background of psychic life. For women, to be like men meant having more.

Men, in contrast, recoiled from their wish to be possessed of breasts, vaginas, and wombs, which connoted sinking into dependency, losing what they already had, and, in ceding their manly privileges, being castrated and disempowered. For men, to be like women meant having less. From a dynamic and defensive point of view, men simply repressed their androgyny and bisexuality more than women did.

In other cultures, for instance China or Tibet, where the Taoist and Tantric mysteries prevail, this was less the case. Ambisexuality and the search for the "eternal feminine" carried with it a sense of dignity and transcendence and represented a quest for power. And it is less true now—in the western world as well—in a society where both men and women work and find themselves on an increasingly equal footing. Ambition no longer means masculinization for successful women, at least not to the same degree as it did for their mothers. Nor do so-called feminine pursuits in men, such as primary childcare, mean abdicating one's masculine status.

Femininity and masculinity are dynamic constructs, in other words, not simply biological givens. They are defined in terms of what they mean consciously and unconsciously to the individual. And, like any dimension of the sense of one's identity, male and female definitions of oneself represent syntheses, as Erikson himself might have noted, of biological disposition and endowment; the identifications and compromises that come with growing up in one particular family environment; and the roles and ideals that are afforded and valued by the surrounding society at any given point in its history. Though there are universal fantasies and wishes in the unconscious, so that a figure such as Oedipus seizes our imagination as he did in Sophocles' day, the meaning of being a woman or a man is complex, contextual, and variable. Being a man now, in 1994, is thus different from what it was for our fathers.

And it will evolve further. Let us reconsider, for example, Maccoby's finding that aggressivity, defined as an aggregate of acts of "intrusive hostility," is a male characteristic. Once embracing this assertion as fact in my theorizing, as a clinician I have been forced to call it into question. In the consulting room, where imagination, thought, and verbalization replace action, it is simply not the case that women are any less hostile than men. Whatever they may do, women's ideation is no less aggressive in intent or form. In their more destructive thoughts and sometimes in their interpersonal dealings and manipulations, women are at least on a par with the so-called male animal. In fact, when it comes to the proverbial war between the sexes, the female partner often seems more likely to lash out directly—in word and deed—against her male counterpart than he against her. And however gentle they may be with their babies, mothers are certainly no less competitive with their blossoming teenaged daughters than men are with their virile young sons. Like men, after all, women do not want to grow old and die.

Although they may not have the same physical strength as males, females can act in less obvious ways to undermine others in the service of themselves. A man's greater aggressivity is a function or corollary of his greater physical power. In the past, in primitive and infrahuman societies, strong males were selected to serve certain gender-specific functions. They warded off predators and competitors, hunted and maintained equilibrating dominance hierarchies while females tended the young. However, as technology takes over for the body, the teleology of both a male's physical strength and his inherent propensity to use it may become less functional and less salient. If aggressivity in men loses its teleological and selective value, it becomes moot whether even this gender difference will survive its obsolescence. How long such a process of "de-selection" might take and just what might be the psychological corollaries also remain uncertain.

A second set of unanswered questions has to do with the degree to which men (and women, for that matter) change during the course of their adult lives and with the ways in which such change takes place. For the most part, concentrating on earlier stages of development, I have not addressed the later phases of the life cycle in this volume: the impact of professional roles, the behavior of a particular spouse, alterations in the structure of a man's family, the death of parents, ageing, illness, divorce, retirement, and other age-specific challenges and idiosyncratic stresses on the individual's masculine identity.[1] But I must add a few words here about the process of psychological change in adult life.

In examining the conflicts a man experiences when he becomes a father, at first I made certain assumptions about the process of personality transformation taking place. With Benedek's work on women, pregnancy, and motherhood as my main model, I delineated a parallel course of development in men and spoke of the "paternal identity crisis." Men, I posited, change in response to gestation, childrearing, and the demands of fatherhood much as women do.

It is a notion I no longer hold. Genuine development is founded on biological maturation. The brain and body must evolve in concert with environmental influence if we are to find a more or less predictable progression in the unfolding of the mind. Development thus proceeds in orderly phases, and there are critical periods after which basic changes cannot take place.

Because they are anatomical and physiological events, a woman's pregnancy, parturition, and lactation (like menopause later on) conform more strictly to this developmental model. Motherhood and the fertility cycle have demonstrable effects on a woman's body and carry the force to restructure her psyche. This is simply not the case with fatherhood or any other aspect of the male condition.

Well-defined sequencing is probably not to be seen in a man's adult life. True, most men fall in love, marry, have children, work, see their children leave home, and retire before dying. But not every man undergoes this life progression. The priest, the exclusive homosexual, or the inveterate bachelor do not marry or have children. But while something may be missing from their lives, they still feel like men. What is more, there is no lockstep timetable and course for an adult man's life. If an individual fails to fall in love at twenty-two, this does not necessarily preclude his doing it later on in midlife. Nor need one fall in love to marry or father a child. And while for most men a work identity is established before finding intimacy, this is not always the case—especially in instances of protracted schooling, long apprenticeships, and career changes.

Perhaps most important, the transformations wrought by these later events seem more arbitrary and tenuous than the developmental milestones of childhood. Becoming a father, for instance, may refigure some men's internal landscapes for better or worse, moving him to progress or miring him in regression. But others, preoccupied with work or absent altogether, may hardly be affected at all. This stands in sharp contrast to the vast majority of mothers for whom a fetus in the womb or a baby at the breast cannot be ignored.

With fathers, then, as with adults in general, it is probably better to speak of adaptation rather than development. The two processes intersect so that some aspects of the one fall within a subset of the other. But the adaptational process does not rely on advances in the individual's psychobiology. In such a perspective, a man adapts to the challenges of his environment by regressing and progressing. He assimilates each new experience to both established and superseded, often unconscious, modes of external action and internal regulation. Usually, since these strategies leave something to be desired, he will have to accommodate to external changes by realigning his existing patterns of reactivity and proactivity.

Such a Piagetian conceptualization is consistent with the views of Hartmann's ego psychology, which emphasized adaptation as the dynamic interaction of organism and environment characterized by allo- and autoplastic adjustments; integration and differentiation; and a general tendency toward increasing internalization. Though physical maturation decreases in pace and extent over the course of life, and though diminution and deterioration become more compelling forces than any expansion of capabilities, adaptational processes characterize a man's functioning from cradle to grave.

So how much does any man grow as he faces life, and why does each man do so differently? These remain the unanswerable questions. In a discipline such as the social science of psychoanalysis, there are just too many variables to consider. In approaching a subject like men and their psychology, the theorist simplifies matters so that he can work logically with them. And since he (or she) cannot begin to identify all the interactive influences involved, this theorist is less able to predict the future from the present than he is capable of reconstructing the past. The psychoanalyst looks for form and meaning at any point in a man's felt life and, like the historian, then retraces his passage to it.

The truism is true: more knowledge only teaches us how little we know. I am more modest now than at the outset of my career in understanding the psychology of men, less willing to generalize, far less prescriptive about what is good and healthy in life. Yet I hope that my efforts have illuminated some central themes in men's inner and past realities. Pursuing what Herman Melville once called "the endless flowing river in the cave of man," I hope that I have alerted my readers to the existence of deepening and sometimes fathomless recesses in any study of what it is that men want.

Works Cited

Abelin, E. (1971). The role of the father in the separation-individuation process. In J. B. McDevitt and C. F. Settlage, eds., *Separation-Individuation.* New York: International Universities Press.

—————— (1975). Some further observations and comments on the earliest role of the father. *Int. J. Psycho-Anal.* 56:293–302.

—————— (1977). Panel, Role of the father in the preoedipal years. Presented at American Psychoanalytic Association, Quebec.

—————— (1980). Triangulation: The role of the father and the origins of core gender identity during the rapprochement subphase. In R. Lax, S. Bach, and J. A. Burland, eds., *Rapprochement: The Critical Subphase of Separation.* New York: Aronson.

Abraham, K. (1920). Manifestations of the female castration complex. In *Selected Papers.* New York: Basic Books, 1953.

—————— (1925a). Character formation on the genital level. In *Selected Papers,* 1942.

—————— (1925b). An infantile sexual theory not hitherto noted. In *Selected Papers.* New York: Basic Books, 1953.

—————— (1942). *Selected Papers.* London: Hogarth Press.

Altman, L. (1977). Some vicissitudes of love. *J. Amer. Psychoanal. Assn.* 25:35–52.

Anderson, R. (1968). Where's dad? Paternal deprivation and delinquency. *Archives, General Psychiat.* 18:641–649.

Anthony, E. J., and T. Benedek, eds. (1970). *Parenthood: Its Psychology and Psychopathology.* Boston: Little, Brown.

Aries, P. (1962). *Centuries of Childhood,* tr. R. Baldick. London: Cape.

Arlow, J. (1969). Unconscious fantasy and conscious experience. *Psychoanal. Quart.* 38:1–27.

—————— (1980). Object concept and object choice. *Psychoanal. Quart.* 49:104–133.

Aronson, G. (1952). Delusion of pregnancy in a male homosexual with an abdominal cancer. *Bull. Menninger Clinic* 16:159–166.

Atkins, N. B. (1970). The Oedipus myth, adolescence, and the succession of generations. *J. Amer. Psychoanal. Assn.* 18:860–875.

Atkins, R. N. (1981). Finding one's father: The mother's contribution to the early representation of the father. *J. Amer. Acad. Psychoanal.* 9:539–559.

—— (1982). Discovering daddy: The mother's role. In S. H. Cath et al., eds., *Father and Child.* Boston: Little, Brown.

—— (1984). Transitive vitalization and its impact on father representation. *Contemp. Psychoanalyst* 20:663–675.

Auden, W. H. (1973). *Forewords and Afterwords.* London: Faber.

—— (1976). *Collected Poems.* New York: Random House.

Bak, R. (1968). The phallic woman: The ubiquitous fantasy in perversions. *Psychoanal. Study Child* 23:15–36.

—— (1973). Being in love and object loss. *Int. J. Psycho-Anal.* 54:1–7.

Balint, M. (1947). "On genital love." In *Primary Love and Psycho-Analytic Technique.* New York: Liveright, 1953.

—— (1956). Perversions and genitality. In S. Lorand, ed., *Perversions, Psychodynamics, and Theory.* New York: Grammercy Books.

Ban, P., and M. Lewis (1976). Mothers and fathers, girls and boys: Attachment behavior in the one-year-old. *Merrill-Palmer Quart.* 20:195–204.

Barclay, A., and D. Cusumano (1967). Father absence, cross-sex identity, and field dependent behavior in male adolescents. *Child Devel.* 38:243–250.

Barnett, M. C. (1966). Vaginal awareness in the infancy and childhood of girls. *J. Amer. Psychoanal. Assn.* 14:129–141.

Barthes, R. (1978). *A Lover's Discourse,* New York: Hill and Wang.

Bell, A. (1968). Additional aspects of passivity and feminine identification in the male. *Int. J. Psycho-Anal.* 49:640–647.

Benedek, T. (1959). Parenthood as a developmental phase. *J. Amer. Psychoanal. Assn.* 7:389–417.

—— (1970a). "Fatherhood and providing." In E. J. Anthony and T. Benedek, eds., *Parenthood: Its Psychology and Psychopathology.* Boston: Little, Brown.

—— (1970b). Parenthood during the life cycle. In Anthony and Benedek, eds., *Parenthood.*

Benjamin, J. (1988). *The Bonds of Love.* New York: Pantheon.

Bergmann, M. S. (1971). Psychoanalytic observations on the capacity to love. In *Separation-Individuation: Essays in Honor of Margaret Mahler,* ed. J. B. McDevitt and C. G. Settlage. New York: International Universities Press.

—— (1980). On the intrapsychic function of falling in love. *Psychoanal. Quart.* 49:56–76.

—— (1986). Transference love and love in real life. *Int. J. Psycho-Anal. Psychotherapy,* 11:27–45.

—— (1987). *The Anatomy of Loving,* New York: Columbia University Press.

—— (1992). *In the Shadow of Moloch: The Sacrifice of Children and Its Impact on Western Religions.* New York: Columbia University Press.

Bernfeld, S. (1949). Freud's scientific beginnings. *Amer. Imago* 8:333.

Bettelheim, B. (1954). *Symbolic Wounds*. Glencoe: Free Press.

Bhavabhuti (1964). *Uttara Rama Carita* (The Later Story of Rama). In *Six Sanskrit Plays*. Bombay: Asia.

Biller, H. (1968a). A multiaspect investigation of masculine development in kindergarten-age boys. *Genetic Psychol. Monographs,* 76:89–139.

——— (1968b). A note on father absence and masculine development in young lower class Negro and white boys. *Child Devel.* 39:10003–10006.

——— (1969). Father absence, maternal encouragement and sex role development in kindergarten age boys. *Child Devel.* 40:539–546.

——— (1970). Father absence and the personality development of the male child. *Devel. Psychol.* 2:181–201.

——— (1971a). Father, child, and sex. Lexington: Heath.

——— (1971b). The mother-child relationship and the father-absent boy's personality development. *Merrill-Palmer Quart.* 17:227–241.

——— (1974). Paternal deprivation, cognitive functioning and the feminized classroom. In A. Davids, ed., *Child Personality and Psychopathology*. New York: Wiley.

Biller, H., and R. Balm (1971). Father absence, perceived maternal behavior and masculinity of self concept among junior high school boys. *Devel. Psychol.* 4:178–181.

Biller, H. and D. Meredith (1974). *Father Power*. New York: McKay.

Biller, H., and S. Weiss (1970). The father-daughter relationship and the personality development of the female. *J. Genetic Psychol.* 116:79–93.

Binstock, W. A. (1973). Two forms of intimacy. *J. Amer. Psychoanal. Assn.* 21:93–107.

Bird, B. (1958). A study of the bisexual meaning of the foreskin. *J. Amer. Psychoanal. Assn.* 6:287–304.

Blanck, G., and R. Blanck (1979). *Ego Psychology*. New York: Columbia University Press.

Blos, P. (1957). Preoedipal factors in the etiology of female delinquency, *Psychoanal. Study Child* 12:229–249.

——— (1962). *On Adolescence,* New York: Free Press.

——— (1963). The concept of acting out in relation to the adolescent process. *J. Amer. Acad. Child Psychiat.* 2:118–143.

——— (1974). The Genealogy of the ego ideal. *Psychoanal. Study Child* 29:43–99.

——— (1980). The life cycle as indicated by the nature of transference in the psychoanalysis of adolescents. *F. J. Psychoanal.* 61:145–152.

——— (1985). *Son and Father*. New York: Free Press.

Blum, H. (1988). Freud and the figure of Moses. *J. Amer. Psychoanal. Assn.* 39:513–536.

Boehm, F. (1930). The femininity complex in men. *Int. J. Psycho-Anal.* 11:444–469.

Bowlby, J. (1958). The nature of the child's tie to its mother. *Int. J. Psycho-Anal.* 39(5):1–23.

———— (1969). *Attachment and Loss.* New York: Basic Books.

Bradley, N. (1961). The doll. *Int. J. Psycho-Anal.* 42:550–556.

Brazelton, T. B., et al. (1975). Early mother-infant reciprocity. In R. Hinde, ed., *Parent-Infant Interaction.* Amsterdam: Elsevier.

———— M. W. Yogman, H. Als, and E. Tronick (1978). The infant as a focus in family reciprocity. In *The Social Network of the Developing Infant,* ed. M. Lewis and L. Rosenblum. New York: Plenum.

Brenner, C. (1951). A case of childhood hallucinosis. *Psychoanal. Study Child* 6:235–243.

Brooks-Gunn, J., and N. Lewis (1975). Person perception and verbal labeling: The development of social labels. Paper at Society for Research in Child Development and Eastern Psychological Association, New York.

Brunswick, R. M. (1940). The preoedipal phase of the libidinal development. *Psychoanal. Quart.* 9:293–319.

Bryan, C. (1930). Bisexuality. *Int. J. Psycho-Anal.* 11:150–166.

Bunker, H. A. (1952). The feast of Tantalus. *Psychoanal. Quart.* 21:355–372.

Burlingham, D. (1935). Child analysis and the mother. *Psychoanal. Quart.* 4:69–92.

———— (1973). The preoedipal infant-father relationship. *Psychoanal. Study Child* 28:00–00.

Cath, S. H. (1962). Grief, loss and emotional disorders in the aging process. In M. A. Berezin and S. H. Cath, eds., *Geriatric Psychiatry.* New York: International Universities Press.

———— (1982). Vicissitudes of grandfatherhood: A Miracle of revitalization? In Cath et al., eds., *Father and Child.* Boston: Little, Brown.

———— (1989). Readiness for grandfatherhood and the shifting tide. In Cath et al., eds., *Fathers and Their Families.* Hillsdale: Analytic Press.

Cath, S. H., A. R. Gurwitt, and J. M. Ross, eds. (1982). *Father and Child: Developmental and Clinical Perspectives.* Boston: Little, Brown.

Chasseguet-Smirgel, J. (1975). A propos du delire transsexuel du President Schreber. *Revue française de la psychoanalyse* 6:1013–1025.

———— (1976). Some thoughts on the ego ideal. *Psychoanal. Quart.* 45:345–373.

———— (1983). Perversions and the universal law. *Int. Rev. Psychoanal.* 10:293–301.

Chodorow, N. (1974). Family structure and feminine personality. In M. Z. Rosaldo and L. Lamphere, eds., *Woman, Culture and Society.* Stanford, Stanford University Press.

———— (1978). *The Reproduction of Mothering.* Berkeley: University of California Press.

Clarke-Stewart, K. A. (1977). The father's impact on mother and child. Paper at Society for Research in Child Development, New Orleans.

Clower, V., reporter (1970). Panel, Development of the child's sense of his sexual identity. *J. Amer. Psychoanal. Assn.* 18:165–176.

Clower, V. (1976). Theoretical implications in current views of masturbation in latency girls. *J. Amer. Psychoanal. Assn.* 24(5):109–125.

Coleridge, S. T. (1817). *Biographia Literaria,* ed. J. Shawcross. New York: Oxford University Press, 1965.

Colman, A., and L. Colman (1971). *Pregnancy: The Psychological Experience.* New York: Herder.

Colarusso, C., and R. Nemiroff (1982). Father in mid-life: Crisis and the growth of paternal identity. In S. H. Cath et al., eds., *Father and Child.* Boston: Little, Brown.

———— eds. (1990). *New Dimensions in Adult Development.* New York: Basic Books.

Conn, J. (1947). Children's awareness of the origins of babies. *J. Child Psychiat.* 1:140–176.

Demos, J. (1982). The changing face of fatherhood In S. H. Cath et al., eds., *Father and Child.* Boston: Little, Brown.

De Rougemont, D. (1956). *Love in the Western World.* New York: Schocken, 1990.

Deutsch, H. (1944). *The Psychology of Women.* New York: Grune and Stratton.

Deutsch, F. (1957). A footnote to Freud's "Fragment of an analysis of a case of hysteria." *Psychoanal. Quart.* 26:159–167.

Devereux, C. (1953). Why Oedipus killed Laius: A note on the complementary Oedipus complex in Greek drama. *Int. J. Psycho-Anal.* 34:132–141.

———— (1963). Sociopolitical functions of the Oedipus myth in early Greece. *Psychoanal. Quart.* 32:205–214.

Diamond, M. (1993). Panel, The Good Enough Father, presented at Div. 39 meetings of American Psychological Association, April 15, 1993.

Dover, K. (1978). *Greek Homosexuality.* Cambridge: Harvard University Press.

Edgcumbe, R., and M. Burgner (1975). The phallic narcissistic phase: A differentiation between preoedipal and oedipal aspects of phallic development. *Psychoanal. Study Child,* 29:161–180.

Eisler, M. J. (1921). A man's unconscious phantasy of pregnancy in the guise of traumatic hysteria. *Int. J. Psycho-Anal.* 2:255–286.

Eissler, K. R. (1951). An unknown autobiographical letter by Freud. *Int. J. Psycho-Anal.* 32:319–324.

Erikson, E. (1959). *Identity and the Life Cycle.* New York: International Universities Press.

———— (1962). Reality and actuality. *J. Amer. Psychoanal. Assn.* 10:451–474.

———— (1963). *Childhood and Society,* New York: Norton.

———— (1964). *Insight and Responsibility.* New York: Norton.

———— (1968). Womanhood and the inner space. In *Identity: Youth and Crisis.* New York: Norton.

———— (1969). *Gandhi's Truty,* New York: Norton.

———— (1980). On the generational cycle: An address. *Int. J. Psycho-Anal.* 61:213–233.

Escalona, S. K. (1968). *The Roots of Individuality: Normal Patterns of Development in Infancy.* Chicago: Aldine.

Esman, A. (1982). Fathers and adolescent sons. In Cath et al., eds., *Father and Child.* Boston: Little, Brown.

Evans, W. N. (1951). Simulated pregnancy in a male. *Psychoanal. Quart.* 20:165–178.

———— (1953). Two kinds of romantic love. *Psychoanal. Quart.* 22:76.

Faber, M. D. (1972). The adolescent suicides of Romeo and Juliet, *Psychoanal. Rev.* 59(2):169–181.

Fairbairn, W. F. (1954). *An Object Relations Theory of the Personality.* New York: Basic Books.

Fast, I. (1984). *Gender Identity: A Differentiation Model.* Hillsdale: Analytic Press.

———— (1985). *Event Theory: A Piaget-Freud Integration.* Hillside: Erlbaum.

Ferenczi, S. (1912). The symbolic representation of the pleasure and the reality principles in the Oedipus myth. In *Sex in Psychoanalysis.* New York: Basic Books, 1950.

———— (1924). *Thalassa: A Theory of Genitality.* New York: Norton, 1968.

———— (1933). Confusion of tongues between the adult and the child. *Int. J. Psycho-Anal.* 30:225–230.

Ferholt, J., and A. R. Gurwitt (1982). Involving fathers in treatment. In Cath et al., eds., *Father and Child.* Boston: Little, Brown.

Fisher, H. E. (1992). *The Anatomy of Love: The Natural History of Monogamy, Adultery, and Divorce.* New York: Norton.

Forrest, T. (1967). The paternal roots of male character development. *Psychoanal. Rev.* 54:81–89.

———— (1969). Treatment of the father in family therapy. *Family Process* 8:106–117.

Fox, R. (1982). Les conditions de l'évolution sexuelle. In *Communications,* no. 35, *Sexualités occidentales.* Paris: Editions du Seuil.

Fraiberg, S. (1969). Libidinal object constancy and mental representations. *Psychoanal. Study Child* 24:9–47.

Freud, A. (1936a). The ego and the mechanisms of defense. In *Writings,* vol. 2 New York: International Universities Press.

———— (1936b). *The Ego and Its Mechanisms of Defense,* tr. Cecil Baines. London: Hogarth Press.

Freud, S. *The Standard Edition of the Complete Psychological Works of Sigmund Freud,* vols. 1–24, ed. J. Strachey. London: Hogarth Press, 1953–1974. Abbrev. *S.E.*

———— (1900). *The Interpretation of Dreams. S.E.* 4–5.

———— (1901). *The Psychopathology of Everyday Life. S.E.* 6.

———— (1905a). Fragment of an analysis of a case of hysteria. *S.E.* 7:7–122.

———— (1905b). *Jokes and Their Relation to the Unconscious. S.E.* 8.

———— (1905c) *Three Essays on the Theory of Sexuality. S.E.* 7:125–245.

———— (1908). On the sexual theories of children. *S.E.* 9:207–226.

———— (1909a). Analysis of a phobia in a five-year-old boy. *S.E.* 10:3–149.

———— (1909b). Notes upon a case of obsessional neurosis. *S.E.* 10:153–230.

———— (1909c). The family romance. *S.E.* 9:236–241.

———— (1910). A special type of choice of object made by men. *S.E.* 11:163–175.

—— (1911a). "Psychoanalytic notes upon an autobiographical account of a case of paranoia." *S.E.* 12:3–82.

—— (1911b). Formulations on the two principles of mental functioning. *S.E.* 12:218–226.

—— (1912–13). *Totem and Taboo. S.E.* 13:1–161.

—— (1913). The disposition to obsessional neurosis. *S.E.* 12:311–326.

—— (1914a). The Moses of Michelangelo. *S.E.* 13:211–238.

—— (1914b). On narcissism: An introduction. *S.E.* 14:69–102.

—— (1914c). Some reflections on schoolboy psychology. *S.E.* 13:239–244.

—— (1915a). Instincts and their vicissitudes. *S.E.* 14:111–140.

—— (1915b). Observations on transference love. *S.E.* 12:157–171.

—— (1916–17). *Introductory Lectures on Psycho-Analysis. S.E.* 15–16.

—— (1917). On transformations of instinct as exemplified in anal eroticism. *S.E.* 17:126–133.

—— (1918a). From the history of an infantile neurosis. *S.E.* 17:3–122.

—— (1918b). Contributions to the psychology of love, III: The taboo of virginity. *S.E.* 17:191–208.

—— (1920). *Beyond the Pleasure Principle. S.E.* 18:3–64.

—— (1921). Group psychology and the analysis of the ego. *S.E.* 18:67–143.

—— (1923a). *The Ego and the Id. S.E.* 19:3–66.

—— (1923b). A seventeenth-century demonological neurosis. *S.E.* 19:69–105.

—— (1923c). The infantile genital organization. *S.E.* 19:141–148.

—— (1924a). The economic problem of masochism. *S.E.* 19:157–170.

—— (1924b). The dissolution of the Oedipus complex. *S.E.* 19:173–179.

—— (1925). Some psychical consequences of the anatomical distinction between the sexes. *S.E.* 19:243–258.

—— (1926). *Inhibitions, Symptoms and Anxiety. S.E.* 20:87–175.

—— (1927a). Fetishism. *S.E.* 21:149–157.

—— (1927b). The future of an illusion. *S.E.* 21:3–56.

—— (1930). *Civilization and Its Discontents. S.E.* 21:59–145.

—— (1931). Female Sexuality. *S.E.* 21:221–243.

—— (1933). *New Introductory Lectures on Psycho-Analysis. S.E.* 22:3–182.

—— (1937a). Analysis terminable and interminable. *S.E.* 23:209–253.

—— (1937b). Construction in analysis. *S.E.* 23:257–269.

—— (1939). *Moses and Monotheism. S.E.* 23:3–137.

—— (1940). Splitting of the ego in the process of defense. *S.E.* 23:273–278.

—— (1954). *The Origins of Psycho-Analysis.* New York: Basic Books.

Freud, S., and J. Breuer (1895). *Studies on Hysteria. S.E.* 2.

Freud, S., and W. Fliess. (1985). *The Complete Letters of Sigmund Freud to Wilhelm Fliess, 1887–1905,* ed. J. M. Masson. Cambridge: Harvard University Press.

Fromm, E. (1943). Sex and character. *Psychiat.* 6:21–91.

Gabbard, G. O. (1993). On hate in love relationships: The narcissism of minor differences revisited. *Psychoanal. Quart.* 58.2:229–238.

———— (1994). On love and lust in the erotic transference, *J. Amer. Psychoanal. Assn.* (in press, 1994).

Galenson, E., and H. Roiphe (1971). The impact of early sexual discovery on mood, defensive organization and symbolization. *Psychoanal. Study Child* 26:195–216.

———— (1976). Early female development. *J. Amer. Psychoanal. Assn.* 24.5:29–58.

———— (1978). The emergence of genital awareness during the second year of life. In R. C. Freidman, R. M. Richart, and R. L. Vande Wiele, eds., *Sex Differences and Behavior.* New York: Wiley.

———— (1982a). Fathers and the preoedipal development of the girl. In Cath et al., eds., *Father and Child.* Boston: Little, Brown.

———— (1982b). "The Preoedipal Relationship of a Father, Mother and Daughter." In Cath et al., eds., *Father and Child.*

Gay, P. (1988) *Freud: A Life for Our Time.* New York: Norton.

Gerson, M. J. (1989). Tomorrow's fathers: The anticipation of fatherhood. In *Fathers and Their Families,* ed. Cath et al. Hillsdale: Analytic Press.

Gillespie, W. H. (1940). A contribution to the study of fetishism. *Int. J. Psycho-Anal.* 21:401–415.

Gilligan, C. (1982). *In a Different Voice: Psychological Theory and Women's Development.* Cambridge: Harvard University Press.

Glenn, J. (1980a). Freud's advice to Hans's father: The first supervisory sessions. In *Freud and His Patients,* ed. M. Kanzer and J. Glenn. New York: Aronson.

———— (1980b). Freud's adolescent patients: Katharina, Dora and the "Homosexual Woman." In *Freud and His Patients.* New York: Aronson.

Graf, H. (1941). *The Opera and Its Future in America.* New York: Norton.

Graf, M. (1942). Reminiscences of Professor Sigmund Freud. *Psychoanal. Quart.* 11.4:465–476.

Greenacre, P. (1950). Special problems of early female sexual development. In *Trauma, Growth and Personality.* New York: International Universities Press.

———— (1953). Certain relationships between fetishism and the faulty development of the body image. *Psychoanal. Study Child* 8:79–98.

———— (1955). Further considerations regarding fetishism. *Psychoanal. Study Child* 10:187–194.

———— (1960). Further notes on fetishism. *Psychoanal. Study Child* 15:191–207.

———— (1966). Problems of overidealization of the analyst and analysis: Their manifestations in the transference and countertransference relationship. In *Emotional Growth,* vol. 2.

———— (1969). The fetish and the transitional object. In *Emotional Growth,* vol. 1.

———— (1971). Perversions: General considerations regarding genetic and dynamic background. In *Emotional Growth,* vol. 1.

———— (1971). *Emotional Growth.* 2 vols. New York: International Universities Press.

Greenberg, M., and N. Morris (1982). Engrossment: The newborn's impact upon the father. In Cath et al., eds., *Father and Child.* Boston: Little, Brown.

Greenson, R. (1968). Disidentifying from mother. *Int. J. Psycho-Anal.* 49:370–374.

Greenspan, S. I. (1932). The second other: The role of the father in early personality formation and the dyadic-phallic phase of development. In Cath et al., *Father and Child.* Boston: Little, Brown.

Griswold, R. (1993). *Fatherhood in America: A History.* New York: Basic Books.

Groddeck, C. (1924). *The Book of the It.* New York: Funk and Wagnalls, 1950.

Grossman, F. K., C. S. Eichler, and X. Winnickoff (1980). *Pregnancy, Birth and Parenthood.* San Francisco: Josey Bass.

Grossman, K. E., and X. Vollkner (1984). Fathers' presence during birth of their infants and paternal involvement. *Int. J. Behav. Dev.* 7:157–165.

Grossman, W. I., and W. A. Stewart (1976). Penis envy as metaphor. *Amer. Psychoanal. Assn.* 24:193–212.

Grunberger, B. (1971). Narcissism. In *Psychoanalytic Essays.* New York: International Universities Press.

———— (1980). The oedipal conflicts of the analyst. *Psychoanal. Quart.* 49:606–630.

Gunsberg, L. (1982). A selected critical review of psychological investigations of the father-infant relationship from six months through the first three years of life. In Cath et al., eds., *Father and Child.* Boston: Little, Brown.

Gurwitt, A. R. (1982). Aspects of prospective fatherhood. In Cath et al., eds., *Father and Child.* Boston: Little, Brown.

———— (1989). Flight from fatherhood. In *Fathers and Their Families,* ed. Cath et al., Hillsdale: Analytic Press.

Hartley, R., F. Hardesty, and D. Gorfein (1962). Children's perceptions and expressions of sex differences. *Child Development* 33:221–227.

Hartmann, H. (1939). *Ego Psychology and the Problem of Adaptation.* New York: International Universities Press.

Hartmann, H., E. Kris, and R. M. Loewenstein (1946). Comments on the formation of psychic structure. *Psychoanal. Study Child,* 2:11–38.

Heimann, P. (1952). A contribution to the re-evaluation of the Oedipus complex: The early stages. *Int. J. Psycho-Anal.* 23:84–92.

Herzog, E., and C. Sudia (1973). Children in fatherless families. In *Review of Child Development Research,* ed. M. Caldwell. Chicago: University of Chicago Press.

Herzog, J. (1979). Attachment, attunement, and abuse. Unpub. ms.

———— (1980). Sleep disturbance and father hunger in 18 to 28-month-old boys: The Erlkonig Syndrome. *Psychoanal. Study Child* 35:219–233.

———— (1982a). On father hunger. In Cath et al., eds., *Father and Child.* Boston: Little, Brown.

———— (1982b). Patterns of expectant fatherhood. In Cath et al., eds., *Father and Child.*

Hetherington, E. (1966). The effects of paternal absence on sex-typed behaviors in negro and white adolescent males. *J. Personality and Social Psychology* 4:87–91.

—— (1972). Effects of father absence on personality development in adolescent daughters. *Developmental Psychology* 7:313–326.

Hite, S. (1976). *The Hite Report on Female Sexuality.* New York: Dell.

—— (1981). *The Hite Report on Male Sexuality.* New York: Random House.

Hoffer, W. (1954). Defensive process and defensive organization. *Int. J. Psycho-Anal.* 35:194–198.

—— (1968). Notes on the theory of defense. *Psychoanal. Study Child* 23:178–188.

Holland, N. (1985). *The Book of the I.* New Haven: Yale University Press.

Horney, K. (1924). On the genesis of the castration complex in women. *Int. J. Psycho-Anal.* 5:50–65.

—— (1926). The flight from womanhood. *Int. J. Psycho-Anal.* 7:324–339.

—— (1932). The dread of woman. *Int. J. Psycho-Anal.* 13:348–366.

—— (1933). Denial of the vagina. *Int. J. Psycho-Anal.* 14:57–70.

Inhelder, B., and J. Piaget (1958). *The Growth of Logical Thinking from Childhood to Adolescency,* tr. A. Parsons and S. Milgram. New York: Basic Books.

Jacobs, T. (1991). *The Use of the Self.* Madison, Conn.: International Universities Press.

Jacobson, E. (1939). On the development of the girl's wishes for a child. *Psychoanal. Quart.* 37:523–538, 1968.

—— (1950). Development of the wish for a child in boys. *Psychoanal. Study Child* 5:139–152.

—— (1964). *The Self and the Object* World. New York: International Universities Press.

—— (1971). *Depression.* New York: International Universities Press.

Jaffe, D. S. (1968). The masculine envy of women's procreative function. *J. Amer. Psychoanal. Assn.* 16:521–548.

Jarvis, W. (1962). Some effects of pregnancy and childbirth on men. *J. Amer. Psychoanal. Assn.* 10:689–700.

Jones, E. (1927). The early development of female sexuality. In *Papers on Psychoanalysis.* Boston: Beacon Press, 1961. pp. 438–451.

—— (1933). The phallic phase. In *Papers on Psychoanalysis,* pp. 452–484. Boston: Beacon Press, 1961.

—— (1953). *The Life and Work of Sigmund Freud,* 3 vols. New York: Basic Books.

—— (1961). "Early Female Sexuality." In *Papers on Psychoanalysis,* pp. 485–495. Boston: Beacon Press.

Jung, C. G. (1912). Symbols of transformation, part 2. In *Collected Works,* vol. 5, tr. R. F. C. Hull. New York: Pantheon, 1956.

Kafka, F. (1919). *Letter to His Father.* New York: Schocken, 1953.

Kakar, S. (1978). *The Inner World: A Psychoanalytic Study of Childhood and Society in India.* New Delhi: Oxford University Press.

———— (1982a) Fathers and sons: An Indian experience. In Cath et al., eds., *Father and Child.* Boston: Little, Brown.

———— (1982b). *Shamans, Mystics and Doctors.* New York: International Universities Press.

Kakar, S., and J. M. Ross (1987). *Tales of Love, Sex and Danger.* New York: Blackwell.

Kanzer, M. (1948). The "passing of the Oedipus complex" in Greek drama. *Int. J. Psycho-Anal.* 29:131–134.

———— (1950). The Oedipus trilogy. *Psychoanal. Quart.* 19:561–572.

———— (1964). On interpreting the Oedipus plays. *Psychoanal. Study of Society* 3:26–38.

Kaufman, I. (1982). Father-daughter incest. In Cath et al., eds., *Father and Child.* Boston: Little, Brown.

Kernberg, O. (1974). Mature love, prerequisites and characteristics. *J. Amer. Psychoanal. Assn.* 22:743–768.

———— (1976). *Object Relations Theory and Clinical Psychoanalysis.* New York: Aronson.

———— (1977). Boundaries and structures in love relations. *J. Amer. Psychoanal. Assn.* 25:81–116.

———— (1991). Aggression and love in the relationship of the couple *J. Amer. Psychoanal. Assn.* 39:45–70.

Kestenberg, J. (1956a). On the development of maternal feelings in early childhood. *Psychoanal. Study Child* 11:257–291.

———— (1956b). Vicissitudes of female sexuality. *J. Amer. Psychoanal. Assn.* 4:453–476.

———— (1968). Outside and inside, male and female. *J. Amer. Psychoanal. Assn.* 16:457–520.

———— (1971). A developmental approach to disturbances of sex-specific identity. *Int. J. Psycho-Anal.* 52:99–102.

———— (1975). *Children and Parents: Psychoanalytic Studies in Development.* New York: Aronson.

Kinsey, A. (1948). *Sexual Behavior in the Human Male,* Philadelphia: Saunders.

Kleeman, J. (1966). Genital self-discovery during a boy's second year. *Psychoanal. Study Child,* 21:358–392.

Klein, M. (1921). The development of a child. In *Contributions to Psycho-Analysis,* London: Hogarth Press, 1948, pp. 13–67.

———— (1923). Infant analysis. In *Contributions to Psycho-Analysis,* London: Hogarth Press, 1948.

———— (1927). Criminal tendencies in normal children. In *Contributions to Psycho-Analysis,* London: Hogarth Press, 1948.

———— (1933). The early development of conscience in the child. In *Contributions to Psycho-Analysis,* London: Hogarth Press, 1948.

———— (1957). *Envy and Gratitude,* London: Tavistock.

Klein, M., and J. Riviere (1937). *Love, Hate and Reparation* London: Hogarth Press.

Kohlberg, L. (1966). A cognitive-developmental analysis of children's sex-role concepts and attitudes. In *The Development of Sex Differences*, ed. E. Macoby. Palo Alto: Stanford University Press.

—— (1967). *Psychosexual Development in Children*. New York: Holt.

—— (1981). *The Philosophy of Moral Development*. San Francisco: Harper and Row.

Kohut, H. (1971). The Analysis of the Self. *Psychoanal. Study Child*, monograph 4.

Kott, J. (1974). *The Eating of the Gods*. New York: Random House.

Kreitler, H., and S. Kreitler (1966). Children's concept of birth and sexuality. *Child Development* 37:363–378.

Kris, E. (1952). *Psychoanalytic Explorations in Art*. New York: International Universities Press.

Kubie, L. (1974). The drive to become both sexes. *Psychoanal. Quart.* 43:349–426.

Lacan, J. (1966). *Ecrits*. Paris: Editions du Seuil.

Lamb, M. (1975). Fathers: Forgotten contributors to child development. *Human Development* 18:245–266.

—— (1976a). The role of the father: An overview. In M. Lamb, ed., *The Role of the Father in Child Development*. New York: Wiley.

—— (1976b). Interactions between two-year-olds and their mothers and fathers. *Psychological Reports* 38:447–450.

—— (1976c). Effects of stress and cohort on mother- and father-infant interaction. *Developmental Psychology* 13:637.

Lampl de Groot, J. (1947). The preoedipal phase in the development of the male child. *Psychoanal. Study Child* 2:75–83.

Lear, J. (1990). *Love and Its Place in Nature: A Philosophical Interpretation of Freudian Psychoanalysis*. New York: Farrar, Straus, Giroux.

Leonard, M. (1966). Fathers and daughters: The significance of "fathering" in the psychosexual development of the girl. *Int. J. Psycho-Anal.* 47:325–334.

Lever, J. (1978). Sex differences in the complexity of children's play and games. *Amer. Socio. Rev.* 43:471–483.

Levine, J. (1976). *Who Will Raise the Children? New Options for Fathers*. Philadelphia: Lippincott.

Levinson, D. J., et al. (1978). *The Seasons of a Man's Life*. New York: Knopf.

Lévi-Strauss, C. (1966). *The Savage Mind*. Chicago: University of Chicago Press.

Lewin, B. D. (1952). The oral triad. In *Selected Papers*, ed. J. A. Arlow. New York: Psychoanalytic Quarterly, 1973.

Lewis, M., and L. Rosenblum (1974). *The Effect of the Infant on Its Caregiver*. New York: Wiley.

Licht, H. (1952). *Sexual Life in Ancient Greece*. New York: Barnes and Noble.

Lidz, R. W., and Lidz, T. (1977). Male menstruation: A ritual alternative to the oedipal transition. *Int. J. Psycho-Anal.* 58:17–31.

—— (1989). *Oedipus in the Stone Age*. Madison, Conn.: International Universities Press.

Liebenberg, B. (1967). Expectant fathers. *Amer. J. Orthopsychiatry* 37:358–359.

Liebert, R. (1986). The history of male homosexuality from ancient Greece through the Renaissance: Implications for psychoanalytic theory. In *The Psychology of Men,* ed. G. I. Fogel, F. M. Lane, and R. S. Liebert. New York: Basic Books.

Loevinger, J., and R. Wessler (1970). *Measuring Ego Development.* San Francisco: Jossey-Bass.

Loewald, H. (1951). Ego and reality. *Int. J. Psycho-Anal.* 32:10–18.

───── (1979). The waning of the Oedipus complex. *J. Amer. Psychoanal. Assn.* 27:751–756.

Lorand, S. (1939). Role of the female penis: Fantasy in male character formation. *Int. J. Psycho-Anal.* 20:171–181.

Lorenz, K. (1966). *On Aggression.* New York: Harcourt, Brace and World.

Lynn, D. (1974). *The Father: His Role in Child Development.* Monterey: Brooks/Cole.

Macalpine, I., and R. Hunter (1954). Observations on the psychoanalytic theory of psychosis. *British J. Med. Psychol.* 27:175–192.

───── eds. (1955). *D. Schreber: Memoirs of My Nervous Illness.* Cambridge, Mass.: Bentley.

Maccoby, E. E., and C. N. Jacklin (1975). *Psychology of Sex Differences.* Stanford: Stanford University Press.

Mahl, G. F. (1982). "Father-son themes in Freud's self-analysis." In *Father and Child,* ed. S. Cath, A. Gurwitt, and J. Ross. Boston: Little, Brown.

Mahler, M. S. (1966). Discussion of P. Greenacre's problems of overidealization of the analyst and analysis. *Psychoanal. Quart.* 36:637.

───── (1974). "Symbiosis and individuation." *Psychoanal. Study Child,* 29:89–106.

Mahler, M. S., and E. Furer (1968). *On Human Symbiosis and the Vicissitudes of Individuation.* New York: International Universities Press.

Mahler, M. S., and B. Gosliner (1955). On symbiotic child psychosis: Genetic, dynamic and restitutive aspects. *Psychoanal. Study Child* 10:195–212.

Mahler, M. S., F. Pine, and A. Bergman (1970). The mother's reaction to her toddler's drive for individuation. In *Parenthood,* ed. E. J. Anthony and T. Benedek. Boston: Little, Brown.

───── (1975). *The Psychological Birth of the Human Infant.* New York: Basic Books.

Malcolm, J. (1981). *Psychoanalysis: The Impossible Profession.* New York: Knopf.

Marcus. I. M., and J. J. Francis (1975). Masturbation: A developmental view. In *Masturbation from Infancy to Senescence,* ed. I. M. Marcus and J. J. Francis. New York: International Universities Press.

Masson, J. M. (1985). *The Assault on Truth: Freud's Suppression of the Seduction Theory.* New York: Farrar, Straus and Giroux.

───── (1988). *A Dark Science: Women, Sexuality and Psychiatry in the Nineteenth Century.* New York: Farrar, Straus and Giroux.

———— (1990). *Final Analysis.* New York: Addison Wesley.

Masters, W. H., and V. E. Johnson (1966). *Human Sexual Response.* Boston: Little, Brown.

Mead, M. (1949). *Male and Female.* New York: Morrow.

Miller, J. B. (1976). *Toward a New Psychology of Women.* Boston: Beacon Press.

Mitchell, G. (1981). *Human Sex Differences: A Primatologist's Perspective.* New York: Van Nostrand Reinhold.

Moore, B., and B. Fine (1990). *A Glossary of Psychoanalytic Terms.* Amer. Psychoanalytic Assoc.

Nabokov, V. (1966). *Speak, Memory.* New York: Perigee.

Nagy, M. (1953). Children's birth theories. *J. Genet. Psychol.* 83:217–226.

Nelson, E., and E. Macoby (1966). The relationship between social development and differential abilities on the Scholastic Aptitude Test. *Merrill-Palmer Quart.* 12:269–284.

Nelson, E., and P. Vangen (1971). The impact of father absence upon heterosexual behaviors and social development of preadolescent girls in ghetto environment. *Proceedings Amer. Psycholog. Assn.* 27:46–49.

Nelson, J. (1956). Anlage of productiveness in boys: Womb envy. In *Childhood Psychopathology,* ed. S. Harrison and J. McDermott, New York: International Universities Press, 1972.

Neubauer, P. B. (1960). "The one-parent child and his oedipal development." *Psychoanal. Study Child* 15:286–309.

Neumann, E. (1949). *The Origins and History of Consciousness,* trans. R. F. C. Hull. New York: Harper and Row, 1962.

Niederland, W. G. (1957). The earliest dreams of a young child. *Psychoanal. Study Child,* 12:190–208.

———— (1959a). The "miracled-up" world of Schreber's childhood. *Psychoanal. Study Child* 14:383–413.

———— (1959b). Schreber. *Psychoanal. Quart.* 28:151–169.

Nizami. *The Story of Layla and Majnun,* tr. R. Gelpke. Boulder, Col.: Shambhala, 1978.

Nunberg, H. (1947). Circumcision and the problems of bisexuality. *Int. J. Psycho-Anal.* 28:145–179.

Ortega y Gasset, J. (1957). *On Love,* tr. T. Talbot, New York: Greenwich Editions.

Parens, H. (1975). Report on workshop: Parenthood as a developmental phase, *J. Amer. Psychoanal. Assn.* 23:154–165.

Parens, H., L. Pollock, J. Stern, and S. Kramer (1976). On the girl's entry into the Oedipus complex. *J. Amer. Psychoanal. Assn.* 24.5:79–108.

Parke, R. (1978). Perspectives on father-infant interaction. In J. D. Osofsky, ed., *Handbook of infancy.* New York: Wiley.

Parke, R., and S. O'Leary (1976). Father-mother-infant interaction in the newborn period. In K. Riegel and J. Meacham, eds., *The Developing Individual in a Changing World,* vol. 2. The Hague: Mouton.

Parke, R., S. O'Leary, and S. West (1972). Mother-father-newborn interaction:

Effects of maternal medication, labor, and sex of infant. *Proceedings Amer. Psychol. Assn.* 28:85–86.

Parke, R., and D. Sawin (1975). Infant characteristics and behavior as eliciters of maternal and paternal responsibility in the newborn period. Paper at Society for Research in Child Development, Denver.

——— (1977). The family in early infancy: Social interactional and attitudinal analyses. Paper at Society for Research in Child Development, New Orleans.

Parsons, T. (1954). The father symbol: An appraisal in the light of psychoanalytic and sociological theory. In L. Bryson et al., eds., *Symbols and Values.* New York: Harper and Row.

——— (1958). Social structure and the development of personality: Freud's contribution to the integration of psychology and sociology. *Psychiatry* 21:321–340.

Parsons, T., and R. Bales (1955). *Family, Socialization and Interaction Process.* Glencoe: Free Press.

Payne, E., and P. Mussen (1956). Parent-child relations and father identification among adolescent boys. *J. Abnormal and Social Psychol.* 52:358–362.

Pedersen, F., P. Anderson, and R. Cain (1977). An approach to understanding linkages between the parent-infant and spouse relationships. Paper at Society for Research in Child Development, New Orleans.

Pedersen, F., and K. Robson (1969). Father participation in infancy. *Amer. J. Orthopsychiatry* 39:466–472.

Pedersen, F., J. Rubinstein, and L. Yarrow (1973). Father absence in infancy. Paper at Society for Research in Child Development, Philadelphia.

Pedersen, F., J. Rubinstein, and L. Yarrow (1978). Infant development in father-absent families. *J. Genetic Psychology* 135:51–61.

Pedersen, F., L. Yarrow, B. Anderson, et al. (1978). Conceptualization of father influences in the infancy period. In M. Lewis and L. Rosenblum, eds., *Social network of the Developing Child.* New York: Plenum.

Person, E. S. (1983). "The erotic Transference in women and men, differences and consequences." Keynote address at American Academy of Psychoanalysis, San Juan, Puerto Rico. Panel report at American Psychoanalytic Association, New York, December 1985.

——— (1988). *Dreams of Love and Fateful Encounters,* New York: Norton.

Piaget, J. (1929). *The Child's Conception of the World.* New York: Harcourt, Brace.

——— (1930). *The Child's Conception of Physical Causality.* New York: Harcourt, Brace.

——— (1932). *The Moral Judgment of the Child.* New York: Free Press, 1965.

Pollock, G. H., and J. M. Ross (1987). *The Oedipus Papers.* Chicago Institute for Psychoanalysis. Madison, Conn.: International Universities Press.

Prall, R. C. (1978). Panel, The role of the father in preoedipal development. *J. Amer. Psychoanal. Assn.* 26:143–162.

Pruett, K. (1983). Infants of primary nurturing fathers. *Psychoanal. Study Child* 38:257–277.

——— (1984). Children of the father-mother: Infants of primary nurturing fathers. In *Frontiers of Infant Psychiatry*, vol. 2, ed. J. Call, E. Galenson, and R. Tyson. New York: Basic Books.

Pruyser, P. (1975). What splits in splitting? *Bull. Meninger Clinic* 39:1–46.

Pumpian-Midlin, E. (1969). Omnipotence, omnipotentiality, conformity and rebellion (abstract). *Bull. Assn. Psychoanal. Medicine* 8(3):31–34.

Rado, S. (1940). A critical examination of the concept of bisexuality. *Psychosom. Medicine* 2:459–467.

Rangell, L. (1953). The interchangeability of phallus and female genital. *J. Amer. Psychoanal. Assn.* 1:504–509.

Rank, O. (1912). *Das Inzestmotiv in Dichtung und Sage*. Leipzig: Deuticke.

——— (1914). The myth of the birth of the hero. In *The Myth of the Birth of the Hero and Other Writings of Otto Rank*, ed. P. Freud. New York: Vintage Books, 1959.

——— (1924). *The Trauma of Birth*. New York: Harper and Row, 1973.

——— (1932). *Modern Education*. New York: Knopf.

Rascovsky, A., and M. Rascovsky (1968). On the genesis of acting out and psychopathic behavior in Sophocles' *Oedipus*. *Int. J. Psycho-Anal.* 49:390–394.

Rebelsky, F., and C. Hanks (1971). Father's verbal interaction with infants in the first three months of life. *Child Development* 42:63–68.

Reik, T. (1920). Oedipus and the sphinx. In *Dogma and Compulsion: Psychoanalytic Studies of Religion and Myth*. New York: International Universities Press, 1951.

——— (1944). *A Psychologist Looks at Love*. New York: Farrar and Rinehart.

——— (1946). *The Psychological Problems of Religion*. New York: Farrar, Strauss.

Reich, W. (1927). *The Function of the Orgasm*. New York: Oregon Institute Press, 1942.

——— (1929). The genital character and the neurotic character. In *The Psychoanalytic Reader*, ed. R. Fliess. New York: International Universities Press.

Roheim, G. (1950). *Psychoanalysis and Anthropology*. New York: International Universities Press.

Rose, G. (1962). Unconscious birth fantasies in the ninth month of treatment. *J. Amer. Psychoanal. Assn.* 10:677–688.

——— (1969). Transference birth fantasies and narcissism. *J. Amer. Psychoanal. Assn.* 17:1015–1029.

Rose, H. (1928). *A Handbook of Greek Mythology*. London: Methuen.

Rosner, H. (1987). Oedipus and his cradle scars. In Pollock, G. H. and J. M. Ross, eds., *The Oedipus Papers*. Madison, Conn.

Ross, J. M. (1974). The children's children: A psychoanalytic study of generativity and nurturance in boys. Diss., New York University (University Microfilms, Ann Arbor).

——— (1975). The development of paternal identity: A critical review of the literature on nurturance and generativity in boys and men. *J. Amer. Psychoanal. Assn.* 23:783–817.

———— (1976). Notes on paternal identity and its developmental line. Lecture at Albert Einstein College of Medicine, New York.

———— (1979a). Fathering: A review of some psychoanalytic contributions on paternity. *Int. J. Psycho-Anal.* 60:317–327.

———— (1979b). The forgotten father. In *Psychosexual Imperatives,* ed. M. C. Nelson and J. Ikenberry. New York: Human Sciences Press.

———— (1990a). The eye of the beholder. In *New Dimensions in Adult Development,* ed. C. Colarusso and R. Nemiroff. New York: Basic Books.

———— (1990b). The role of the father representation in romantic love. Paper at Denver Psychoanalytic Society, March 31.

———— (1992). *The Male Paradox.* New York: Simon and Schuster.

Ross, J. M., and P. B. Dunn. (1980). Notes on the genesis of pathological splitting. *Int. J. Psychoanal.* 61:335–349.

Ross, J. M., and J. Herzog (1985). The sins of the father. In *Parental Influences in Health and Disease,* ed. T. J. Anthony and G. H. Pollock. Boston: Little, Brown., pp. 477–510.

Ross, N. (1960). Rivalry with the product. *J. Amer. Psychoanal. Assn.* 8:450–463.

———— (1970). "The primacy of sexuality in the light of ego psychology." *J. Amer. Psychoanal. Assn.* 18:267–284.

———— (1982). Domination-submission patterns in the patriarchal family structure. In Cath et al., eds., *Father and Child.* Cath. Boston: Little, Brown.

Samaraweera, S., and C. Cath (1982). Fostering the consolidation of paternal identity. In Cath et al., eds., *Father and Child.* Boston: Little, Brown.

Santrock, J. (1970a). Paternal absence, sex-typing and identification. *Developmental Psychology* 2:264–272.

———— (1970b). Influence of onset and type of paternal absence on the first four Eriksonian developmental crises. *Developmental Psychology* 3:273–274.

———— (1972). The relation of type and onset of father absence of cognitive development. *Child Development* 43:455–469.

Sassen, G. (1980). Success anxiety in women: A constructivist interpretation of its sources and its significance. *Harvard Education Rev.* 50:13–25.

Schafer, R. (1974). Problems in Freud's psychology of women. *J. Amer. Psychoanal. Assn.,* 22:459–487.

———— (1992). *Retelling a Life: Narration and Dialog in Psychoanalysis.* New York: Basic Books.

Scherfey, M. J. (1966). The evolution and nature of female sexuality in relation to psychoanalytic theory. *J. Amer. Psychoanal. Assn.* 14:28–128.

Schreber, D. (1903). *Memoirs of My Nervous Illness.* London: Dawson, 1955.

Seides, S. W. (1987). Discussion, "The riddle of Little Hans." Presented at Psychoanalytic Association of New York, January.

Sennett, R. (1992). *The Uses of Disorder: Personal Identity and City Life.* New York: Norton.

Settlage, C. F. et al. (1988). Conceptualizing adult development. *J. Amer. Psychoanal. Assn.* 36:347–370.

Shapiro, E. R., R. L. Shapiro, J. Zinner, and D. A. Berkowitz (1977). The border-line ego and the working alliance. *Int. J. Psycho-Anal.* 58:77–87.

Sheleff, L. (1981). *Generations Apart.* New York: McGraw-Hill.

Shengold, L. (1978). Assault on a child's individuality. *Psychoanal. Quart.* 47:419–424.

——— (1988). *Soul Murder.* New Haven: Yale University Press.

Slater, P. (1971). *The Glory of Hera.* Boston: Beacon Press.

Silverman, M. (1980). "A fresh look at the case of Little Hans." In *Freud and His Patients,* ed. M. Kanzer and J. Glenn. New York: Aronson.

Simenauer, E. (1954). "Pregnancy envy" in Rainer Maria Rilke. *Amer. Imago 2* 11:235–248.

Slap, J. (1961). Little Hans's tonsillectomy. *Psychoanal. Quart.* 30:259–261.

Socarides, C. W. (1960). The development of a fetishist perversion. *J. Amer. Psychoanal. Assn.* 8:281–311.

——— (1968). *The Overt Homosexual.* New York: Grune and Stratton.

——— (1970). A psycho-analytic study of the desire for sexual transformation (transsexualism). *Int. J. Psycho-Anal.* 51:341–350.

——— (1978). *Homosexuality.* New York: Aronson.

——— (1982). Abdicating fathers, homosexual sons. In Cath et al., eds., *Father and Child.* Boston: Little. Brown.

Sperling, M. (1964). A case of ophidiophilia. *Int. J. Psycho-Anal.* 45:227–236.

Spitz, R. A. (1945, 1946). Hospitalism: An inquiry into the genesis of psychiatric conditions in early childhood. *Psychoanal. Study Child* 1:53–74; 2:113–117.

——— (1965). *The First Year of Life.* New York: International Universities Press.

Sprey, J. (1967). The study of single parenthood. *Family Life Coordinator* 16:29–35.

Staver, N. (1944). The use of a child guidance clinic by mother-dominant families. *Smith College Studies in Social Work* 14:367–388.

Stendhal (1842). *On Love,* 3rd ed. New York: Liveright, 1947.

Stephens, W. (1961). Judgments by social workers on boys and mothers in father-less families. *J. Genetic Psychol.* 99:59–64.

Steele, B. F. (1970). Parental abuse of infants and small children. In *Parenthood,* ed. E. J. Anthony and T. Benedek. Boston: Little, Brown.

——— (1982). Abusive fathers. In Cath et al., eds., *Father and Child.* Boston: Little, Brown, pp. 481–490.

Stern, D. N. (1974). The goal and structure of mother-infant play. *J. Amer. Acad. Child Psychiat.* 13:402–421.

——— (1977). *The First Relationship: Infant and Mother.* Cambridge: Harvard University Press.

——— (1985). *The Interpersonal World of the Infant.* New York: Basic Books.

Sternberg, H. (1951). Fathers who apply for child guidance. *Smith College Studies in Social Work* 22:53–68.

Stoller, R. J. (1968). *Sex and Gender.* New York: Science House.

——— (1975). Healthiest parental influences on the earliest development of masculinity in baby boys. *Psychoanal. Forum* 5:232–262.

——— (1976). Primary femininity. *Amer. Psychoanal. Assn.* 24.5:59–78.

——— (1979). *Sexual Excitement.* New York: Pantheon Books.

——— (1985). *Observing the Erotic Imagination.* New Haven: Yale University Press.

Stoller, R. J., and G. Herdt (1982). The development of masculinity: A cross-cultural contribution. *J. Amer. Psychoanal. Assn.* 30:29–59.

Sullerot, E. (1979). *Women on Love: Eight Centuries of Feminine Writing.* New York: Doubleday.

Teilhard de Chardin, P. (1972). *On Love.* New York: Harper and Row.

Tessman, L. (1982). A note on the father's contribution to his daughter's ways of working and loving In Cath, et al., eds., *Father and Child.* Boston: Little, Brown.

Trehowan, W. (1965). The couvade syndrome. *Brit. J. Psychiatry* 111:57–66.

Tripp, E. (1970). *Crowell's Handbook of Classical Mythology.* New York: Crowell.

Tyson, P. (1982). The role of the father in gender identity, urethral erotism, and phallic narcissism. In Cath et al., eds., *Father and Child.* Boston: Little, Brown.

Valliant, G. (1977). *Adaptation to Life.* Boston: Little, Brown.

Van der Leeuw, P. J. (1958). The preoedipal phase of the male. *Psychoanal. Study Child* 13:552–374.

Van der Waals, H. G. (1965). Problems of narcissism, *Bull. Menninger Clinic* 29:243–275.

Van Leeuwen, K. (1966). Pregnancy envy in the male. *Int. J. Psycho-Anal.* 47:319–324.

Waelder, R. (1936). The principle of multiple function. *Psychoanal. Quart.* 5:45–62.

Wainwright, W. H. (1966). Fatherhood as a precipitant of mental illness. *Amer. J. Psychiatry* 123:40–44.

Wallerstein, J., and J. Kelly (1982). Divorcing fathers. In Cath et al., eds., *Father and Child.* Boston: Little, Brown.

Weber, M. (1947). *The Theory of Economic and Social Organization.* New York: Free Press.

Weissman, P. (1963). The effects of preoedipal paternal attitudes on development and character. *Int. J. Psycho-Anal.* 44:121–131.

White, R. W. (1959). Motivation reconsidered: The concept of competence. *Psychological Review,* 66:297–333.

Winnicott, D. W. (1953). Transitional objects and transitional phenomena. *Int. J. Psycho-Anal.* 34:89–97.

——— (1957). *Mother and Child.* New York: Basic Books.

——— (1958). *Collected Papers.* New York: Basic Books.

——— (1963). Communicating and not communicating leading to study of certain opposites. In *The Maturational Processes and the Facilitating Environment,* ed. Winnicott. New York: International Universities Press.

Wisdom, J. O. (1976). The role of the father in the mind of the parents, in psychoanalytic theory, and in the life of the infant. *Int. Rev. Psychoanal.* 3,2:231–240.

Wolff, P. (1965). The development of attention in young infants. *Annual, New York Academy of Science* 118:815–830.

Wolff, W. (1950). *The Threshold of the Abnormal.* New York: Hermitage.

Yogman, M. (1977). The goals and structure of face-to-face interaction between infants and fathers. Paper at Society for Research in Child Development. New Orleans.

———— (1982). Observations on the father-infant relationship. In Cath et al., eds., *Father and Child.* Boston: Little, Brown.

Yogman, M., et al. (1977a). Development of social interaction of infants with fathers. Paper at Eastern Psychological Association, New York.

———— (1977b). Parent-infant interaction under stress: The study of a temperamentally difficult infant. Paper at American Academy of Child Psychiatry, Toronto.

Zelazo, P., et al. (1977). Fathers and sons: An experimental facilitation of attachment behaviors. Paper at Society for Research in Child Development, New Orleans.

Zilboorg, G. (1931). Depressive reactions related to parenthood. *Amer. J. Psychiatry* 10:927–962.

———— (1944). Masculine and feminine. *Psychiatry* 7:257–296.

Notes

1. Studying Men

1. In 1966, in the tradition of Karen Horney (1924, 1932, 1933) before she left the Freudian fold, Mary Jane Scherfey published an article in the *Journal of the American Psychoanalytic Association* in which she argued that, like other men, most psychoanalytic theorists had succumbed to the typical male fear of female sexuality. Stressing penis envy, which Horney believed to be a secondary and largely defensive phenomenon in girls, they constructed convoluted theories of female development that were really apologia for a misogynistic social order and male supremacy.

Scherfey's contribution proved to be the first in a series of more or less official responses to the new feminism and to women's growing impatience with the sexism in psychoanalytic circles. Other reactions followed, all of them challenging the equation of "normal femininity" with passivity, masochism, moral dependency, and so-called acceptance of castration—characteristics that analysts, foremost among them Helene Deutsch (1944), had hitherto attributed to the normal woman's lot. Schafer (1974), Stoller (1968, 1976), Grossman and Stewart (1976), Clower (1970, 1976), and many others began to consider the politics of penis envy, that is, the role of social constraints in accentuating a genuine but not necessarily organizing aspect of a woman's infantile libidinal life. Like Horney and Jones (1927), they argued the existence of what Stoller termed "primary femininity" (1976). Girls will be girls, analysts began to recognize—not boys. And in 1976, in a special supplement for the journal in which Scherfey's piece had appeared ten years earlier, editor Harold Blum collected these revised views on womanhood.

Yet another implication of this shift in perspective on gender relations was the reconsideration of the psychology of men. Freud had constructed his own notions of male development as the paradigmatic course in an oddly circuitous fashion. Deriving his inferences from clinical work with mostly female hysterical patients, he proceeded to outline a more or less linear progression for an ideal type of male, whom he saw as phallic-minded from cradle to grave. The subsequent contributions of Edith Jacobson (1964) and Margaret Mahler (1975), stressing the origins of both sexes in the orbit of their mothers, seemed to point to a more complex and ambiguous evolution of male identity. Apart from the contributions of Stoller (1968) and Ralph Greenson (1968) on the boy's disidentification from his mother, psychoanalysts had generally ignored such vagaries. It was these vagaries that I would pursue over the next two decades.

2. I have reviewed these evolving contributions in Ross, 1975. The major essays include Freud, 1905c, 1908, 1909a, 1914b, 1917, 1918a, 1923, 1924a,b, 1925, 1931, 1933; Rank, 1914; Jung, 1912; Neumann, 1949; Klein, 1921, 1923, 1927, 1933; Klein and Riviere, 1927; Fromm, 1943; Zilboorg, 1944; Jacobson, 1950; Stoller and Herdt, 1982; Lidz and Lidz, 1989; MacAlpine and Hunter, 1954, 1955; Winnicott, 1953; Mahler, Pine, and Bergmann, 1975; Kestenberg, 1956; 1968, 1971; Blos, 1962; Nelson, 1956; Van der Leeuw, 1958; Stoller, 1975; Herzog, 1982, Gurwitt, 1976, and Benjamin, 1988.

3. In Ross, 1979a, I have summarized psychoanalysis' fitful appreciation of the father's role in his sons' and daughters' development. In this article, I show how slow the field has been to complement the "father of the Oedipus complex" with a view of a man's sex-specific and facilitating contributions to vital aspects of his children's emotional well-being and cognitive growth. Long before he becomes cast as the punitive castrator and emulated because he is feared, the male parent's presence and nurturing serve to enhance the unfolding of separation-in-dividuation; self-identity; core gender, sexual identity, and sexual-object choice; drive modulation; impulse control; the internalization of an ego ideal; and more. What is more, according to Blos (1985), the father's influence continues, exerting pressure on sons and daughters during their adolescence and young adulthood (see Chapter 9). The major analytic texts include Freud 1900, 1909a,b, 1912, 1920, 1921, 1930, 1932, 1939; Loewald, 1951; Greenson, 1968; Greenacre, 1966; Mahler and Gosliner, 1955; Mahler, Pine, and Bergman, 1975; Stoller, 1968, 1975, 1976; Jacobson, 1964; Benedek, 1970a,b; Abelin, 1971, 1975, 1977, 1981; Herzog, 1980, 1982a; Lacan, 1966; Ross, 1979a,b; Grossman, Eichler, and Winnicott, 1980; Grossman and Volkner, 1984; Gerson, 1989; Cath, Gurwitt, and Gunsberg, 1989. Outside the field of psychoanalysis, major studies of the father's role in development have been published by Lamb, Yogman and Brazelton, Pruett, Levine, and others.

4. John Demos would have us speak instead of a "renewed fatherhood." In a study of fatherhood in America (1982), Demos, a family historian, reconstructed the gradual disengagement of men from home and family. Images of the father's role have changed over the past 300 years with industrialization, and, I would add, first, the mushrooming, in the mid-20th century, of a technological and corporate society and, then, its deterorization. Prior to these developments, when men worked at or near the home, often in a family business, fathers were held to be a child's primary caretaker, responsible for his or her emotional and, above all, moral development. Mothers were regarded as ancillary figures, serving basically to help implement a father's guidance. As a man's hours away from the family

increased, he became essentially an external protector and material provider, with the mother becoming more exclusively involved with their offspring's upbringing. Changes in child-custody laws followed suit. (Also see Griswold, 1993).

3. Becoming a Father

1. For notions on the adaptational phase of parenthood, see Kestenberg, 1975; Benedek, 1959, 1970; Erikson, 1963, 1964; Colarusso and Nemiroff, 1990; Levinson et al., 1978.

4. Fathers in Action

1. On the failures of fatherhood, see Biller 1968a,b, 1969, 1970, 1974; Hetherington, 1966; Santrock; Barclay and Cusumano, 1967; Nelson and Vangen, 1971; Nelson and Macoby, 1966; Herzog and Sudia, 1973.

2. On infants' social interactions, see Lamb, 1975; Pedersen, Rubinstein, and Yarrow, 1973, 1978; Pederson, Anderson, and Cain, 1977; Pederson et al., 1978; Parke, 1978; Parke, O'Leary, and West, 1972; Parke and Sawin, 1975; Parke and O'Leary, 1976; Yogman, 1977, 1982; Yogman et al., 1977.

5. Oedipus Revisited

1. For overviews of facilitative fathering, see Diamond, 1993; Cath et al., 1982, 1992.

2. For further psychoanalytic perspectives on filicidal impulses in fathers and mothers, see Ferenczi, 1933; Shengold, 1988; Schreber, 1903; Niederland, 1959a,b; N. Ross, 1982; Socarides, 1982.

3. For analytic interpretations of the Oedipus myth, see Pollock and Ross, 1987; Rank, 1912, 1932; Reik, 1920; Kanzer, 1948, 1950, 1964; Licht, 1952; Devereux, 1953, 1963; Erikson, 1980; Grunberger, 1980; Sheleff, 1981.

4. Please refer to the following classical scholars: Rose, 1928; Licht, 1952: Tripp, 1970; Dover, 1978; Bunker, 1952; Kott, 1974.

5. For further comment on Greek pederasty, see Slater, 1971; Dover, 1978; Liebert, 1986.

6. For references to new fatherhood as a time of psychopathological risk, see Zilboorg, 1931; Jarvis, 1962; Wainright, 1966; Herzog, 1982b.

7. For Freud's notes about universal fantasy, see Freud, 1900, 1913, 1927a, 1930.

8. For references to the negative Oedipus, see Freud, 1909b,c, 1918a; Blos, 1985.

9. For parent-child studies and family intervention programs, see Spitz, 1965; Brazelton et al., 1978; Stern, 1977, 1985; Mahler, Pine, and Bergman, 1975; Shapiro et al., 1977; Kestenberg, 1975; Samaraweera and Cath, 1982; Kaufman, 1982; Steele, 1970, 1982; Ross and Dunn, 1980; Ferholt and Gurwitt, 1982.

10. For countertransferential issues, filicidal and otherwise, see N. Atkins, 1970; Grunberger, 1980; Jacobs, 1991.

8. Young Love

1. For psychoanalytic books on love, see Benjamin, 1988; Bergmann, 1987; Kakar and Ross, 1987; Kernberg, in preparation; Person, 1988.

2. On romantic love, see Altman, 1977; Bergmann, 1971, 1980, 1986; Van der Waals, 1965; Balint 1947; Chasseguet-Smirgel, 1983; Kernberg, 1974, 1977; Kakar and Ross, 1987.

A Modest Conclusion

1. For work on later stages of the male life cycle, see Ross, 1992; Erikson, 1959, 1963, Valliant, 1977; Levinson et al., 1978; Settlage et al., 1988.

Acknowledgments

There are many individuals, foundations, and academic institutions, too numerous to cite here, to whom I am indebted in the preparation of this book. As far as past mentors and collaborators are concerned, let me single out the following: my father Nathaniel Ross, Erik Erikson, Arthur Couch, George Klein, Robert Holt, Sudhir Kakar, Peter Blos Sr., Judith Kestenberg, Louise Kaplan, Paulina Kernberg, Harold Blum, James Herzog, Stanley Cath, Alan Gurwitt, Pamela Daniels, Richard Atkins, George Pollock, and Stanley Cath.

My acquiring editor at Harvard University Press, Angela von der Lippe, has been instrumental in inspiring this volume. At Harvard, Joyce Backman shaped the final manuscript with her unfailing elegance and sense of logical simplicity. Keith Bradley and Grissel Bordoni-Seijo, my administrative assistants, gave its preparation the most thoughtful attention. Barbara Fisher was a patient and loving presence throughout the course of my work.

I am indebted to the Rockefeller Foundation for awarding me a residency at the Bellagio Study and Conference Center for June 1993, when I completed the revisions of the manuscript.

This book is revised from my work published elsewhere, and I would like to thank the original publishers: Chapter 2: "Toward Fatherhood: The Epigenesis of Paternal Identity during a Boy's First Decade," *International Review of Psychoanalysis* 4(1977), 327–347. I have also interpolated examples of my research from "Father to the Child: Psychoanalytic Reflections," *Psychoanalytic Review* 70.5 (1987).

Chapter 3: "Paternal Identity: A Personal Equation of Manhood and

Fatherhood," in *On Sexuality: Psychoanalytic Observations,* ed. C. W. Socarides and T. B. Karasu (New York: International Universities Press, 1979). Excerpts have also been taken from "The Forgotten Father," in *Psychosexual Imperatives,* ed. M. C. Nelson and J. Ikenbery (New York: Human Sciences Press, 1979).

Chapter 4: "Fathers in Development," in *Parenthood: A Psychodynamic Perspective,* ed. Rebecca S. Cohen, Bertram J. Cohler, and Sidney H. Weissman (New York: Guilford Press, 1984). This chapter also incorporates material from "The Forgotten Father."

Chapter 5: "Oedipus Revisited: Laius and the Laius Complex," *Psychoanalytic Study of the Child* 37 (1982). Material is also drawn from "The Darker Side of Fatherhood: Paternal Aggression in Practice," *International Journal of Psychoanalytic Psychotherapy* 11 (1985).

Chapter 6: "The Riddle of Little Hans: An Invasion of Psychic Privacy," in *Fathers and Their Families,* ed. Stanley H. Cath, Alan Gurwitt, and Linda Gunsberg (New York: Analytic Press, 1989).

Chapter 7: "Beyond the Phallic Illusion," in *The Psychology of Men,* ed. Robert S. Liebert, Frederick M. Lane, and Gerald I. Fogel (New York: Basic Books, 1986).

Chapter 8: "An Essay on Romantic, Erotic Love," in Supplement on Affects, *Journal of the American Psychoanalytic Association* 39 (1991).

Chapter 9: The Peter Blos Lecture, 1991.

Index